ARMENIAN FOLKLORE BIBLIOGRAPHY

Armenian Folklore Bibliography

ANNE M. AVAKIAN

UNIVERSITY OF CALIFORNIA PRESS

Berkeley   Los Angeles   London

UNIVERSITY OF CALIFORNIA PUBLICATIONS:
CATALOGS AND BIBLIOGRAPHIES

Volume 11

UNIVERSITY OF CALIFORNIA PRESS
BERKELEY AND LOS ANGELES, CALIFORNIA

UNIVERSITY OF CALIFORNIA PRESS, LTD.
LONDON, ENGLAND

Library of Congress Cataloging-in-Publication Data

Avakian, Anne M., 1906–
    Armenian folklore bibliography / Anne M. Avakian.
        p.   cm.—(University of California publications. Catalogs
    and bibliographies ; v. 11)
    Includes index.
    ISBN 0-520-09794-7 (alk. paper)
    1. Folklore—Armenia—Bibliography. 2. Armenia—Social life and
customs—Bibliography. I. Title. II. Series.
Z5984.A75A93   1994
[GR203.12]
016.398'09566'2—dc20   94-13033
                                                                  CIP

The paper used in this publication meets the minimum requirements of
American National Standard for Information Sciences—Permanence of
Paper for Printed Library Materials, ANSI Z39.48-1984.

For Professor Alan Dundes who persuaded me to compile this bibliography. I have learned things about my culture that I would not have known if I had retired to a comfortable retirement home to await transport to a distant galaxy.

For the memory of my mother who taught me to read the Armenian language.

Contents

Foreword

The Armenians are a truly ancient people with a language and culture dating back to many centuries before the Christian era. They lived in their homeland in Anatolia, but for several hundreds of years they were subject to Ottoman rule. During World War I, the Armenians were decimated by massacres and deportations, all of which amounted to virtual genocide. From that time on, the Armenian people—those who survived—were forced to live in exile. Refugees from the 1915 disaster either went to Armenian communities in Russia or to sanctuaries farther abroad. So whereas before World War I, an Armenian ethnographic society had flourished and part of its efforts included the collection of folklore, the work of this society came to an end during World War I.

A glimmer of hope for those espousing a nationalistic reestablishment of an Armenian state or homeland occurred with the creation of the Republic of Armenia (1918–20) in Erevan, but that dream was short-lived because Armenia became a part of the Soviet Union in 1921. The situation remained unchanged until September of 1991 when the Republic of Armenia emerged again, this time as a member of the Commonwealth of Independent States (CIS).

Despite the undoubted antiquity of Armenian folklore, most 20th-century folklorists know relatively little about it. There are several reasons for this. Armenian folklorists have tended to write about their folklore in Armenian and few non-Armenian folklorists can read that language. In addition, because of the enforced Armenian diaspora, Armenian folklore has been reported in a variety of languages. This is why only a polyglot who could read Armenian among other languages—including Russian, French, and German—could have any idea of the incredible richness of Armenian folklore and the substantial scholarship devoted to it.

Fortunately, Anne M. Avakian, a retired professional librarian and a woman very much devoted to the study of Armenian culture, has undertaken to survey Armenian folklore scholarship and has thereby opened up what has hitherto been a closed book. Born in 1906 in Fresno, California, a city justly famous for its significant Armenian population, Anne Avakian grew up on a farm surrounded by many varieties of fruit trees. Her parents, both Armenians from Palu, Turkey, instilled in her a lifelong love for things Armenian. After earning an elementary school teaching credential from Fresno State College, she enrolled at Pomona College where she received her B.A. in English in 1930, graduating magna cum laude and a member of Phi Beta Kappa. Several years later, she studied at the School of Librarianship at the University of California, Berkeley, obtaining a certificate in 1932 which was essentially the equivalent of what was later called a Masters in Library Science. From 1934 to 1971, Anne Avakian worked for the U.S. Civil Service as a librarian for various offices of the U.S. Department of Agriculture. For example, from 1943 to 1971, she served as librarian for the Western Regional Research Laboratory of the U.S. Agricultural Research Service in Albany, California.

Some years ago after her retirement, while in her seventies, Anne Avakian began auditing my folklore courses on the Berkeley campus. Her presence was much appreciated by me and by my students. She became more and more interested in folklore in general and Armenian folklore in particular. She had long been engaged in quilting and needlepoint. She took special pleasure in keeping me informed of current publications in folklore. I often first learned of new books in the field through her periodic gift-packages of three-by-five slips with valuable bibliographical information on them. She made a point of reading library acquisition serials in order to cull titles relevant to Armenian culture and to folklore. Once when I suggested to her that she ought to compile a bibliography of Armenian folklore, she replied that she was too old to do so and that some young folklorist should be encouraged to put in the many hours of labor in the library required to assemble a comprehensive bibliography of that sort. Finally, I did prevail and she, somewhat reluctantly at first, agreed to accept the challenge.

Anne Avakian is a member of many organizations including library associations, the American Name Society, the American Folklore Society, the California Folklore Society, the California Historical Society, the Armenian Genealogical Society, the Armenian Library and Museum of America, and the Society for Armenian Studies. The chronology of her publications runs from 1938 to 1992. They include *Armenia and the Armenians in Academic Dissertations: A Bibliography* (Berkeley: Professional Press, 1974), and Supplement 1 (1987); "Three Apples Fell from Heaven," *Folklore*, 94 (1987), 95–98; and more than 250 reviews of books by or about Armenians for the *California Courier*, an American-Armenian weekly.

The field of folkloristics is surely indebted to Anne Avakian for having unearthed so many references on Armenian folklore. Her admirably succinct annotations are sufficient to allow the non-Armenian reader access to the contents of the books and articles she has listed. Her coverage of Armenian folklife runs the gamut from the famous epic of David of Sassoun to the traditional symbolic motifs found in Armenian rugs. She has also wrestled successfully with the daunting transcription/transliteration variations in Armenian names.

Not many individuals in their eighties would even have considered attempting such an ambitious project, but as should be obvious, Anne Avakian is no ordinary individual. Her unflagging energy coupled with her professional expertise in librarianship and her genuine knowledge of folklore have made it possible for her to complete this first real survey of Armenian folklore scholarship. It is an important contribution to world folkloristics and will surely be hailed by folklorists and specialists in Armenian studies alike. I consider it a rare honor to have been invited to write this foreword for such a valuable compilation by a truly remarkable woman.

Alan Dundes
Berkeley, California

Preface and Acknowledgments

This bibliography was undertaken very late in my retirement, so it is necessary to declare its limitations. These 1375 citations would have expanded considerably if I had been able to travel to large libraries in the United States and abroad, especially to the outstanding Armenian collections in Erevan, Venice, Vienna, and Jerusalem. My citations are derived from Berkeley libraries: the Graduate Theological Union, and most of all from the University of California. The latter has also extended its Interlibrary Borrowing Service, which has brought me items from other libraries through careful computer searches by Dr. Leon Megrian. I owe special thanks to the University of New Mexico library, which ordinarily does not circulate periodicals, yet made available to me its limited file of *Azgagrakan Handes*. For the missing issues I have depended on the detailed table of contents of that journal as well as that of *Eminian Azgagrakan Zhoghovatsu*, published by the Armenian State Museum of Ethnography. Mr. Artashes Nazinian, the current folklorist at Erevan, supplied those to me, and he also sent a number of Armenian books unavailable in libraries in the United States. Virginia Fox gave me the Wilson and Covington article (1991) with a misleading title in an obscure publication. I cannot overlook the constant encouragement of Prof. Alan Dundes.

Anyone who works on a bibliography that includes several languages encounters the jungle of transliteration. I have tried to follow the U.S. Library of Congress transliteration table of 1987. In Armenian there is the problem of two dialects, the Eastern used in Russia, later the Soviet Union, and the Western used elsewhere. I was faced with a dilemma: should I adopt one or the other. I finally decided to use both, without diacritical marks, depending on the origin of the publication. Yet even that was a problem: sometimes an Armenian wrote in Lebanon, then moved to Erevan where he did some writing, and finally wrote in the United States. What dialect form does one use?

Then there is the question of names. Usually Armenian surnames end in "ian," even though transliteration in either dialect, before the spelling reform of 1922, would render it as "ean." Long ago the U.S. Library of Congress adopted the "ian" ending because that form was generally used by Armenians and still is today. In Armenia "yan" is the present accepted form, but with some exceptions I use the "ian" ending in the bibliography. The "yan" ending is used in the United States for some names that have three vowels in succession, thus the name Saroyan instead of Saroian. However, there are persons who prefer to retain the triple vowels, as does Prof. Nina Garsoian. Another reason I have tended to use the "ian" ending even for Eastern Armenian authors is that many of their articles have Russian summaries, and the Russian transliteration of the Armenian name comes out with the "ian" ending. But to complicate matters further, the Russian language does not use the letter "H" so that a problem arises with the name itself—Hagopian becomes Agopian, and Ohannesian becomes Oganesian. Other unexpected forms also occur. Zabelle C. Boyajian's mother was English, her father was Armenian; she always wrote in English as Zabelle C. Boyajian. Yet one important library calls her Zapel C. Poyachean. Another bibliographical work comes up with Phaphazian; further search reveals that this is not a misprint but stands for the name Papazian.

I can still hear the caution from Prof. Della Sisler of my library school days when she gave an exception to a cataloging rule, then introduced us to "an exception to an exception." I admit that I have made some arbitrary decisions in this compilation, but I can safely say that my inconsistencies are consistent. Before going further, take a look at the variant spellings of the surname of the father of Armenian folklore, Servantsian, the form I have chosen from the following variations that I encountered in the preparation of this bibliography. I have made a cross reference only from the one form used by the Library of Congress: Srowandztiants.

Here are the variants of the Servantsian name:

Serouantstiants	Sruandztian
Serowantstiantz	Sruanjteanc
Servandstiants	Sruanjtreanc
Servandztiantz	Sruanztiianz
Servanstiantz	Srvandzdyants
Servanstianz	Srvandzian
Servantiants	Srvandztian
Servantsdiantz	Srvandztiants
Servantsediants	Srvandztiyants
Servantsian	Srvanjteanc
Servantstian	Srvanjtyanc
Servantstiants	Srvanstyanc
Servantzdian	Srvantsdyants
Servantzdiantz	Srvantsian
Serwantzdian	Srvantsiants
Sirvantziants	Srvantsyants
Srawantzdiants	Srvantziantz
Srouandziants	Srwajteanc
Srowandztiants	Srwandztiants
Sruandzteants	

Another problem encountered in the preparation of this bibliography is the lack of cumulative indexes. A compilation covering three time periods of journals exists, but I was unable to locate a copy of even one of the volumes. Sometimes individual journals issue a cumulative index to a group of volumes, but the forms of entry change, and one also discovers that the listings are selective. This has meant that I have had to leaf page by page through periodicals such as *Bazmavep* (1843 to date) and others to discover articles about folklore. International bibliographies seldom include Armenian periodicals, and even if they do the citation gives the Russian form of the journal title without a cross reference from the Armenian title.

Armenian folklore terminology has complexities too numerous to explain. It is gratifying that more recent articles have adopted the English "folklore" (in Armenian transliteration to be sure) instead of using the confusing terminology of earlier years. In my index I have tried to give preference to English equivalents, such as "dragon" instead of *vishap*. But I have not found a suitable equivalent for *bantukht*, which primarily means pilgrim. Among Armenians a youth or a young married man went to Constantinople or some other large city to work a few months or longer to augment the family income. He was not really a pilgrim, nor was he a migratory worker, a term commonly used in America. Many *bantukht* songs exist that express the loneliness of the worker in the big city and the longing of the families at home who await his return. Hence my decision to use the Armenian term.

Despite the complications encountered, I hope that this bibliography will serve as an introduction to a neglected subject. May this beginning be followed in the future by another bibliographer who can extend what is here and perhaps include the folklore of Georgia and other areas of the Caucasus.

A.M.A.
July 10, 1992

Introduction

Folklore is part of Armenian culture. But who are the Armenians? When and where did they appear on the earth? What did they do? And why do we need to give attention to Armenian folklore?[1]

According to some scholars, Armenians are an Indo-European people; others believe that they are a mixture of people who came from Thrace, crossed over to Phrygia, and moved eastwards to the Anatolian area where they occupied Urartu, which had fallen from power. The Armenians call themselves Hay (pronounced "high") and their country Hayastan (Haiasdan). When we name old Armenia we cannot point to a place that had a fixed boundary over the centuries of its existence. The historic home comprises the area from 39° to 49° east longitude, and 37.5° to 41.5° north latitude. The present Armenian Republic is a fraction of that area, a little larger than the state of Maryland.

Armenia is mentioned in the Bible (II Kings 9:17; Isa. 37:38) as is Ararat (Gen. 8:4; Jer. 51:27). Some scholars consider Ararat (Urartu) the precursor of Armenia.

Armenians look upon Mt. Ararat, which they also call Masis, as the symbol of Armenia. Hecataeus of Miletus, the Greek historian (c. 500 B.C.) notes the Armenoi. On the rock face of Behistun in Persia is an inscription in which Darius I (520 B.C.) lists his victories and names Armenia as one of his satrapies. The *History* of Herodotus also speaks of the Armenians, but of special interest to our subject is Xenophon's *Anabasis* (c. 400 B.C.) in which he gives a glimpse of Armenian life—the dwellings, the plenty and variety of food and wine—and adds that Armenians drank beverages through a straw.

Armenian history has been marked by periods of independence and subjugation: its history reveals the names of Medes, Parthians, Persians, Greeks, Arabs, Georgians, Mongols, Kurds, Jews, Russians, Turks, Crusaders, and missionaries from European countries and the United States. During the Crusades there was a Cilician Armenia bordering on part of the Mediterranean. That kingdom ended in 1375.

All the peoples named above brought about population movements within the country as well as to outside countries. Thus developed the Armenian diaspora that extends over many parts of the world. All these contacts and movements should be borne in mind when folklore dispersion is considered. But many Armenians remained in their historic homeland, a rugged country with cold winters. In the small mountain villages where topography permitted, the Armenians engaged in agriculture and a variety of crafts. They were also the leading traders in Anatolia. Thus politics, history, and economics are

---

[1] Sirarpie Der Nersessian's *The Armenians* (New York: Praeger, 1970, 216 pp.) gives some history as well as cultural information as does Ara Baliozian's *The Armenians* (Saddle Brook, New Jersey: A.G.B.U., Ararat Press, 1985, 191 pp.). H.F.B. Lynch's *Armenia, Travels and Studies* (London: Longmans, 1901, 2 v.) covers both the Turkish and Russian provinces. The work has much descriptive material accompanied by many photographs and maps. His journeys took place from August 1893 to March 1894, and again from May to September 1898. Many places described are now obliterated or renamed.

disciplines that should be studied to understand the folklore of all peoples, including the Armenians.

Two important events in Armenian history should be emphasized. The first was the adoption of Christianity in A.D. 301 when King Tiridates III (Trdat) became a Christian through the teaching of Gregory the Illuminator. The other was the invention of the Armenian alphabet early in the first century A.D. in order to introduce writing as a unifying element in the spread of Christianity.

Mesrop Mashtots, with the support of Catholicos Sahag, undertook the task of devising the alphabet of 36 letters in a distinctive script. Two more letters were added later. The alphabet stimulated scholars to translate a number of Greek philosophical works into classical Armenian, and some religious works were translated from the Syriac. By 466 the Bible was translated from Greek into Armenian.

This dedication to the language was to have far-reaching influence in the latter part of the 19th century when a number of Armenian periodicals appeared that covered a variety of subjects, including a bit of folklore. A reading public was created that became informed about events at home and abroad. Most important was the idea of reforms. Some persons even thought of nationalism.

The Ottoman government introduced strict censorship and thus began more repressive measures that brought on the massacre of 1895. That was followed by the Adana massacre of 1909. Last of all came the premeditated policy to exterminate the Armenians by genocide in 1915. So ended the continuation of Armenian culture and folklore in the areas of Turkey once occupied by Armenians.

After the translation period Armenian histories appeared. Among the best known was the *History of the Armenians* by Moses of Khoren. This has been attributed to the fifth century, but some scholars maintain that it belongs to a later period because some events in the book happened at a later date. The question may well be raised whether modern standards of historiography can be applied to any early histories that went through the hands of copyists. Despite disputes, what is important is that the *History* of Moses of Khoren and other early works arose from the oral tradition.[2]

In the early Armenian histories one finds myths, legends, heroic tales, etc. that are part of what we call folklore. Religious writings were popular, but later other subjects appeared. Armenian writing developed a group of scribes and illustrators who produced

---

[2]Moses of Khoren's *History* speaks of the singers of the province of Goghtn. They sang about the heroic characters of Armenian history. In later times singers were known as *gusans*, a word said to come from Pahlevi, one of the Persian languages; it is also said to be of Parthian origin. Another word for minstrel is the Arabic *ashugh*, a word that refers to love, and this word was commonly used by Armenians. But the Armenian minstrel's songs were not exclusively devoted to love, and they were more often connected with the folk than with courtly circles. The minstrel sang some folk songs, but he also created some songs of his own about events, hardships, and economic conditions. Some minstrels were blind, and went from village to village as entertainers. Payment was voluntary. They also engaged in contests; the loser had to give up his musical instrument, the *saz*, to the winner.

There were hundreds of Armenian minstrels. The most famous was Sayat-Nova (1712?–95). He sang in Armenian, Georgian, and Azerbaijani, and for awhile was connected with the Georgian court. Some of his songs have been preserved and articles have been written about the hidden meanings of some of his songs. Scores of pages have been written about the date of his birth. He was married and had a family, but in later years became a priest assigned to Haghbat Monastery near the Georgian border. It is said that when he heard about a contest to be held in Tiflis, he shed his clerical garb and hastened to join it. Armenian minstrels were quite active in Persia during the 19th century.

thousands of manuscripts in medieval times. Even though invaders and conquerors destroyed many manuscripts, many still survive in prominent libraries of the world. The Armenian nobility or men of wealth commissioned the preparation of manuscripts for themselves or as gifts. Many of the texts were religious, but the decorations and illustrations show costumes, furnishings, plants, animals, birds (some with human heads). Some show masks and musical instruments. All may properly be called visual folklore. From Avedis K. Sanjian's book, *Colophons of Armenian Manuscripts, 1301–1480* (Cambridge: Harvard University Press, 1969, 459 pp.) we learn of the conditions under which the manuscripts were prepared.

Much of the lore in the old histories was derived from oral transmission. The Bible was the source of many manuscript texts, and the artist provided illustrations he considered acceptable for the texts. Observation of nature provided many decorative motifs, and the imagination supplied the fantastic figures in the manuscripts. Only the wealthy could afford manuscripts, and aside from that, because the texts were in classical Armenian, only the educated could read them.

Among the common people was a wealth of folklore that was a part of daily life. There were tales, anecdotes, fables; there were thousands of proverbs, oaths, curses, blessings, and prayers; there were songs for work and festive occasions; there was no lack of superstition, and magic, and other lore. Yet most of this wealth was secluded in the villages. But time brought technological and educational progress. Printing replaced manuscripts, and some of the monasteries and churches established schools where the popular language gained dominance. New currents were astir in the 19th century. Father Alishan (1852) published a slim book of popular songs in Armenian and English. In St. Petersburg, Miansarov Miansarian (1868) compiled a book of Armenian literature and devoted a small section to songs and proverbs.

It has been said that there is an association of folklore with nationalism. Nowhere was this more apparent than in the Armenian papers that proliferated in Armenian communities in Turkey and Russia. Writers contributed articles about literature, but there were also articles about political matters, especially the need for reforms. Some space was given to folklore, and thus nationalism and folklore became companions on the printed page. Although censorship limited the life of most of these publications, they had a part in drawing attention to folklore.

Armenian folklore attracted the interest of some travelers, a topic that deserves separate study. However, here is one example. August von Haxthausen was exploring Transcaucasia, and in Tiflis met Khachatur Abovian (1805?–48), who described some Armenian customs and also told him some tales. Haxthausen (1856) included these in his book and thus introduced Armenian folklore to German readers.

Abovian had received his education at the Echmiadzin Seminary and also at the Nersessian school in Tiflis. His life took an unexpected turn when he met Prof. J. J. F. Parrot (some cite him as Friedrich Parrot) in Erevan. Parrot was to lead an expedition to Mt. Ararat and chose Abovian as his interpreter or guide. Parrot was so impressed by Abovian that he offered him a scholarship to study at the University of Dorpat. Abovian spent several years there, becoming interested in Western ideas and nationalism. On his return home he wrote a novel, *Verk Hayasdani* (The Wounds of Armenia), the first Armenian novel written in the vernacular. The book's background featured the suffering endured by Armenians under Persian domination in the early 19th century. Included were some folklore items. Abovian never saw the book in print because one day in 1848 he left his house and was never seen again. Whether he was the victim of political foul play remains a question. His book was published in 1858, but has never been translated. Abovian influenced some future Armenian novelists to introduce folklore in their works.

The person recognized as the father of Armenian folklore is Bishop Karekin (christened Hovhannes) Servantsian (1840–92).[3] He was born in Van, a town on the eastern shore of Lake Van. After finishing at the local school Hovhannes went to Varag (Varak) Monastery for further education at the school established by Khrimian Hayrig.[4] There Hovhannes read Eghishe's account of the Battle of Avarayr (A.D. 451) when a vast Persian army tried to impose Zoroastrianism on the Armenians. In one of the very bloody phases of the battle, several heroic martyrs fell. Hovhannes was so impressed that he dropped his name and called himself Karekin Servantsian after one of the martyrs. Even though the Armenians lost the battle, they were able to retain their Christian faith.

Khrimian Hayrig began publishing a paper called *Ardzvi Vaspuragan* (The Eagle of Vaspuragan), and Servantsian helped with its production. When Khrimian decided to seek funds elsewhere to continue publishing, he took Servantsian with him to Erevan, Echmiadzin, Tiflis, and a small area of Persia. After returning, they later went to St. Garabed Monastery in Mush and started the paper *Darono Ardzvik* (Eaglet of Daron). Both publications included articles about nationalism, and Servantsian contributed items of folklore. Neither paper survived very long because of censorship. Khrimian Hayrig went on to higher responsibilities, first as the Armenian Patriarch in Constantinople, and later becoming Catholicos of the Armenian church in Echmiadzin.

Servantsian continued his clerical duties, which consumed much of his time as his work took him to Mush, Van, Erzerum, and Constantinople. As he went from place to place, he observed and noted many things, but he admitted losing some of the material. Drawing on his remarkable memory, he decided to publish what he recalled. The result was *Krots u Prots* (Written and Unwritten, often cited as *Krots-Prots*), published in 1874 under a Constantinople imprint. In this slim volume Servantsian included *Sasuntsi Davit gam Mheri Tur* (David of Sassoun or Mher's Door), which he had heard about while traveling from village to village in the course of his clerical duties.[5] Seeking a narrator wherever he went, after three years he finally located Grbo, a villager near Mush, who could tell the story. Servantsian transcribed it as he heard it, and thus came to light a version of the Armenian epic, David of Sassoun. Servantsian was not sure how it would be received, but noted that he would be satisfied if only 20 persons understood and approved what he had transcribed.

In the various commentaries about Servantsian's book most attention is given to the epic. Little has been said about the longer portion of the book, which consists of brief, picturesque descriptions of places and the traditions or folkways connected with each place. He left no guideline for collecting folklore, but his method is clear: observe and

---

[3]The original surname of the family has not appeared in any of the articles I have seen about Servantsian. The family home was situated directly opposite a large *sant* (mortar) where women came to grind wheat. So the dwelling was called *Santents Dun* (The Mortar House). We have only the name of the father, Avedis, who lived there with several sons, the youngest being Hovhannes.

[4]Mgrdich Khrimian (1820–1907) entered the priesthood after his wife and only child died. He was dedicated to the idea of education for both sexes, and he longed for reforms that would alleviate the suffering of the people. He was so beloved by all Armenians that they called him Khrimian Hayrig (Little Father).

[5]Actually the tale had been afloat for a long time. Two 16th-century Portuguese travelers mentioned it in their itineraries as they went through Armenia on their way to India. (See A. Baião, 1923.)

listen. He also noted by name a number of clergymen who were collecting folklore that had not been published at the time he wrote *Krots-Prots*. A search through a later bibliography (Ghanalanian, 1985) does not reveal any of these names.

Servantsian wrote other books besides *Krots-Prots*, but I have been able to see only *Manana* (Manna), *Hamov-Hodov* (With Flavor and Fragrance), and *Toros Akhpar* (Brother Toros) (this last not a collection of folklore). When the Armenian Patriarch of Constantinople sent Servantsian, with others, to survey the condition of the Armenian communities in Turkey after the Russo-Turkish war of 1877–78, Servantsian noted that certain places still followed old customs and that someone should contact the people there and record the folklore. In both *Manana* and *Hamov-Hodov*, Servantsian not only recorded folktales but also included a wide variety of genres of folklore. It is from these two volumes that F. Macler translated some tales into French and J. S. Wingate made some translations into English. Later some prominent Armenian writers, e.g., H. Tumanian and A. Isahakian, "improved" items taken from Servantsian, a disappointment for those familiar with the Servantsian transcriptions.

There are no original transcriptions of the folklore that Servantsian collected, but some of his letters are in the archives at Erevan. Servantsian was active during a period of repression, especially the reign of Sultan Abdul Hamid II, who was in power from 1875 to 1909. There was much suspicion and considerable censorship in the printing of certain words and even "certain chemical formulas," according to R. H. Davison's book *Turkey* (Englewood Cliffs, N.J.: Prentice-Hall, 1968, p. 96). It was during this period that American Protestant missionaries had established Armenia College in Kharpert, but they had to change the name to Euphrates College. In his later years Servantsian remained in Constantinople because he felt that he was under surveillance.

Servantsian loved the common folk and felt that their lore was a treasure worthy of preservation. Though his life was brief, he left a lasting impression on later folklore collectors.

Sarkis (Sargis) Haykuni (1838–1908) was born in a village near Trebizond. His original surname was Ghazarian, but when and why he took the name Haykuni I do not know. In his early years he was dedicated to the improvement of the lot of Armenians in Turkey. His nationalist interests led to his imprisonment for short periods in Turkey and Russia. He was a contemporary of Servantsian, and it is on record that they met in 1878; they may have discussed politics as well as folklore.

A teacher by profession, Haykuni also collected folklore in various places in the local dialects. He had the reputation of being a careful collector. He collected some Kurdish lore as well and requested the important folk song collector Komitas to supply the musical notation of several Kurdish songs. He contributed articles to Armenian periodicals, but much of his folklore material was published in several volumes of *Eminian Azgagrakan Zhoghovatsu* (Eminian Ethnographic Collection). I have been able to see only the second volume, which is devoted mostly to folktales. The table of contents of that periodical shows that Haykuni collected other genres of folklore as well.

Today when Armenian folk songs are mentioned, Komitas (Gomidas) (1869–1935) takes first place. Much has been written about him and his work, but H. Begian (1964) states in his thesis that S. Poladian (1942) gives the best account in English. The current authority on Komitas is R. A. Atayan of Erevan. Komitas was a native of Kutahya (Kutaiah) Turkey. He was orphaned early in life, and after some schooling in his native town, attended the Gevorgian Seminary (sometimes called Academy) at Echmiadzin. There he became a priest and taught liturgical music. He transcribed some folk songs his pupils knew, but he was also very active in collecting folk songs from many villages. It has been estimated that he collected from 3000 to 5000 songs, but today only 1200 (another estimate is 1000) of his transcriptions remain in the archives at Erevan.

Through the generosity of a wealthy Armenian (A. Mantashev [Mantashian]), Komitas studied music in Berlin from 1896 to 1899. He received his doctoral degree for his thesis on Kurdish music, but according to Begian no copy of the thesis exists. He returned to Echmiadzin and gave concerts there, and later went to Berlin, Paris, and Switzerland where he introduced Armenian folk music. In 1910 he moved to Constantinople and continued his concerts. There was a complaint that some of his folk music included nationalistic elements, and that may have been the reason that in 1915 the Turkish government exiled him along with about 100 Armenian intellectuals. Through great effort and intervention he was released, but he was a broken man, having seen too much torture and terror used on his compatriots. He spent the rest of his life in a Paris hospital where he died in 1935.

Komitas believed that folk music was derived from the village folk and did not think that any folk music originated in urban areas. When he was in Erevan he met Manuk Abeghian, and they published a collection of song texts (Komitas and M. Abeghian, 1904). Abeghian among other things was a linguist, and he made changes in the text of some folk songs to make them more literary. It is difficult to understand why Komitas agreed to these changes.

The Servantsian influence touched Dikran (Tigran) Navasardian (1861–1927), a native of Vagharshabad near Erevan. At age 12 he was sent to the Nersessian school in Tiflis where he became interested in various Armenian and Russian papers that had liberal political views. He came under surveillance and in 1879 was arrested for distributing a song that suggested freedom. He had also distributed a picture of Michael Nalbandian, a liberal thinker and activist in Russia. Navasardian was imprisoned, but with outside help was released in 1880. He then worked under an assumed name as a translator in a hospital. In 1885 he went to Geneva, studied engineering, and then returned to Tiflis where he worked on underground conduits.

Given such a background one may wonder how Navasardian came to have a place in Armenian folklore. No doubt his early acquaintance with various Armenian papers introduced him to folklore items that appeared there. From the age of 15 he collected folklore during his school holidays. He felt a close tie to the people and wanted to preserve their heritage. From 1882 to 1903 he published 10 volumes of *Hay Zhoghovrdakan Hekiatner* (Armenian Folk Tales), although this is really a misnomer because the volumes included several genres of folklore. How did Navasardian assemble all this material? Only some of it was his own work. He organized a group of 40 field workers and sent them out to collect folklore. What instructions he gave them is not certain, but a brief article about P. Muradian, one of his collectors (see S. A. Vardanian, 1980) perhaps gives some clue. Muradian indicated the narrator's name, age, sex, and origin, and also noted the narrator's skill as well as the quality of memory. We might assume that Navasardian instructed the field workers to cover these points, but we do not know. An attempt to locate even one volume of Navasardian's work has ended in failure. Despite Navasardian's extended project, only one article has appeared about him (S. A. Vardanian, 1974). Nothing has been noted about his activities from 1903 to the time of his death in 1927, a curious gap in the literature.

We now turn to folklorists whose work was not interrupted by surveillance, imprisonment, or exile. One person who stands out is Grigor Khalatian (1858–1912), a native of Alexandropol (earlier Gumri, later Leninakan, once again Gumri). After his early education in his home town he went to Moscow to study medicine. There he met Mkrtich Emin,[6] who was on the faculty of the Lazarian Institute for the Study of Oriental Languages. Emin persuaded him to study Armenian history and literature. Khalatian went to Germany for further study and upon his return to Moscow was invited to teach Armenian literature at the Lazarian Institute, where he eventually became head of the history and literature department.

Khalatian was aware that the publication of Servantsian's works had stimulated interest in the collection of folklore, but he observed that some collectors did not know what to collect and that some lacked a sense of order. So he prepared a guide to introduce some uniformity, which he called *Plan for Armenian Ethnography and Ethnic Judicial Customs* (translated title) (see G. Khalatian, 1887). The *Plan* has 10 divisions: (1) Geography and history; (2) Anthropological information; (3) Dwellings; (4) Costume and adornment; (5) Food and drink; (6) Mode of life and occupations; (7) Family life, customs, and national characteristics; (8) Beliefs; (9) Language, writing, and art; (10) Kinds of folk and oral literature. The second part of the book is concerned with domestic law and is divided as follows: (1) The general situation and administrative judgment; (2) Civil law; (3) Criminal law.

The *Plan* tells the collector how to talk to the informant, how to transcribe, and how to classify the results. It stresses the importance of attending to collecting material as soon as possible and of writing down what is presented, not what should be. It then points out that collected material should be published. Thus the collection of ethnographic and folklore material was placed on a scientific basis.

Although Khalatian lived in Moscow, he maintained close ties with Armenians in Constantinople, Erevan, and areas in the Caucasus where Armenians lived. He served as editor of *Eminian Azgagrakan Zhoghovatsu* (Eminian Ethnographic Collection) from 1901 to 1912, vols. 1–8. Volume 9, the final one, was edited by K. Kostanian.

Another leading folklorist was Ervand Lalayan (1864–1931). He too was a native of Alexandropol, but the origin of the family is traced to Karabagh, an area recently in the news. Lalayan received his education at the Nersessian school in Tiflis, and he later taught school for several years in Alexandropol. In 1890, together with his wife, he went abroad for higher education in Geneva and Lausanne. For a short time, in 1894, he worked at the Mekhitarist Congregation in Vienna. From there he went to Paris to attend anthropological lectures. While in Paris he was accepted as a contributing member of the Anthropological Society.

When Lalayan returned home to Alexandropol, he devoted his time to teaching. Inspired by Khalatian's *Plan*, he began collecting folklore even though he continued to

---

[6]Mkrtich Emin (1815–90) is cited by the French as Jean-Baptiste Emin because Mkrtich means the baptizer. Emin also used the initials N. O. for which there is no explanation. However, there is circumstantial evidence that he used those initials when he wrote in Russian. Emin was born in Persia and educated in India. Later he served on the faculty of the Lazarian Institute, a school established by the Lazarian family. The school flourished for 100 years. Emin was interested in languages, literature, and folklore. When he died he left 10,000 rubles, the income of which was to be used for publishing ethnographic articles. Out of this fund came the publication of the periodical *Eminian Azgagrakan Zhoghovatsu* (Eminian Ethnographic Collection, 1901–1913).

teach. No doubt his foreign contacts also influenced his interest in folklore in a way that had not been considered earlier by Armenian folklorists. In 1895 (usually noted incorrectly as 1896) he established a journal called *Azgagrakan Handes* (Ethnographic Review) which was to continue through 1916. The first volume was published in Shushi in Karabagh and later volumes in Tiflis. He edited this publication and also contributed many articles to it. Then in 1901 he organized the Armenian Ethnographic Society (translated title), which had 174 members and a few honorary members that included the Catholicos of the Armenian church and N. Marr. The aim of the society was to promote ethnographic and archeological work, protect the antiquities of the Caucasus, establish a museum and library, present lectures, and establish prizes for the best studies in the subject area of the society. Aside from this he encouraged the publication of books and Armenian inscriptions.

Lalayan worked with enthusiasm, going around with a camera and taking pictures to accompany some of the articles in *Azgagrakan Handes*. He made personal investigations and transcribed folk material, and also organized expedition groups. One very important contribution he made was to seek out Armenians who had fled from Turkey in 1915. From them he collected folktales and thus saved versions that would have been lost forever. In 1914–15 he published three volumes of folktales called *Margaritner* (Pearls), which he had started to collect in 1912. It has been impossible to locate any volume of this set. Lalayan's works are being collected, but up to now only two are available: *Javakhk* (1983), and *Artsakh* (1988) (Artsakh is another name for what is called Karabagh today). The Khalatian *Plan* was familiar to Lalayan, but he noted that it should be enlarged and extended to meet new demands. There is no evidence that this suggestion has been followed.

Among the more recent figures in Armenian folklore was Manuk Abeghian (1865–1944). After his early education in Artapat, his native village in Vaspurakan, he attended the Gevorgian Seminary in Echmiadzin. Later he studied in Germany (1893–98) where he received his doctoral degree from the University of Jena for his thesis *Das Armenische Volkesglaube* (1898). After a short visit to Paris he returned to Tiflis and Erevan. By profession a teacher, he eventually became a professor at the University of Erevan. He also became a member of the Armenian Academy of Sciences. His linguistic knowledge involved him in the Armenian spelling reform adopted in 1922. He wrote many articles in Armenian papers and a two-volume work on the history of Armenian literature in which he gave special attention to Armenian fabulists. Abeghian's interest in folklore is evident in his thesis topic, as noted above, and in later writings. The minstrel tradition attracted Abeghian; he was very familiar with Moses of Khoren's *History* in which the Goghtn singers were recognized as the singers of tales. Minstrelsy was popular for centuries, and Abeghian's particular interest was in the metrical structure, rhythm, and the language of the minstrel songs.

Abeghian's principal folklore focus was on the epic David of Sassoun. He transcribed a version in 1885 and in later years made a critical study of the epic's locale, events, and characters, comparing them with the actual place names, historical events, and persons of the mid-10th century when the epic was said to have originated. In 1936 Abeghian and K. Melik-Ohanjanian undertook an ambitious project—to compile the extant versions of this epic. From the various titles of the variants, they selected the title *Sasna Tsrer* (Daredevils of Sassoun). I was able to borrow the first volume of this compilation, but unfortunately 60 pages of the introduction were missing. But from the remaining fragment I learned that the compilation is arranged by region and does not follow the first version that Servantsian transcribed. Thus the 1885 transcription appears first in volume one. The second volume was published in two parts, 1944 and 1951, respectively. I learned recently that volumes three and four have been published, and that volume five is in preparation. Obviously other editors undertook the later compilations.

Another significant date for this epic is 1939, when the 1000th anniversary was celebrated with the publication of the unified, or combined, text. The Institute of Language and Literature of the Armenian Academy of Sciences commissioned the work with I. (or H.) Orbeli as editor-in-chief. The task was assigned to Prof. Abeghian, Prof. K. Abov, and A. Ghanalanian, who selected 50 variants of the epic from which they put together the episodes that represented the story of the several generations in the epic. The Ararat dialect was chosen to express the equivalents of dialect words of the original transcriptions. From this edition came several translations and adaptations of the epic. Thus Abeghian contributed to Armenian folklore from Tsarist times through part of the Soviet period.

When we come to Aram T. Ghanalanian (1909–83), we meet a 20th century folklorist. He would have received his education from 19th-century–educated teachers, but as a child he would have heard from his elders of the 1914–18 war during which the Russian revolution ended the Tsarist regime in 1917, of Armenia's brief independence in 1918–20, and of Armenia's emergence as a Soviet Republic in 1921.

Ghanalanian was born in Akhaltskha, Georgia, where there was (and still is) a large Armenian community. After his early education there he went to an industrial school in Tiflis. In 1927 he entered the University of Erevan, majoring in Armenian language and literature. One of his teachers was Manuk Abeghian, who advised him to take an interest in folklore and even suggested that he compile a bibliography. This eventually came to fruition as a chronological list of well over 1000 items arranged chronologically from 1830 to 1982 and indexed by author and topic (Ghanalanian, 1985). The list includes many citations to brief folklore items that appeared in various Armenian papers that were popular in the late 19th century. Though these papers do not turn up on U.S. computer databases, access to old Armenian papers is possible in Armenian libraries abroad (in Erevan, Venice, Vienna).

After completing his university studies Ghanalanian taught for a year and then had the task of looking over about 1000 transcriptions of folktales collected by Lalayan in 1915–16. He was supposed to abridge these tales with the idea of preparing a concordance, but if the work was ever completed there is no mention of it in his bibliography or anywhere else.

It was in the mid-1930s that something new appeared in Soviet folklore. Frank J. Miller, in his book *Folklore for Stalin* (Armonk, N.Y.: M. R. Sharpe, 1990, 192 pp.) describes and gives examples of what he calls a new genre, pseudo-folklore. His book does not mention Armenians, but we have evidence from Ghanalanian's bibliography that G. Tarverdian and A. Ghanalanian published *Lenine Hay Folklori Mej* (Lenin in Armenian Folklore, Erevan, 1936). K. Melik-Ohanjanian edited and wrote the introduction for the book. It has been impossible to locate a copy to find out what the erudite editor had to say about the new genre. The index to the present volume notes works in which excerpts of the Lenin material appear. What is fascinating is the striking parallels to the Biblical flight to Egypt as well as to the discovery of a narrator who reminds us of the peasant who told the epic David of Sassoun to Servantsian. For example, when Lenin was a baby, a threat to his life was disclosed, so his parents took him to a distant land. As for the David of Sassoun parallel, we have two itinerant wool carders who meet a peasant who recites a narrative about Lenin and his heroic deeds. It seems that under the Soviet regime it was helpful to use old models to add to Lenin's legitimacy.

It is appropriate to note here that users of this bibliography should not be surprised to encounter authors who mention Marx, Engels, or Lenin or quote them directly. Such recognition was undoubtedly helpful for writers.

The scope of Ghanalanian's publications is evident in the bibliography. He wanted to broaden the field of folklore studies, and for him Armenian folklore revealed a democratic world view in the works of Armenian writers. He intended to write a book on this subject, but died before he could undertake the project. He did live long enough to edit the first two volumes of Abeghian's works, now in eight volumes.

Armenian folklore is old, but only in the latter part of the 19th century did Bishop Servantsian's pioneer work give it recognition as a national treasure that should be collected and published. It is noteworthy that before World War I the Armenians, a tiny fraction of the world population, published more than a score of books of folklore as well as many articles in Armenian periodicals. Beyond that, G. Khalatian published his *Plan* as a guide for folklore collectors, and E. Lalayan organized the Armenian Ethnographic Society.

Then the historical events of World War I laid a destructive hand on folklore. The Armenian communities in Turkey were eliminated. Armenian communities in the Russian provinces experienced losses of another kind: the periodicals *Azgagrakan Handes* (AH; Ethnographic Review) and *Eminian Azgagrakan Zhoghovatsu* (EAZh; Eminian Ethnographic Collection) ceased publication and were never revived. The Armenian Ethnographic Society, which had many long-range plans, did not survive. Place names changed in both Turkey and Russia. A list of these changes, together with a map, should be made for provenance of folklore transcriptions.

Very little folklore material was published in Soviet Armenia after the Russian revolution. However, in 1936 the first volume of variants of David of Sassoun was published, followed in 1944 with the first part of volume two. In 1939 the unified text of David of Sassoun was published, but on the whole, the years of World War II were lean ones for publication. It was not until the 1950s that books and articles appeared with some frequency. In 1959 the first volume of *Hay Zhoghovrdakan Hekiatner* (Armenian Folk Tales) was published. The series is still in progress, and volume 13 (1985) is the most recent. This series includes tales collected in earlier years by Lalayan, Navasardian, Haykuni, and others. Arrangement is regional, and for each tale there is a note that gives the name of the collector, narrator, date, and place of transcription. The first three volumes include tales collected in villages of the Ararat area. Motifs are listed at the end of volume three, but functions are not noted. For example, there are over four dozen references to the word "apple," but nothing indicates whether the fruit is a symbol of love, fertility, or immortality. Here it is appropriate to mention that only quite recently have Soviet Armenian folklorists become aware of the Stith Thompson *Motif-Index of Folk-Literature* and the A. Aarne–Stith Thompson *The Types of the Folktale*. When the *Hay Zhoghovrdakan Hekiatner* series is completed, it would be very useful to have a more suitable motif index as well as a tale type index.

Other projects are the publication of the complete works of several authors, e.g., Abeghian's complete works in eight volumes, Servantsian's works in two volumes, and Lalayan's works in five volumes, of which two are in print.

Armenian folklore in translation has reached foreign readers in books and periodicals since the latter part of the 19th century. But the very first book devoted exclusively to folktales was published in English in the United States in 1898 by A. G. Seklemian (1864?–1920). His book, *The Golden Maiden*, contained tales he had heard in childhood and later, and some were translated from Servantsian's works. A native of Bitias, a village of the Musa Dagh area, Seklemian was educated at Central Turkey College, a school established in Aintab by American missionaries. While teaching school in Erzerum for several years, he developed an interest in folktales, and he intended to publish a book of tales. His views were considered harmful to the young, however, so he was arrested and spent 13 months in prison. Thus his publication plan had to be postponed until he came to the United States. *The Golden Maiden* is out of print, but selections from it have been reprinted in *Armenia* and *New Armenia* (see entries in the bibliography).

A particularly significant book, *100 Armenian Tales*, was published by Susie Hoogasian Villa in 1966. Ten immigrant Armenians living in the industrial Delray section of Detroit, Michigan, narrated to her tales they recalled from the old country. Thanks to her expertise in shorthand and her ability to translate simultaneously, she transcribed many tales from which she selected the ones for her book. Included for each tale is comparative material from tales of other nationalities. Also provided in the book are a motif index based on Thompson's *Motif-Index* and short biographical sketches of the narrators.

Perhaps the time has come for some kind of folklore survey from Armenian immigrants of the period after World War II. A large community of immigrants from Lebanon, Iran, Egypt, and the Soviet Union has settled in the Los Angeles area, and before too much acculturation takes place their folkways should be recorded. Folklore studies should also be conducted in the large Armenian communities in South America and Australia.

We must now consider the problem of the language barrier. In this bibliography most of the citations are in Armenian, but if Armenian folklore is to reach western folklorists, some avenue of access is necessary. First of all, there must be easy access to the ethnographic journals mentioned earlier. Few libraries have these journals, and those that do will not lend them. It is imperative that reprints be made so that many libraries and perhaps even some folklorists can buy them. Through the index to this bibliography items for translation can be selected. Aside from commercial translation agencies, there are other potential sources for translation. Several universities in the United States have Armenian Studies programs, so it would be possible to enlist students for translation work. Another potential source of translators is the American University of Armenia, which was established in Erevan in 1991. Most of the student body is Armenian, but all classes are given in English. At present the curriculum is limited to Business Administration and Engineering, but the long-term plan includes expansion into departments in Agriculture as well as the Humanities. No doubt there will be Armenian students who will be willing to do some translation work.

Since folklore is our theme, we cannot help but think of the fairy godmother in her beautiful gown and the magic wand she holds. But is this her only guise? When the Armenian alphabet was devised early in the 5th century, did not Armenian scholars translate Greek philosophical works and Syriac religious texts into Armenian? Later did not the wealthy Lazarian family establish the Lazarian Institute for the Study of Oriental Languages that survived in Moscow for one hundred years? Did not Prof. Emin of that institution leave a bequest of 10,000 rubles for the publication of ethnographic articles? Did not Mantashev (Mantashian) grant a scholarship to Komitas to study in Berlin? Let us keep our faith in the fairy godmother; she can fulfill a wish or two.

Now we return to the initial question. Why should attention be given to Armenian folklore? There may be connections with other folklore. For example, the Roman geographer Solinus of the third century observes that there are no snakes in Ireland. We have heard that St. Patrick expelled the snakes from that land. Then there is St. Epipan, who worked among Armenians who had reverted to paganism in order to bring them back to Christianity. He took some disciples to a Greek island where there were many poisonous snakes and other harmful creatures. When he set foot on the island, all the harmful creatures vanished. What, if any, are the connections? In folklore no stone should be left unturned—there may be something there.

Anne M. Avakian
July 10, 1992
Berkeley, California

Abbreviations

The following abbreviations are used for frequently cited periodicals:

AH	*Azgagrakan Handes*
B	*Bazmavep*
H	*Hairenik*
HA	*Handes Amsorya*
L	*Lraber*
PH	*Patma-Banasirakan Handes*
REA	*Revue des Études Arméniennes*

ARMENIAN FOLKLORE BIBLIOGRAPHY

A., N. *See* Aginian, N.

Abeghian, Ardashes
1900–1901   "Tlvat-Davit." [David of Sassoun.] *AH* 6:159–192; 7–8:103–112.
  A variant form of the epic in verse form. Collected in 1899 from a narrator of Moks.

1902   "Sasnay Tsrer." [Daredevils of Sassoun.] *AH* 9:117–143.
  Four branches of the epic in prose form; told in 1899 in Ararat dialect.

1913   "H. F. B. Lynch." *AH* 25:226–228.
  Obituary of famous traveler who wrote *Armenia: Travels and Studies.* London. 1901, 2 v.

1931–32   "Azkakrutiune Hayots mech." [Ethnography Among Armenians.] *H* 9(11):109–119; 9(12):122–133; 10(1):129–140; 10(2):136–148; 10(5):87–99.
  History of ethnography from olden times to last 100 years. Includes folklore and mentions Grimm.

1932   "Azkakragan arasbelagan darre Movses Khorenatsu badmutean mech." [The Ethnographic Mythological Element in the History of Moses of Khoren.] *H* 10(9):137–150.
  Discusses heroic figures, their treatment, and value for the Armenian nation.

1940   "Hay zhoghovrtagan vebe." [The Armenian Folk Epic.] *H* 18(10):106–110.
  About variants of the epic David of Sassoun. Some believe it has 40 parts, but it really has four. Origin may have been during Arab domination of Armenia (7th–9th centuries).

1948   "Manug Abeghian (1865–1944)." *H* 26(3):90–101.
  Biographical sketch including work in folklore.

Abeghian, Ardashes *(continued)*
1955   "Manug Abeghian." *H* 33(1):23–28; 33(2):46–56; 33(3):72–77; 33(4):93–99;
            33(6):69–80; 33(7)87–95: 33(9):83–94; 33(10):88–94; 33(11):69–76.
            Study of life and work as educator, linguist, literary historian, and
            folklorist.

Abeghian, Hasmik
1975   *Isahakyane ev zhoghovrdakan epose.* [Isahakian and the Folk Epic.] Erevan,
            HSSR, GA Hrat. 187 pp. port., il.
            History of Isahakian's poem "Sasma Mher." [Mher of Sassoun.]
            Development of idea of Mher as lover of freedom who had social
            conscience and enlarged world view. Based on manuscript and published
            versions.

Abeghian, Manuk
1899   *Der armenische Volksglaube.* Leipzig, W. Drugulin. 127 pp. Dissertation,
            Jena, 1898.
            Armenian beliefs about soul and death, light and darkness, fate, various
            nature cults, spirits, and magic. Armenian translation is in his *Erker*
            [Works] vol. 7:11–102, and German original appears in same volume pp.
            449–579. Erevan, 1975. Extended review in *Globus* (1900) 78:238–293
            by Julius von Negelein.

1906–8   "Hay zhoghovrdakan vepe." [The Armenian Folk Epic.] *AH* 13:5–36; 14:39–
            68; 15:5–32; 6:69–117; 17:5–36; 18:5 –24.
            About David of Sassoun, its locale, style of people, historical aspects of
            tale and traditional influences, remnants of old myths, religious and moral
            ideas, worship of dead, meaning of "Tsrer."

1940   *Gusanakan zhoghovrdakan dagher, hayrenner ev antuniner.* [Minstrel Folk
            Songs, Ballads and Emigré Songs.] Erevan, Izd-vo Armfan-a. 339 pp.
            Includes a short Russian summary (pp. 37–39). Variety of folk songs.
            Gives manuscript sources of songs. Notes and vocabulary included.

1948   *Istoriia drevnearmianskoi literatury.* [History of Ancient Armenian Literature.]
            Erevan, Izd-vo Akad. Nauk, Armianskoi SSR. Vol. 1 (523 pp.)
            Have seen only vol. 1. Includes myths, historical heroes, the Persian war,
            and some material on folklore. Includes bibliography of 218 items.

1966   *Hay vipakan banahyusutyun.* [Armenian Narrative Folklore.] Erevan, HSSH,
            GA Hrat. 570 pp. port. (His *Erker* [Works], v. 1). Russian summary.
            Discussion of terminology, collecting folklore. Includes early legends and
            myths, heroic tales, Persian war, Daron war. Large part is critical study of
            David of Sassoun.

1967   *Hay knarakan banahyusutyun.* [Armenian Lyrical Folklore.] Erevan, HSSH, GA Hrat. 387 pp. (His *Erker* [Works], v. 2). Russian summary.

First part (pp. 9–280), called "Hin gusanakan erger" [Old Armenian Minstrel Folk Songs], gives detailed analysis of the metrical structure, rhythm, language of songs. Second part (pp. 283–383), called "Zhoghovrdakan khaghikner" [Folk Dances], gives examples of types of songs and their structure.

1968   *Hayots hin grakanutyan patmutyun.* [History of Ancient Armenian Literature.] Erevan, HSSH, GA Hrat. (His *Erker* [Works], v. 3).

Covers from beginning to 10th century; pp. 17–80 give some superstitions, legends, heroic tales, pagan gods.

1970   *Hayots hin grakanutyan patmutyun.* [History of Ancient Armenian Literature.] Erevan, HSSH, GA Hrat. (His *Erker* [Works], v. 4).

Covers period from 10th to 15th centuries. Of special interest, pp. 171–189 about fables of Mkhitar Gosh; pp. 189–228 about fables of Vartan. Some examples are given.

1975   "Hishoghutyunner Komitasi masin." [Reminiscences About Komitas.] In his *Erker* [Works]. Erevan, HSSH, GA Hrat, v. 7:431–439.

Activities of Komitas in Echmiadzin and how author and Komitas compiled the book *Hazar u mi dagh* [A Thousand and One Songs.] Mentions that Komitas had transcribed 3000–4000 folk songs.

1975   "Komitas Vardapet ev yur gortse." [Komitas Vardapet and His Work.] In his *Erker* [Works], Erevan, HSSH, GA Hrat. pp. 420–430.

Objects to article in *Nor Dar* no. 110 (no date) by contributor (not named) about work of Komitas in Echmiadzin. Supposedly Komitas pursued love songs.

1975   "Zhoghovrdakan ergaran ev 'Hazar u mi khagh.' " [Folk Song Book and "A Thousand and One Songs."] In his *Erker* [Works], Erevan, HSSH, GA Hrat. v. 7:406–419.

Originally appeared in *Murch* no. 11 of 1903 which was not available to me. Critic not identified. Abeghian defends editing songs of Komitas so they will be edifying to public.

1985   "Azkayin vep." [National Epic.] In his *Erker* [Works], Erevan, HSSH, GA Hrat. v. 8:12–65.

Essay on David of Sassoun first published by K. Servantsian in 1874. Compares with an 1889 version called "David and Mher," half historical, half mythical.

Abeghian, Manuk *(continued)*
1985   "Hay zhoghovrdakan araspelnere M. Khorenatsu Hayots patmutyan mej."
            [The Armenian Myths in Moses of Khoren's *History of the Armenians*] In his
            Erker [Works], Erevan, HSSH, GA Hrat, v. 8, pp. 66–272.
                A critical study of mythical tales, heroic tales, and legends. Beliefs based
                on real events, not artificial creations.

Abeghian, Manuk, and Melik-Ohanjanian, K.
1936–   *Sasna Tsrer.* [Daredevils of Sassoun.] Erevan, Bedagan Hrad. [State
            Publishing House.]
                This compilation gives all the versions known of the epic David of
                Sassoun. Unfortunately I was able to see only vol. 1 (1936) but most of
                the introduction of many pages was missing; of the little that remained I
                learned that the arrangement is regional not chronological. I was unable to
                locate a copy of vol. 2, part 1, but did see part 2, but it had a very limited
                introduction. According to Mr. A. Nazinian of Erevan the project of
                compilation continues; volumes 3 and 4 have been published and another
                volume is in preparation. Above I have given the names of the original
                compilers; other persons have been involved since.

Abegian. *See* Abeghian

Ablian, Eprem
1895   "Badmutiun Drtaday Etovbiaren." [Story of Drtad (Tiridates) in Ethiopian.] *B*
            53:71–76.
                A translation of René Basset's French translation from Ethiopian. No
                information given on Basset article or where it was published.

Abov, G. A.
1964   "Hay zhoghovrti mets banasteghtse." [The Great Poet of the Armenian
            People.] *PH* 3:3–16.
                About Sayat-Nova, Armenian minstrel of 18th century who wrote and
                performed ballads in Armenian, Georgian, and Azerbaijani. Songs about
                rights of peasants; against oppression.

Abrahamian, A. A., et al.
1963   *Sayat Nova.* Erevan, HSSH. 231 pp.
                A collection of eight articles about various aspects of Sayat-Nova's work.

Abramian, L. A.
1977   "Ob idee dvoinichestva po nekotorye etnograficheskim i folklornym
            dannym." [The Idea of Duality According to Some Ethnographic and
            Folklorist Data.] *PH* 2:177–190. Armenian summary.
                Examines duality structure, e.g., heroes of David of Sassoun as well as
                Armenian folk portrayal, with examples. Study of mechanism, similarity,
                and symbolism.

Abramian, L. A., and Demirkhanian, A. R.
1985   "Mifologema bliznetsov i mirovoe derevo." [Mythology of Twins and the
            Cosmic Tree.] *PH* 4:66–84. Armenian summary.
                About meaning of a group of images in ancient Armenian rock art. Based
                on mythological and artistic elements.

Acharian, Hr.
1902   "Turkeren pokhareal parer Hayereni mej." [Turkish Words Borrowed in
            Armenian.] *Eminian Azgagrakan Zhoghovatsu* 3:1–381.
                Title gives scope; dictionary of borrowed words follows, pp. 59–377.

1911   "Hay barbaragitutyan urvagits ev dasavorutyun Hay barbarneri." [Outline of
            Armenian Dialectology and Study of Armenian Dialects.] *Eminian
            Azgagrakan Zhoghovatsu* 8:1–306, with a dialect map.
                The "um," "ke" (or "ge"), and "el" branches of dialects are presented in
                the study.

1913   "Hayeren gavarakan bararan." [Dictionary of Armenian Provincial Dialect.]
            Eminian Azgagrakan Zhoghovatsu 9:1–1141.
                After some introductory material on various dialects, pp. 43–1141 is a
                dictionary of dialect words.

Acharian, Hr., and Acharian, Armenuhi
1902   "Havakatsoy Bolshay ramkakan angir grakanutean." [Collection of
            Constantinople Armenian Peasant Oral literature.] *AH* 9:160–196.
                Notes that 13 tales collected by his sister, but none appears. Includes
                prayers, songs, games, riddles, proverbs and sayings, etc.

Adam, Paul
1906   "Armenian Popular Songs." *Armenia* 2(4):23–28; 2(6):24.
                Abbreviated preface of Arshag Chobanian's book about Armenian folk
                songs. Title of book not given. Descriptive information and emphasis on
                spirit of songs. Gives examples.

Adamian, A.
1962   "Haykakan mi avandutyun Petros Arajini veraberyal." [An Armenian legend
            about Peter I.] *PH* 4:248–250.
                Peter I imprisoned in Holland. An Armenian Margos Mirzakian enters
                prison, exchanges clothes with Peter who goes to Russia. Armenian later
                released, meets Peter I at Astrakhan who promises to take some
                Armenians to Moscow or Petersburg.

Adontz, N.
1927   "Tarkou chez les anciens arméniennes." *REA* 7:185–194.
                Ancient god-hero; supernatural huge figure connected with lightning and
                thunder; sometimes characterized as eagle or vulture.

Adontz, N. *(continued)*
1927–28   "Les fêtes et les saints de l'église arménienne." *Revue de l'Orient chrétien*
             26:74–104, 225–278.
                 Various festivals and saints of the Armenian church. Notes that article to
                 be continued, but learned from another source that the continuation not
                 published because of some imperfections. *See* Renoux, Ch., 1980–81.

1930   "Les fonds historiques de l'épopée byzantine Digenis Akritas." *Byzantinische
             Zeitschrift* 29:193–227.
                 Notes that Byzantine epic Digenis Akritas has some relationship to the
                 Armenian David of Sassoun—time, geography, and twin heroes.

1934   "Les légendes de Maurice et de Constantin V empereurs de Byzance."
             *Brussels. Université. Institut de Philologie et d'Histoire Orientales. Annuaire
             Mélanges Bidez* 2:1–12.
                 Armenian Byzantine emperor, Maurice, of lowly birth, son of gardener.

Adoyan, A. G.
1965   "Haykakan amusna-entanakan haraberutyunnere mijnadaryan orenknerum."
             [Armenian Marriage-Family Relations in Medieval Laws.] *PH* 3:49–66.
             Russian summary.
                 Based principally on book of justice by Mkhitar Gosh.

Adrbed (pseud.). *See* Mubayajian, Sargis

Agathangelos
1976   *History of the Armenians.* Translation and commentary by R. W. Thomson.
             Albany, State University of New York Press. 527 pp. fold. map. Text in
             Armenian and English.
                 Includes embedded items of folklore interest, e.g., legend of Ripsime and
                 Gaiane, King Tiridates' transformation into boar, and some information
                 about pagan Armenia.

Agayan, Gaiane
1978   "Epos 'David Sasunskii' i Armianskaia klassicheskaia literatura v otsenke A.
             Fadeeva." [The Epic of "David of Sassoun" and Armenian Classical
             Literature in the Estimation of A. Fadeev.] *L* 5:71–82. Armenian summary.
                 Fadeev's various articles in journals show esteem he has for the epic and
                 also for such authors as Raffi, Abovian, Isahakian, and others.

Aghaton, Ervant
1932   *Oktagar kidelikner ev kordznagan khradner Hay ergrakordznerun.* [Helpful
             Information and Practical Advice for Armenian Farmers.] Vienna, Mkhitarian
             Dbaran. 181 pp. port.
                 Of special folk interest are several plants useful for folk medicine.

Aghayan, M.
1950   "Komitasi erazhshtakan katarman arveste." [The Art of Musical Performances
         of Komitas.] *L* 9:71–76. Russian summary.
         Aside from collecting folk songs, Komitas was a performer. He had a
         tenor/baritone voice and sang in Berlin while studying there. He was also
         a choral director and composer.

1959   *Hay gusannere ev gusana-ashughakan arveste.* [Armenian Minstrels and the
         Minstrel Art.] Erevan, Haypethrat. 65 pp.
         Includes music with words for 17 songs. Defines *gusan,* a Pahlavi word
         meaning poet, or folk musician. In Arabic known as *ashugh,* the word for
         love. Notes terminology and variant meanings, places of performance.
         About contests and themes: love, religion, advice, social conditions,
         history.

Aghbalian, N.
1927   "Koghtan erkeri masin." [About the Koghtan Songs.] *H* 5(9):46–52;
         5(10):45–54.
         Pagan songs of Koghtan (Goghtn) area. Meter of songs needs further
         study.

1979   "Moses Khorenatsi." Trans. by Armine Manoukian Saroyan. *Armenian
         Review* 12(2):152–162.
         Biographical information about Moses of Khoren and his place in
         Armenian history. No exact citation of original except that it is from
         Aghbalian's history of Armenian literature, vol. 4.

Aginian, N.
1893   "Mheri turn—Dosbyants grone." [Mher's Door—The Religion of Dosp.] *HA*
         7:239–242.
         Physical feature of rock of Van known as Mher's Door, its name and
         origin and inscriptions on it. Evidence of animal sacrifices there. Legends
         about it.

1894   "Azkayin erker hin Hayots." [National Songs of Ancient Armenia.] *HA*
         8:133–137, 165–170, 197–200, 329–333.
         A translation of Fetter's "Die nationalen Gesange der alten Armenier."
         Full name of Fetter not given, hence listed under translator's name. Does
         not note when and where original appeared. Gives examples of Koghtan
         (Goghtn) songs.

1931   "Ervant Lalayan." *HA* 45:289–294. port.
         Biographical sketch of Lalayan and his work in folklore.

Aharonian, A.
1897   "Surmelui zhoghovrdakan erger." [Folk Songs of Surmelu.] *AH* 2:321–347.
             Songs from province on right bank of Arax River. Mixed population.
             Credits minstrels and young girls for preserving songs. Describes village
             musical life; minstrel songs of past and present. Girls sing alternate
             quatrains, sometimes have contests. Mostly love songs (122) pp. 339–
             347.

1913   *Les anciennes croyances arméniennes (D'après de folk-lore arménien).*
             Geneva, Impr. Jent. 71 pp. Dissertation, Univ. de Lausanne.
             Special attention to hearth (fire) that represents life of family. Role of
             women to maintain hearth through administration of household. Worship
             of fire, sun, moon. Protective spirits of hearth. Care of dead and
             remembrance of them. *See* S. Z. Markarian thesis, 1931. An Armenian
             translation with title "Haygagan hin havadalikner" [Ancient Armenian
             Beliefs] appeared in *H* (1939–40)18(1):1–4; 18(2):80–90; 18(3):112–117;
             18(4):9–13; 18(7):51–57; 18(6):155–162; 18(7):160–164; 18(8):121–
             125. Translator's name not given.

1960   "Hay gine ev Anahide." [The Armenian Woman and Anahid.] *H* 38(4):1–3.
             Contrasts Anahid the mother goddess of Armenians with the Persian
             Anahid goddess of love.

Aharonian, G. H.
1965   *Hiusenig.* Boston, "Hairenik." 251 pp. il.
             Most of text about village is in Armenian, but James H. Tashjian has an
             English section, pp. 227–231. In Armenian text there is a section on
             weddings (pp. 119–121). Some songs and ballads and special festivals
             (pp. 122–132). Some pictures show crafts, bread baking, and making of
             confection *rojig.*

Aharonian, V.
1937   "Sasnay Tzrer." [Daredevils of Sassoun] *H* 15(6):171–173.
             This is a review of vol. 1 of David of Sassoun, published in Erevan in
             1936. Later volumes planned to include all variant versions.

1940   "Sasuntsi Tavit" [David of Sassoun.] *H* 19(2):159–165.
             This is a review of the epic David of Sassoun that appeared in Armenian
             in 1939. This edition is known as the unified text, composed from various
             versions.

1954   "Sayeat Novayi masin." [About Sayat-Nova.] *H* 32(8):92–93.
             Reply to S. Saharuni who noted in a column of various items that Sayat-
             Nova was buried in Khachavank. Aharonian reports that Khachavank in
             Tiflis has no burial yard. Sayat-Nova was buried at Medz Pert (Great
             Fort) church of St. George. See *H* (1953) 31(8):106–108.

Ahian, Stepan
1985   " 'Sasna Tsrer' Haykakan epose ev hndevropakan erek fenktsiannere." [The
        Armenian Epic "Sasna Tsrer" and the three Indo-European functions. *PH*
        1:32–46.
            According to G. Dumézil the three functions are: supreme sovereignty,
        martial spirit, variety of representation. David of Sassoun reveals these
        functions.

Ahikar. *See index*, Ahikar

Airuni. *See* Hayruni

Ajarian. *See* Acharian

Ajello, Roberto, and Borghini, Alberto
1989   "Il serpente e l'abbondanze: a propisito di un passo di Eznik di Kolb." *B*
        147:259–279. Armenian summary.
            Snake a symbol of wealth and spirit of the home and place.

Ajemian, Hovhannes
1955   *Harsnajghya havakadzoy Hay zhogh., erkere Chmshgadzakashrchanneren.*
        [Collection of Armenian Wedding Folk Songs from Chmshgadzak and
        Surroundings.] Paris, P. Adjemian. 94 pp.
            Aside from wedding songs, includes work, love, and dance songs with
        some descriptive notes, list of dialect words. A review by H. Boghosian
        appeared in *HA* (1955) 69:285–286.

Akhian. *See* Ahian

Akhverdian, Georg
1903   *Hay ashughner.* [Armenian Minstrels.] Tiflis, M. Martirosiants. 527 pp.
            There are 59 minstrels representing dialects of Ararat, Kantsak, Tiflis, and
        Hashtarkhan. Songs of some given. No dates of minstrels. Glossary at
        end of volume. Sayat-Nova not included because a separate volume
        devoted to him, but I have not been able to locate a copy.

Akopian. *See* Hakobian

Alboyajian, Arshag
1937   *Badmutiun Hay Gesarioy, deghakragan, badmagan ev azgakragan
        usumnasirutiun.* [History of Armenian Caesarea; Topographical, Historical,
        and Ethnographical Study.] Cairo, H. Papazian. 2 v. il., maps. Paged
        continuously.
            Vol. 2, pp. 1594–1836 devoted to ethnography and folklore: home life,
        customs relating to weddings, births, deaths, amusements, festivals,
        beliefs of old women, protective prayers, superstitions, proverbs and

Alboyajian, Arshag *(continued)*
sayings, songs, etc. Not many examples because area Turkish speaking.
Examples of stories in dialect.

1952   *Badmutiun Evdokioy Hayots.* [History of Armenians of Tokat.] Cairo, Nor
            Asdgh. 1751 pp. and 105 pp. il.
            Topographical, historical, and ethnographic information. Ethnography pp.
            1349–1560. Includes proverbs and sayings, anecdotes (in dialect),
            customs, ornaments and dress, food and drink, marriage, birth and care
            of children, entertainment, folk medicine, superstitions. Includes story of
            lazy bride, p. 1455.

1961   *Badmutiun Malatioy Hayots; deghakragan, badmagan ev azgakragan.*
            [History of Malatia Armenians; Topographical, Historical, and
            Ethnographical.] Beirut, Sevan. 1536 pp.
            Ethnographic section pp. 1097–1208. Family life, customs relating to
            weddings, birth, death; superstitions, fables, riddles, anecdotes, curses,
            oaths, blessings and prayers. Some children's songs and lullabies.

1961   *Hushamadean Kutinahayeru.* [Memorial Book of Kutahya Armenians.]
            Beirut, Donikian. 231 pp. il., map.
            Of folklore interest, pp. 147–177. Camp life in nearby areas. Home town
            of Komitas who visited there and organized choir for entertainment. Name
            day parties held for all having same name. Brief information on baptisms,
            weddings; coins dropped from above, children pick coins. Turkish-
            speaking community but includes 600 Armenian words given as
            examples. Diminutive names.

Alishan, Ghevont
1848   "Gaghant, nor darvoy sovorutiun." [Gaghant, New Year's Custom.] *B*
            6:407.
            Word *gaghant* from Roman calends. Gives ancient Armenian calendar
            when New Year began Aug. 1, *Vartavar*, the water festival and first fruits.

1850–51   "Azkayin vibasanutiun." [National Narrative.] *B* 8:356–361 (not pp. 340–345
            as printed; pages out of order), 9:6–9. [Second part signed A.M.]
            Notes some of heroic tales embedded in Moses of Khoren's *History*.
            Notes that some early material lost because not written, and later ones
            suppressed with advent of Christianity to exclude pagan material.

1852   *Armenian Popular Songs.* Venice, St. Lazar, Mkhitarist Congregation. 85 pp.
            English and Armenian on opposite pages. Derived from manuscripts
            13th–18th centuries.

1891–95   "Hin havadk Hayots." [Ancient Beliefs of Armenians.] *See* his *Hin Havadk*
            (1910).

1895 *Hay pusag, gam Haykakan pusapanutiun.* [Armenian Plants, or Armenian Botany.] Venice, St. Lazar, Mkhitarist Congregation. 647 pp. il.

  Although 3,239 plants listed, some are cross references. Arranged alphabetically by common names. There is a scientific name index and some Turkish and Arabic names. Quotations from old Armenian works given for many items, and medicinal uses sometimes noted as well as special connections with tradition.

1910 *Hin havadk, gam hetanosagan gronk.* [Old beliefs, or Pagan religion.] Venice, St. Lazar, Mkhitarist Congregation. 557 pp. il.

  Originally published anonymously with the title "Hin havadk Hayots" in *B* in 1894–95: 52:5–8, 49–53, 97–104, 145–152, 193–197, 241–248, 259–301, 337–345, 385–390, 433–438, 481–490, 528–533. (1894) 53:8–12, 53–57, 97–104, 149–153, 193–197, 241–250, 289–296, 337–346, 385–389, 433–442, 481–486. 1895. Covers worship of nature, celestial bodies, special gods, spirits, etc.

Alishan, Leo M. *See* Alishan, Ghevont

Alishan, Leonardo P.

1985–86 "The Sacred World of Sasna Tsrer: Steps Toward an Understanding." *Society for Armenian Studies. Journal* 2:107–139.

  Interpretation of the epic David of Sassoun from some of its sacred aspects.

Allahverdian, Aramayis

1933 "Ashugh Pagher Oghli." [The Minstrel Pagher Oghli.] *H* 11(7):114–121.

  About an Armenian 17th century minstrel of Julfa. Only 13 of his songs survive in written form.

Alojian, H

1909 "Arevabashdutiun ev gragabashdutiun." [Sun Worship and Fire Worship.] *B* 67:393–399.

  Besides other peoples, in early times Armenians worshipped the sun. Introduces some historical evidence.

1910 "Gragabashtutiune enthanur askerits ev Hayots mech." [Fire Worship Among Nations in General and Armenians.] *B* 68:13–21.

  In early days Persians were fire worshippers; some Armenian customs similar to Persian practices suggest Persian derivation.

Altunian, Tatul

1931 *Haykakan zhoghovrdakan erger.* [Armenian Folk Songs.] Erevan, "Sovetakan Grogh." 151 pp.

  Includes musical notations. There are 42 songs; some texts identified by names of poets, others not. No introduction or information on sources. Music for dance and song ensembles.

Amirbakian, R. J.
1989   "K voprosy o nekotorykh zoomorfnykh simbolakh v iskusstvo vostoka." [On
              the Question of Some Zoomorphic Symbols in Eastern Art.] *PH* 1:65–78.
              Armenian summary.
                   In medieval art Orientals have distinct artistic models of animal figures;
                   snake and peacock appear in Byzantine, Armenian, Persian, Central
                   Asian, Indian Art as symbols.

Amirian, Lemyel
1981   "From Pazyryk to Dragon Rugs and Kum Kapu: Armenians and the Oriental
              Rug." *Armenian Review* 34:348–358.
                   Explains reasons for ascribing rugs noted in title as Armenian rugs. Paper
                   presented at Symposium on Armenian Rugs at Wash., D. C., on Oct. 18,
                   1980.

Amirkhanian, M. D.
1971   "Armianskaia narodnaia pesniia v Russkikh perevodakh." [Armenian Folk
              Songs in Russian Translation.] *PH* 3:223–225. Armenian summary.
                   With minor exceptions, these are work songs. Some examples are
                   bilingual.

Amsler, Jean
1978–79   " 'Dawit de Sasun' et les 'Niebelungen.' " *REA*, n.s. 13:187–195.
                   Analysis of parallel features of the Armenian and German epics named in
                   title; comparisons more numerous at beginnings and endings.

Amurian, A.
1961   "Semiramis." *H* 39(2):41–44.
                   Legend of the Armenian "Ara the Beautiful" and Assyrian queen. When
                   Ara killed in battle, the queen calls on gods to lick Ara's wounds to revive
                   him. No success.

Ananikian, Mardiros H.
1964   "Armenian Mythology." In *The Mythology of all Races*. N.Y., Cooper
              Square Publishers, pp. 1–100, and notes, pp. 379–397. Plates I–VI and
              frontis.
                   Armenian pagan deities a mixture of native, Iranian, and Semitic elements.
                   Worship of heavenly bodies, fire, water, mountains, trees, and plants.
                   Also about spirits, monsters, our betters, death, cosmogony.

Anderson, E. R.
1978–79   "The Armenian Sassoun Cycle: Folk Epic Structure and Theme." *REA* 13,
              n.s. 175–186.
                   David of Sassoun epic is history of a family. Each generation goes
                   through hero life pattern. Ritual use of language, use of word magic.
                   Charisma of clan maintained makes for success of Armenian experience.

1986–87   "Myth on the Way to Romance—the Sassoun Cycle." *REA* 20, n.s. 271–275.
> Theory of epic; considers epic as a process of myth displacement in a point between myth and romance. Uses David of Sassoun as example of myth displacement.

Andreasian, Sarkis
1979   *Hay erki 2 husganer; Sayat Nova, Gomidas Vartabed.* [Two Giants of Armenian song; Sayat-Nova and Gomidas Vartabed.] Chicago, Ill. (1353 Catalpa Ave., 60640). 183 pp. il.
> Biographies of 18th century Armenian minstrel, Sayat-Nova, and Armenian folk-song collector, Komitas Vardapet. Includes comments by various persons about them. Special note made of origin and meaning of Sayat-Nova's name and question of date of his death.

Anetsi, Hovh.
1895   "Transilvanioy Hayots mayrakaghake." [The Capital of Transylvania Armenians.] *HA* 9:239–246, 278–285.
> First part describes Gerla, the capital. Gives 108 sayings used there. Second part gives some dance songs with music. Also two tales: "The Cow" and "The Mother, Son, and Dragon."

Anonymous
1833   "An Armenian Marriage at Constantinople." *Penney Magazine* 2:439–440.
> Describes ceremony and ritual in house (not church) but priest performs old customs strictly. Service according to Armenian church, not Armenian Catholic.

1843   "Azkayin erkeru ev avantneru vray." [About Folk Songs and Traditions.] *B* 1:332–334.
> Gives a folk song relating to Lake Van and explains significance of some expressions.

1846–51   "Hanelug." [Riddle.] *B*.
> A riddle in single issues of several volumes beginning with vol. 4 (1846) through vol. 9 (1851), a total of about 90 riddles. Answers given in issue following one in which riddle was noted.

1847   "Grung." [Crane.] *B* 5:95–97.
> Describes bird and its habits and migration to distant places. The song "Grung" appealed to Armenians who left home to work [*bantukhts*]. Ten stanzas are noted. Not mentioned here, but there has been some dispute about whether the song is a rural folk song.

1847   "Ramgagan aragavor khoskov." [Peasant Proverbial Sayings.] *B* 5:259–260.
> Proverbs reflect character of people; some of the 21 proverbs in Turkish.

Anonymous *(continued)*

1847   "Zuarjali tibuadzner." [Pleasant Encounters.] *B* 5:16, 76.
               Couple of jokes in each section.

1848   "Khelatsi aragner." [Wise Proverbs.] *B* 6:336.
               A list of 17 adages, proverbs.

1849–56   "Aragk." [Fables.] *B* beginning with vol. 7 (1849), 8 (1850), 13 (1855), and
               14 (1856), fables (i.e., proverbs) are given in various issues.

1850   "Basilikos gam arkayig ots." [The Basilisk or King Serpent.] *B* 8:140–142.
               il.
               Conception of ancient folk about animals which burn, poison, or turn to
               skeletons whatever they meet or touch. Beliefs relate to Armenians also.

1850   "Vanetsots erk gakavu." [Partridge Song of Van.] *B* 8:230.
               In dialect of Van about favorite bird, the partridge.

1850–51   "Azkayin, gam Hayakhos aradzk." [National or Armenian Speech Proverbs.]
               B 8:32, 96, 128, 160, 192, 224, 288, 352; 9:112, 160, 223, 370.
               A total of 140 proverbs.

1855   "A Visit to the Yezedis, or Devil Worshipers in Armenia." *Frasers Magazine*
               51:587–592 .
               Traveler, not named, visited Yezedis. Yezdan the name used in adoration
               of supreme being, the Devil. Armenians not followers, but some groups
               in Armenian territory follow the cult. I may add a personal note that there
               was a well-known tailor in Fresno, Calif. whose surname was Yezdan.

1865   "Arag." [Fable.] *B* 23:96.
               Fable "The Hornbeam and the String Bean," but no source given.

1867   "Hantes harsaneats Mush kavarin mech." [Wedding Ceremony in Province of
               Mush.] *B* 25:307–313.
               Marriage ages, asking for girl, engagement, dancing, ceremony, etc.

1868   "Hampartsman donin hantese Mush kavarin mech." [Celebration of the
               Ascension Day Festival in the Province of Mush.] *B* 26:129–130.
               A spring festival. Describes special food *samir* (ground millet, butter,
               milk). Girls dress in festive garb, decorate black/white ox with flowers,
               take ox from door to door and collect eggs, butter.

1875   "Aradzk azkayink." [National Proverbs.] *B* 35:40, 125–126, 246.
               Total of 130 proverbs in alphabetical order.

1881   "Pank vasn khapogh aghuesin ev charutean nra." [Words About the Deceptive Fox and its Mischief.] *B* 39:193–198.
> A fable taken from a 17th century manuscript. How the fox finds tempting bait in a trap and tricks wolf who gets caught in trap and fox gets bait. Farmer kills wolf and skins it.

1883   "Aragk." [Fables.] *B* 41:61–62.
> Gives three fables, but no source indicated.

1884   "Erk sireliots." [Song of Lovers.] *B* 42:134.
> Folk song, but no designation of place.

1887   "Aradzk Khodorchartsiots" [Proverbs of Khodrchur Armenians.] *HA* 1:175, 197–198.
> Proverbs (67) collected from residents; many dialect words explained.

1887   "Erk Vanetsots." [A Song of Van Armenians.] *B* 45:16.
> A song of several stanzas and refrain used for Ascension Day festival (*vijag*). Notes tying of floral bouquet with basil.

1889   "Nakhgin azkayin sovorutiunk harsaneats." [Former National Wedding Customs.] *B* 47:232–234 .
> Lists 21 customs briefly, e.g., engagement is a seal of approval that cannot be broken.

1890   "Antradarutiun." [Anagram.] *HA* 4:164.
> Gives two stanzas of anagrams.

1890   "Vererkutiun." [Palindrome.] *HA* 4:164.
> Incorrectly designated in English as palindrome; it is an anagram, and gives example: Van—Nav. [NB: Van is name of town; nav means ship.—AMA].

1891   "Mgrdich Emin." *HA* 5:51–53. port.
> About life and work of Emin, who was a linguist and also interested in folklore.

1893   "Arag. Manuk ev sheram." [Fable. Spider and Silkworm.] *B* 51:328.
> Source of fable not given.

1893   "Azkayin gorusdner." [National Losses.] *HA* 7:22–23.
> Of the three obituaries only one related to folklorist K. Servantsian.

1895   "Peasant Life in Armenia." *Outlook* 51:671.
> Report of a correspondent of London "Telegraph," but no name or date. About Sassoun folk who keep strict rules of fast. Gives fragments of folk songs, epics, legends. Mixture of pagan and Christian elements.

Anonymous *(continued)*

1902   "Kavarats aghchgan erke." [The Peasant Girl's Song.] *B* 60:481–482.
            First song: "Mother They Have Come After Me." Second song: "Mother
            Don't Give me to—" in which she enumerates an artisan in each stanza.

1902   "The Past in the Present." *Journal of American Folklore* 15:192.
            About *kelek* still used in Armenia. A raft made of reeds and inflated
            animal skins. Also use of inflated skin on which man sits astride.

1906   "Aradzk-nakhniats." [Traditional proverbs.] *B* 64:104, 243, 293, 375.
            A total of 17 proverbs.

1911   "Hin aradzner." [Old Proverbs.] *B* 69:182, 257.
            A total of seven proverbs.

1912   "Armenian Folk-tales. The Sea-Maiden." *Armenia* 6:154–155.
            Gives no translator or narrator.

1912   "The Armenian Handkerchief. How They Are Made." *Children's Star* 9:151.
            il.
            Armenian needle lace edgings on handkerchiefs.

1912   "Krikor Khalatiants." *B* 70:13 4–135.
            Obituary notes his education and activity in folklore.

1913   "The Bird Sahak, an Armenian Legend." *Armenia* 6:269
            Bird said to have been human once.

1913   "Vanetsots siro erg." [Love Song of Van Armenians.] *AH* 25:108.
            First line of song: "The Rose has Opened on Vartavar Sunday."

1917–19   "Armenian Proverbs." *New Armenia* 9:361; 10:39, 121, 164, 11:4.
            A total of 17 proverbs; no name of translator.

1929   "Armenian Proverbs." *New Armenia* 21:14, 30.
            Translated by Robert Arnot; 28 proverbs.

1948   "Hay-roofed Houses of Chubukhli, a Soviet Armenian Valley Town."
            Geographical Journal Bulletin, series 2, vol. 27, Bulletin 10:2. il.
            This is a picture that shows practice of piling hay on roofs for animal feed;
            by spring roofs are cleared.

1969   "Hay azkayin erazhshtutian himnadire." [The Founder of Armenian National
            Music.] *L* 1:3–6.
            On occasion of 100th anniversary of the birth of Komitas and his studies
            in Berlin. His purpose to show special characteristics of Armenian folk
            music.

Antepian, Paylak
1985   *Mussaler.* [Mount of Moses.] Erevan, HSSH, Hrat. 215 pp. (Hayagrutyan ev
        banahyusutyan . . . no. 16). *L* 2:91–93.
            Not seen, so listed under reviewer. No author indicated. Mentions I.
            Levin's methodology. Includes 55 folktales; songs, traditions, fables,
            anecdotes, riddles, curses, blessings, oaths, 680 proverbs. Examples of
            songs in dialect and standard Armenian.

Antreassian, Alice
1975   *Armenian Cooking Today.* New York, St. Vartan Press, 189 pp. il.
            Arranged by types of food; special section on Lenten foods, pp. 161–169.
            Includes glossary, index, and sources of ingredients.

Antreassian, Alice, and Jebejian, Mariam
1981   *Classic Armenian Recipes: Cooking Without Meat.* New York, Ashod Press.
        308, xxxi pp. il.
            Vegetarian. End pages give menu suggestions, sources of ingredients,
            notes, hints, and index.

Antrig[ian], N.
1905   "Tidoghutiun me Oghimbionu aragnerun vray." [An Observation on the
        Fables of Olympianos.] *B* 61:9–13.
            Olympianos probably copied 15 fables from Aesop. Gives example of a
            fable in three versions that belong to Greek tradition.

1906   "Koghtean erkeru vray." [About the Koghtan songs.] *B* 64:105–107.
            Much written about Koghtan (Goghtn) songs, but few songs exist. New
            questions arise relating to certain words.

1907   "Titsapanagan tidoghutiunner." [Mythological Observations.] *B* 65:106–109
            About some ancient Armenian gods—Mard, Zadig, Astkhig. Also
            temples.

Apkarian, D.
1964   "Endanagan park Nor Chughayi." [Family Customs of New Julfa.] *HA*
        78:245–256, 403–406.
            Many customs Europeanized except weddings and some relating to birth.
            Includes very old song (17 stanzas) used on occasion of tying the green
            and red ribbon across groom's breast. Second part about beliefs and
            superstitions about pregnancy and birth.

1964   "Havadalikner Nor Chughayi mech." [Beliefs in New Julfa.] *HA* 78:549–
        554.
            Armenians lost large part of their beliefs, but kept a few firmly, e.g.,
            magic and superstitions.

Apkarian, D. *(continued)*
1964–65   "Nor Chughayi aradznere." [Proverbs of New Julfa.] *HA* 78:549–554, 79:111–120, 283–290, 395–404.
In dialect of New Julfa, 970 proverbs listed in alphabetical order.

1965   "Nor Chughayi orhnutiunnere ev anetsknere." [Blessings and Curses of New Julfa.] *HA* 79:515–524.
Blessings (172), curses (220) in alphabetical order.

Aprahamian, R.
1939   "Sayat-Novayi dagheri klkhavor kegharvestagan kdzere." [The Main Lines of Creativity in Sayat-Nova's Lyrics.] *H* 17(7):104–110.
Analysis of Sayat-Nova's prosody to suit his musical instrument.

Apresian, G. Z.
1968   "Estetika eposa David Sasunskii." [Aesthetics of the Epic David of Sassoun.] *Banber Erevani Hamalsarani* 2:89–108.
Real beauty of the world and its inner harmonies; man and nature one.

Arabian, Tovmas K.
1971   "Hushamadean Severagi." [Memorial of Severag.] Beirut, Sevan Press, 504 pp. il., map.
Of folklore interest, pp. 429–452. In Severag wedding horses for bride and groom arranged in advance. Bride's horse decorated with needlework, etc. All decorations go to owner of horse, plus a gift. Examples of various kinds of songs, some sayings with meanings; Lent and foods; beliefs.

Arakelian, B. N.
1956   "Razvitie remesla i tovarnogo proizvodstva v Armenii v IX–XIII vekakh." [Development of Handicrafts and Goods Made in Armenia in the 9th–13th Centuries.] *Sovetskaia Arkheologii* 26:118–152. il.
Variety of crafts and metal working, ceramics, bookbinding, etc. Of special interest to designers.

1977   "Akademikos Hovsep Orbeli." [Academician Hovsep Orbeli.] *PH* 1:19–30. port. Russian summary.
On occasion of Orbeli's 90th birthday. Orbeli student of art; antiquities division of Hermitage. Also a folklorist.

1978   "Armenian Mosaic of the Early Middle Ages." *Simposia Internationale di Arte Armena*, 1st, Bergamo, 28–30, June 1975. *Atti* 1–18. Venice, St. Lazar.
Illustrations of special interest since they show motifs used in decoration—grapes and varieties of birds.

1987 "Akademikos Hovsep Orbeli." *L* 10:3–13. port.

On occasion of 100th year of Orbeli's birth. Versatile man: archeologist, Caucasus specialist, Armenologist, compiler of Kurdish-Russian dictionary. During World War II directed move of Hermitage treasures to safety. In 1939 in charge of Russian translation of David of Sassoun and prepared introduction; in 1956 compiled medieval Armenian proverbs.

Arakelian, B. N., and Ioannisian, A. R.

1951 *Istoriia armianskogo naroda.* [History of the Armenian People.] Erevan, Haypethrat. vol. 1, il. (part col.).

Only first volume seen. Includes some pictures of implements and head dress.

Arakelian, Gohar

1988 "Nerkararutyun arevelyan Hayastanum." [Dyeing in Eastern Armenia.] *L* 3:49–55. Russian summary.

Up to second half of 19th century dyeing done in villages. Plant and animal sources for color; formulas often secret of women. Color specialties of some villages.

Arakelian, H.

1898 "Kiurdere irants tune." [The Kurds in Their Home.] *AH* 4:144–158..

Notes that since some Kurds live in Armenian areas, it is well to give brief information about tribes, occupations, customs, etc.

Aramian, Garabed [also called Aramian, Charles Garabed]

1952 *Zaveshtakirk ev erazahan.* [Book of Humor and Dream Interpretation.] New York, Yeprad Press. 223 pp. English title page gives title as *Armenian Droll Stories and Dream Book.*

Dream portion, pp. 127–222, is arranged alphabetically by object seen in dream, followed by one or two line interpretation.

Arkayik [no first name]

1908–10 "Ghapani avandutiunnerits." [From the Traditions of Ghapan.] *AH* 18:106–108; 19:90–94.

Traditions about occupations and Christ and science.

1910 "Ghapani banavor grakanutyunits." [From the Oral Literature of Ghapan.] *AH* 20:112–114.

Gives first lines of 25 *jangyulum* in dialect and 10 prayers. The *jangyulum* is a special quatrain verse form used in fortune songs.

Armen, Marka

1937 "Hay erazhshdutiune." [Armenian Music.] *H* 15(3):71–89; 15(4):109–129.

Historical view starting with pre-Christian times through minstrels. Section on Komitas and his collection of folk songs.

Armenian Relief Society. Western Section. Sophia Chapter.
1985?   *Armenian Costume Through the Centuries*. Fresno, Calif. 107 pp. col. il.
               Title page and introduction in English, Armenian, and French. Most
               costumes copied from pictures from historical sources shown in
               publication of "Hay Guin" Society of Teheran, but fabrics and colors not
               identical. Models wearing costumes are named local persons.

Arnag [no first name]
1936   "Gomidas Vartabed." *H* 14(3):73–85. il.
               About life and work of Komitas, the Armenian folk song collector who
               studied in Erevan, Tiflis, and Germany. Illustration shows his choral
               group in Constantinople.

Arnag [no first name] *(continued)*
1937   "Gudina" [Kutahya.] *H* 15(9):97–106. il.
               Mostly description of locality, and some history. Of interest, pp. 104–105
               about wedding.

Arnot, Robert
1901   *Armenian Literature, Comprising Poetry, Drama, Folk Lore and Classic
               Traditions*. Rev. ed. London and New York, The Colonial Press. 142 pp.
               Bound with *Babylonian and Armenian Literature*. Only part of book
               includes folklore: some proverbs on pp. 1–6, an unspecified version of
               David of Sassoun, in prose, on pp. 55–79, as well as a couple of folktales
               on pp. 7–44, all trans. by F. B. Collins.

Aroutyounian. *See also* Arutiunian and Harutyunian.

Aroutyounian, S. R., and Sahakian, A. S.
1975–76   "Nouveaux enregistrements de l'épopée 'David de Sasun.' " *REA* n.s.
               11:255–267.
               Tabulates number of versions discovered in various districts in 1971,
               1972, 1973. First time four women narrators. Article first appeared in *PH*
               1973(1):224–233 with title "Sasna Tsrer zhoghovrdakan vepi norahayt
               patumnere," by S. Harutyunian and A. Sahakian, then in Russian in
               Sovetskaia Etnografia 1975(2):80–86, with title "Novye zapisi eposa
               'David Sasunski,' " by S. Arutiunian and A. Sh. Saakian.

Arsharuni, A.
1961   *Hay zhoghovrdakan taterakhagher*. [Armenian Folk Theatrical Plays.]
               Erevan, Haypethrat. 339 pp.
               Celebrations of certain Armenian festivals are considered as theatrical
               productions, e.g., Shrovetide, *vijag* (fortune game). Much attention given
               to weddings, not only description but also typical conversations when
               asking for hand of girl. Includes notes.

Arutiunian. *See also* Aroutyounian and Harutyunian

Arutiunian, S. B.
1969   "Otrazhenie drevnevostochnoi zhatvennoi mifologii v zagadke o paenitse."
    [The Reflection of Old Oriental Narrative Literature About Harvesting in the
    Wheat Riddle.] *L* 11:67–77. Armenian summary.
        Wheat riddle appears in Armenian tradition, folklore, and literature as well
        as in European folklore. Notes that Archer Taylor found its roots in
        Christ's life and suffering. Author believes founded on Oriental motifs
        about death and resurrection of Gods.

1971   "Relikty blagoslovenii pri obshchestvennoe zhertvopoedanii." [Relics of
    blessings offered at public gatherings.] *PH* 3:256–262.
        Notes toasts in 15 languages and Armenian; such sayings as "To your
        health," etc.

1976   "Mifologicheskii obraz solntsa zagadke o lampade." [Mythological Image of
    the Sun in the Icon Lamp Riddle.] *PH* 1:237–242. Armenian summary.
        The riddle: "The snake in the sea, precious stone in its jaw." There are 50
        variants in Eastern and Western Armenian. Examination of riddle reveals a
        substitute foundation of riddle as portrayal of sun in ancient fables.

Arutiunov, S. A.
1979   "Analiz i otsenka izbeganiia" [Analysis and Appraisal of Avoidance]
    Sovetskaia Etnografiia 1:53–56. English summary.
        Avoidance should be linked with traditions of different groups to fill
        social and psychological practices. Ethical evaluation with social and
        historical context. Disagrees with Ia. S. Smirnova and A. I. Pershits,
        same journal 1973(6). Gives no pages.

Arutiunov, S. A., and Mkrtumian, Iu. I.
1981   "Problema klassifikatsii elementov kultury." [The Problem of Culture
    Classification.] *Sovetskaia Etnografiia* 4:3–15.
        About Armenian Food System classed with Near East: milk, subclass
        grain and cattle class of grain subtype within agricultural type. Meat
        products limited to ritual consumption or special events.

Arvanian, Veronica
1954   "The Living Cult of the Great Mother Anahit." *Armenian Review* 7(2):25–32.
        Anahit, the Armenian goddess of virtue, purity, charity helps at child
        birth, protects Armenian people. Connected with mother earth, growth of
        wheat. Certain expressions still reminders of Great Mother and use of
        certain wheat foods used on special occasions. Gives examples. Armenian
        translation in *H* (1956) 34(4):32–40 with title "Gentani bashdamunke
        Anahid Mayr astvadzdzuhiun."

Asadourian, Hagop H.
1962   *Gomidas Vartabed ev Hay Erke*. [Gomidas Vartabed and the Armenian
            Song.] [Printed in Beirut by "Ani."] 89 pp. ports.
            Collection of author's writings that appeared in various papers.
            Accomplishments of Komitas as collector of folk music; also as
            composer. Author supports editing some texts of songs; gives examples.

Asatrian, As., et al.
1954   *Hay Grakanutiun*. [Armenian Literature.] Erevan, HSSR, GA Hrat. 3 v.
            Of folklore interest: v. 1:20–37 about Armenian myths and legends; brief
            summary of David of Sassoun, pp. 84–103; about minstrel Sayat-Nova,
            pp. 203–211. Vol. 2:122–142, various kinds of folk songs, with
            examples.

Ashot, Ashugh [Ashot Dadalian]
1946   *Ashughakan erger*. [Minstrel Songs.] Erevan, Haypethrat. 33 pp.
            Of the 27 songs the first is "Stalin." Most are love songs. The minstrel
            was from Zangezur.

Aslanian, H. Jack
1986   "Armenian Healers and their Métier." *Armenian Review* 39(2):1–26.
            Designates healers; materia medica 5th–17th centuries.

Aslanian, Vahe
1950   *A Comparative Analysis of the Sharagan and Folk Song and Their Role in
            Armenian Culture*. 121 pp. M.A. Thesis, Claremont Graduate School.
            Not seen.

Astuatsaturian, Georg
1903   "Sayat-Novayi anhayt ergerits." [From the Unknown Songs of Sayat-Nova.]
            AH 10:94–112.
            Songs found in Georgian archives of Academy of Sciences in St.
            Petersburg. Texts are given.

Ataian, Robert. *See* Atayan, R. A.

Atayan, R. A.
1961   "Hay zhoghovrdakan erazhshtutyan usumnasirutyan mi kani hartser." [A Few
            Problems About the Study of Armenian Folk Music.] *PH* 3–4:39–57.
            Soviet Armenian folk music collecting behind what Komitas had done
            alone. Collecting should go on, and work should be done on
            methodology of collecting by experts.

1964   "Komitas-sobiratel' armianskii narodnoi pesni." [Komitas—Collector of
        Armenian Folk Music.] *Congrès International des Sciences Anthropologique
        et Ethnologique*, 7th, Moscow, 3–10 Aug. 1964. *Actes*, v. 7:329–333.
        Information on collection of folk music by Komitas. Pp. 527–529 give
        musical notation of seven songs.

1969   "Les chants des maitres arméniens de moyen-age." *Musica Antiqua* 2:121–
        345. Polish summary.
        Covers from ancient period to middle ages, *gusans* (minstrels), work
        songs; also some church music.

1969   "Hay kaghakayin zhoghovrdakan erge Komitasi steghtsagortsutyan mej."
        [Urban Armenian Folk Music in the Work of Komitas.] *L* 11:27–34.
        Komitas believed that no true Armenian folk music ever created in the
        towns. But he was aware that rising feeling of nationalism inspired some
        music in towns. He transcribed some into musical notations. Some music
        included.

1969   "Komitase Hay zhoghovrdakan ergeri havakogh." [Komitas Collector of
        Armenian Folk Songs.] *Banber Erevani Hamalsarani* 2:143–152.
        Komitas lived and worked in villages, took part in social life to collect
        songs. Kinds of folk songs given with example of each kind by name and
        its special features. Collected 4000 folk songs of which over 1000 now
        exist. Outstanding contribution to folk music.

1969   "Komitasi erazhshtakan azgagrakan zharangutyunen." [From the Legacy of
        Komitas's Ethnomusicology.] *PH* 2:43–62. Russian summary.
        Summary of collections of various kinds of manuscripts. Komitas
        collected 4000 folk songs. Words of songs reflect history, spirit of
        people. Only 1200 songs vocalized. Much of Komitas material scattered
        or lost because of his exile in 1915 and his illness.

1969   "Komitasi steghtsagortsakan zharangutyan mi kani hartser." [A Number of
        Questions Relating to the Creative Legacy of Komitas.] *PH* 4:15–29. Russian
        summary.
        Songs published at various periods and variants that show polyphony.
        Specifies 70 songs with 100 variants that have been published in three
        volumes.

1978   "Element der Mehrstimmgkeit in der armenischen Volksmusik." In *Essays in
        Armenian Music*, ed. by Vrej Nersessian, London, Kahn Averill, pp. 179–
        188. English summary on p. 188 incorrect; see summary right after table of
        contents.
        Armenian music usually considered monodic, and the polyphonic is
        neglected, but Komitas pointed out polyphonic best represented in folk
        songs. Includes musical notations. Article also published in *Beiträge zur
        Musikgeschichte Östeuropa*, 1977:428–437.

Atayan, R. A. *(continued)*
1980   "Komitas [Gomidas] Soghomonian [Soghomon]." In *The New Grove Dictionary of Music and Musicians*. London, Macmillan, vol. 10:166–168.
            Survey of life of Komitas, education, and study in Berlin. Collected folk music, was a composer, ethnomusicologist, choral director, teacher. Led choirs in Istanbul, Smyrna, Alexandria, Cairo. List of his works.

1988   "The Horovels [plowing songs] of Karabagh in Komitas's Musical Notations." *Kroonk* 7:26–27.
            Komitas made notation of plowman's song, "Draw, Pull off." Not certain if he was ever in Karabagh, but he discovered the song and wrote it down in 1890.

1988   "Komitasi usumnarutyune Berlinum." [The Education of Komitas in Berlin.] *PH* 2:48–59. Russian summary.
            Komitas studied music in Berlin from 1896–1899. Gives courses studied and names of teachers.

Atrpet. *See* Mubayajian, Sargis

Avagian. *See* Avakian

Avakian, Anne M.
1987   "Three Apples Fell From Heaven." *Folklore* 98:95–98.
            About terminal formula of many Armenian folktales. Title of paper is the formula; explanation is given of probable origin.

Avakian, Hovh.
1925   "Karekin eb. Srvantsdiants." [Bishop Karekin.] In his *Kragan temker*. [Literary Portrayals.] New York. pp. 115–123.
            Biographical sketch, and about survey of Armenian provinces in latter part of 19th century.

Avakian, N. K.
1967   "Haykakan gulpanern u srnapannere ev nrants zardanakhshere." [Armenian Socks and Gaiters and their Designs.] *PH* 4:250–257. il.
            Until 20th century, girls knitted socks and gaiters for their hope chests. Designs often local. Wool, and sometimes silk used, latter for women. One-color or multi-colored, natural motifs, some embroidered.

1970   "Sebastiayi ev shrchaka kyugheri zhoghovrdakan taraze XIX darum ev XX dari skzbin." [The Folk Costume of Sebastia and Environs in the 19th Century and beginning of 20th Century.] *PH* 2:223–232. il.
            Gives pattern outlines of underwear and outer garments. Photos of embroidered aprons and vests.

1971   "Bartsr Hayki zhoghovrdakan taraze XIX darum ev XX dari skzbin." [The Folk Costume of Upper Armenia in the 19th Century and beginning of 20th Century. *PH* 4:183–196. il. Russian summary.

     Gives outline drawings of garments, quantity of fabric needed, kinds of fabric used. Pictures of sashes with woven designs—each area has distinctive design.

1972   "Sposoby ornamentatsii traditsionnoi odezhdy Armian v XIX–XX vekakh." [Modes of Ornamentation of Traditional Armenian Costumes in the 19th and 20th Centuries. *Sovetskaia Etnografiia* 4:108–117. il.

     Shows embroidered belts, and other decoration on costumes. One piece of jewelry illustrated. Costumes for men and women included from various areas.

1975   "Aparani ev Aragatsi shrjanneri zhoghovrdakan taraze XIX dari verjin ev XX dari skzbin." [The Folk Costume of the Aparan and Aragats Areas in the Latter 19th Century and Beginning of 20th Century.] *PH* 2:245–253. il.

     Types of fabric used. Also pictures of garments. One plate shows elaborate embroidery on cap and other items.

1976   "Ob Areslakh narodnogo kostuma Armian (XIX–nachalno XXv." [About the Arealak Folk Costumes 19th to Beginning of 20th Century.] *Kavkazskii Etnograficheskii Sbornik* 6:188–201. il. (part col.)

     Descriptive information; includes line drawings as well as pictures of costume for men and women of Arealak area.

1983   *Haykakan zhoghovrdakan taraze, XIX d.–XX d.skizp.* [Armenian Folk Costume, 19th Century–Beginning of 20th Century.] Erevan, HSSH, GA. 109 pp. il.

     Black and white designs in text; 66 figures in plates at end, jewelry included. Also a glossary.

Avdalbekian, S. T.
1964   "Buyseri pashtamunki azdetsutyune Haykakan mi kani teghanunneri vra." [The Influence of Plant Worship on Some Armenian Place Names.] *PH* 4:223–225.

     Worship of certain trees in pagan times has remained in the names of villages and later on church monasteries.

1976   "Patmut'iun hamaspiur tsaghkin." [Story of the Flower Campion.] *PH* 1:258–259.

     A wonder-working flower, e.g., a snake gains extra strength from the flower. Mkhitar Gosh refers to the flower in his fable 26. Flower belongs to the genus Lychnis. It has been said that a snake on a rampart looked down on Alexander's army and 300 died.

Axon, William A. E.
1881   "An Armenian Legend." *Notes and Queries*, 6th series 4:147.
                About place name Lezk based on legend of "Ara the beautiful," king of
                Armenia, and Semiramis.

Ayvazian, Abraham H.
1893   *Shar Hay gensakruteants*. [A Series of Armenian Biographies.]
                Constantinople, K. Baghdadian. 3 v. in 1.
                Vol. 1:74–112 about Matevos Tbir of 18th century and early 19th century
                who prepared something like an almanac that gave advice—what to eat,
                etc. Vol. 3:209–215 about a minister, M. K. Chafrasdjian, who used
                certain expletives when he became angry.

Ayvisun, Hripsime
1956   "Haygagan barere." [Armenian Dances.] *H* 34:74–73.
                Describes kinds of dances, including those that involve songs. Examples
                of songs are given.

Azadian, T.
1943   *Agn ev Agntsik*. [Agn and the Agn Folk.] Istanbul, H. Aprahamian. 130 pp.
                il.
                Short historical, ethnographic, and biographical compilation. Devotes pp.
                14–28 to G. Janigian's work on Agn folklore with some examples of
                songs. Includes some lullabies, wedding songs, love songs, songs of
                longing, laments. Bibliography of Agn, pp. 119–130.

B., C. C.
1888   "Armenian Christmas." *Notes and Queries* 7th series, 5:236.
                Notes January 6 is date of Christmas. Cites Morer's Dictionary, 1694.

Babakhanian, Arakel
1916   "Avedik Ezekyan." *AH* 26:220.
                Obituary.

Babayan, F. S.
1967   "Mijnadaryan jnarakats mi kani nmushneri masin." [About a Few examples of
                Medieval Glazed Earthenware.] *PH* 1:147–151. il.
                Examples from Dvin and Ani. Of interest for designs; notes symbolism of
                animal figures from 11th–13th centuries.

Babayan, L.
1897   " 'Khalder' anune." [The Name "Khalder."] *AH* 2:300–306.
                Extended summary of article in *Zeitschrift für Ethnologie* about Urartian
                name Khaldi. No specific citation is given of the original article.

1907   "Hamurabii orenagirke." [Hamurabi's Law Book.] *AH* 15:53–61.
        Old laws reflect Babylonian culture. Comparisons should be made with
        Biblical laws.

1907   "Parskastani krakapashtnere." [The Fire Worshippers of Persia.] *AH* 18:37–
        58.
        Historical information about beliefs and religious rites and customs.

Badmakrian. *See* Patmagrian

Badrik. *See* Patrik

Baghdasarian, V. S.
1979   "Sayat-Novayi davtari ev mi kani khagheri masin." [About Notebook and
        Some Songs of Sayat-Nova.] *PH* 1:233–243. Russian summary.
        Sayat-Nova's notebook reveals that some songs are in cipher in form of
        alphabet rhymes.

Baghdasarian-Tapaltsian, S. H.
1958   *Msho barbare.* [The Dialect of Mush.] Erevan, HSSH, GA Hrat, 276 pp.
        This dialect study has supplement that has 15 stories and anecdotes in
        dialect. Also 710 proverbs and sayings, and some blessings. A dialect
        word list and a classified Armenian word list followed by equivalents in
        Mush dialect.

Baghdigian, S. A.
1934   *Arabgir ev shrchagayi kiughere.* [Arabgir and its Neighboring Villages.]
        Beirut, "Vahakn." 156 pp. il .
        Of special interest pp. 44–122: domestic architecture, food, festival days,
        home remedies, death and burial, proverbs and sayings, curses,
        blessings. Examples of songs for special events (some in Turkish). Page
        65 describes meeting groom-to-be with lights and music when invited to
        dinner on the Saturday after engagement.

Baghramian, Rh. H.
1960   *Dersimi barbarayin kartese.* [Dialect Map of Dersim.] Erevan, HSSH, GA
        Hrat. 177 pp. 3 fold. maps.
        Dialects from some Kharpert-Erzingan area villages. Grammatical
        explanations and examples of stories, anecdotes, sayings of specific
        villages. Word lists included.

Baião, Antonio
1923   *Itenerarios da India a Portugal por terra.* Coimbra, Impr. da Universidade.
        xxxvii, 309 pp. 6th ed.
        Itinerary of Antonio Tenreiro and Mestre Afonso of 16th century. This
        work makes earliest mention of Armenian epic David of Sassoun (see pp.
        217, 226–228.) *See* R. Gulbenkian and H. Berberian, 1971.

Bakalian, Amy
1985   "The Armenian Family and Related Topics; a Bibliography." *Armenian Review* 38(4):23–40.
              Includes some folklore material. Most of items in English or European languages, and some in Russian.

Bakhchinian, H. G.
1975   "Sayat-Novayi erek tsatskagri vertsanutyune." [Deciphering Three Cryptograms of Sayat-Nova.] *PH* 4:169–173. Russian summary.
              Generally believed that Sayat-Nova composed nothing after 1759, but the deciphered cryptograms are proof that they date from 1792.

1986   "Ditoghutyunner Sayat-Novayi Davtari Veraperyal." [Observations on Sayat-Nova's Notebook.] *PH* 3:209–221.
              The Notebook is a reconstruction of original book of songs from which some pages lost. Compares some of changes in songs.

1987   "Sayat-Novayi dzadzgakire." [Sayat-Nova's Secret Writing.] *HA* 101:833–839.
              Author quotes from Sayat-Nova's songs in Armenian, Georgian, and Azerbaijani and states there are clues in them of birth date and name of his wife.

1987   "Sayat-Novayi Vratseren khagheri lezun." [The Language of Sayat-Nova's Georgian Songs.] *L* 12:21–26. Russian summary.
              On occasion of 275th year of minstrel's birth. Sayat-Nova's language close to the people, and not the courtly language assumed. Gives examples.

1988   *Sayat-Nova, kianke ev gortse.* [Sayat-Nova, his Life and Work.] Erevan, H. Kh.S.H., GA Hrat. 350 pp.
              Have seen review only. Reviewed in *Banber Erevani Hamalsarani* 1989(3):213–215, by A. G. Madoyan. A detailed account of Sayat-Nova's songs and dances in three languages—Armenian, Georgian, Azerbaijani.

Bamberger, Joan
1986–87   "Family and Kinship in an Armenian-American Community." *Journal of Armenian Studies* 3:77–86.
              Notes that some of old customs of engagements and wedding rituals persist today.

Bampukchinian, G.
1980   " 'Krunk' ergin hnaguyn bnagire." [The Earliest Version of the Song "Krunk."] *PH* 2:105–109.
              Various 18th century printed versions, but notes that there was a 1639 copy existing. The 12-stanza version of mid-17th century is given in text.

Although not stated here, it is believed it is not a folk song despite contrary idea held by some. Krunk (Grung) means crane.

Barakian, V. J.
1921   *Paroyalits zaveshdner.* [Pleasant Jests.] Fresno, Calif., Bedros R. Torosian. 161 pp.
         Probably the first collection of jokes published by an Armenian in California. Some of jokes are general, some distinctly Armenian. One concerns Armenians in San Francisco in 1860.

1922   *Khohanotsi kirk.* [Cookbook.] Fresno, Calif., "Nor Giank-Aror." 119 pp.
         Includes 182 recipes of which 71 are Armenian. Interesting to note food acculturation. Non-Armenian recipes include cakes, pies, candies. Some household hints included. No alphabetical index.

Barseghian, L. A.
1967   "Gegham lerneri 'vishapnere.' " [The Serpents (or Dragons) of the Gegham Mountains.] *PH* 4:181–188. il. Russian summary.
         Fishlike monuments found in several localities. A French translation of this article appears in *REA* n.s. 5:289–293. il. 1968. Translated by Martiros Minassian with the title "Les višaps des monts Guegham."

Bartikian, H.
1962   "Aghtamar ev 'Digenes Akritase.' " [Aghtamar and "Digenes Akritas."] *PH* 3:256–257.
         Commentary on article by A. A. M. Bryer in *Antiquity* (1960) 34:295–297. Bryer should have seen greater relationship to David of Sassoun.

1963   "Byuzandakan 'Digenis Akritasi' vipergutyune ev nra nshanakutyune hayagitutyan hamar." [The Byzantine epic "Digenis Akritas" and its significance in Armenology.] *PH* 3:185–194. Russian summary.
         Important to compare this Byzantine epic with David of Sassoun since about same period, 9th–10th centuries.

1963   "Tork (Turk) Angeghi araspeli veraprumnere 'Sherefname'um." [Vestiges of Turk Angegh in "Sherif-name."] *PH* 2:294–295.
         Tale related to Angegh family; used much among Armenians that it moved into Muslim world of Kurds.

Basmadjian, Garig
1976   "76 Armenian Proverbs and Sayings." *Ararat* 17(1):25–26.

1978   "More Armenian Proverbs and Sayings." *Ararat* 19(2):47.
         A list of 22 proverbs and sayings.

Basmajian, K. H.
1890   *Social and Religious Life in the Orient.* New York, American Tract Society.
            247 pp. il.
                 Of Armenian folklore interest, pp. 156–163 about engagements and
                 weddings, dowry, and life of bride in father-in-law's house.

1907   "Zvartnots beveragri aritov." [About the Inscription of Zvartnots.] *AH*
            16:210–211.
                 About reading of cuneiform inscription of ruined Zvartnots church.

Basset, René
1896   "Les anciens chants historiques et les traditions populaires des l'Arménie."
            Revue des Traditions Populaires 11:323.
                 About date of Moses of Khoren's *History*—not 5th century, but 8th
                 century. Commentary on article by E. L Lalayan in same journal, pp.
                 129–138 .

1921   "Le folklore dans le 'Journal Asiatique.' " *Revue Africaine*, no. 306–7:15–
            46.
                 Useful bibliographic information, but Armenian section brief, pp. 30–31.

Batikian, Levon
1971   "Mkrtich Emin (1815–1890)." *Erevani Hamalsarani Lratu* 10:42. port.
            Russian summary.
                 Biographical sketch. Emin was interested in foreign languages and
                 literature at Lazarian Institute.

1974   "Mkrtich Emin Hay hetanosakan mshakuyti masin." [Mkrtich Emin About
            Pagan Armenian Culture.] *Banber Erevani Hamalsarani* 1:206–214. Russian
            summary.
                 Author confirms idea that Emin was the first who studied Armenian and
                 foreign manuscripts to show importance of Armenian pantheon and its
                 role and meaning in Armenian pagan life.

Bayan, G.
1909   *Armenian Proverbs and Sayings.* Venice, Academy of St. Lazar. 52 pp.
                 The 254 proverbs and sayings given in Armenian are followed by English
                 translation. Not in alphabetical or topical order. There are several editions
                 of this work dating from 1888 to 1922.

Bdoyan, V.
1956   "Harsnakan tseseri u sovoruytneri nkaragir, gratsvats 14-rd darum."
            [Description of wedding rites and customs as written in the 14th century.]
            Banber Madenadarani 1:53–56.
                 Of special interest since wedding information usually dated in more recent
                 times.

1964   "Sharatsan sisteme Vana lchi avazanum." [The System of Drill Sowing in the Lake Van Basin.] *PH* 1:242–257. il.
        Explains methods of sowing and gives illustrations of implements.

1968   "Hundzi gortsiknere Hayastanum." [Harvesting Implements in Armenia.] *PH* 3:182–190. il.
        Shows pictures of sickles, scythes, forks, etc. from 9th–8th centuries B.C. from excavations. Some items still used in recent times.

1971   "Pontosi Hayeri varogh gortsiknere." [The Tilling Implements of the Pontic Armenians.] *PH* 4:197–205.
        Black Sea area implements and tools for tilling the soil in 6th–8th centuries.

1972   *Erkragortsakan mshakuyte Hayastanum.* [Agriculture in Armenia.] Erevan, HSSH, CA, Hrat. 508 pp. il.(part col.)
        Describes and illustrates agricultural tools and implements and their use. Of special interest, pp. 415–501 about the agricultural year and special rituals connected with festivals and their significance.

1974   *Hay azgagrutyun; hamarot uruagits.* [Armenian Ethnography; a Brief Outline.] Erevan, Erevani Hamalsarani Hrat. 287 pp. il.
        Brief biographical information on Armenian ethnographers; some collected a little folklore. Pictures of folk life, e.g., methods of moving heavy things. Extensive bibliographies for each chapter. Reviewed by S. Nahapetian in *Banber Erevani Hamalsarani* 1975(1):227–229.

1976   "Entrutyan ev amusnutyan dzever 'Sasuntsi Davit' eposum." [Forms of Selection and Marriage in the Epic "David of Sassoun."] *Banber Erevani Hamalsarani* 1:84–99. Russian summary.
        Describes primitive selection of husband and wife and forms of marriage in matriarchal and patriarchal family in epic David of Sassoun.

1977   "Vanatur ev Amanor astvatsutyunneri tsptyal pashtamunkneri hartsi shurje." [About the Question of Disguised Ceremonies of the gods Vanatur and Amanor.] *Banber Erevani Hamalsarani* 2:146–161. il. Russian summary.
        Vanatur and Amanor protective gods of agriculture. During celebrations scarecrowlike figures used in ceremonies. With advent of Christianity appeared under various names. Bagrint province.

Bedickian, S. V.
1906   "Feet Washing Ceremony in the Orient." *Armenia* 2(8):46–48.
        Describes ceremony in an Armenian settlement (not named). Article taken from *The Presbyterian*, but issue not specified.

Bedickian, S. V. *(continued)*
1906   "How the Armenians Keep the New Year and Christmas." *Armenia* 3(2):8–12.
    "Gaghant Bab" of New Year described as giver of gifts. Aside from going to church, Christmas observed by visiting friends. Gift to godfather. [Note: Armenian Christmas is on Jan. 6.]

Bedoukian, Harold
1982   "Natural Dyes in Caucasian Rugs." *Armenian Review* 36:398–404.
    Describes sources of dyes used—kermis, cochineal, madder, indigo, saffron. Paper presented at 3rd Annual Symposium of the Armenian Rug Society, Sept. 25, 1982.

Bedrosian, Robert
1984   " 'Dayeakut'iun' in Ancient Armenia." *Armenian Review* 37(2):23–47.
    About boys reared by adoption until around puberty. Intended to protect children of nobility. Popular term of practice is "wet nurse": also known as tutor, governess. Breast kissing establishes relationship of mother and child.

Begian, Harry
1964   *Gomidas Vartabed: His Life and Importance to Armenian Music*. Thesis, Ed.D., University of Michigan. 267 pp.
    Notes this is first presentation in English aside from brief essays not always reliable. Makes exception to S. Poladian's work. Author uses historical approach to Komitas as folk song collector, performer, director, teacher, researcher, appearances abroad. Komitas received Ph.D. on Kurdish music in 1899, but thesis not available. See *Dissertation Abstracts* 26:1683.

Beglarian, Hrachya
1987   "Hatsagortsutyune mijnadaryan Hayastanum." [Bread Baking in Medieval Armenia.] *L* 5:72–78. Russian summary.
    Archeological discoveries reveal kinds of grains used for bread. Information also from notes in manuscripts. End of article names kinds of bread. Flour used for making puddinglike food. Grains also used for making beer.

Bénard, Auguste
1904   "Littérature populaire arméniennes." *L'Arménie* no. 188:3.
    Few folk songs from various places. Notes difficulty of revealing spirit of some in translation.

Benneyan, Garabed

1899   *Malatioy deghakragan ev azkakragan ashkhadaserutyune.* [A Work about Malatia's Topography and Ethnography.] [No place], Malatioy Grtasirats Ungeruteon Harazad Haduadzi Getronagan Varchutean. [Authorized Section of the Malatia Cultural Association's Central Committee.] 278 pp.

        Of special folklore interest are pp. 83–214, which give special attention to weddings, and some information on birth, death, burial, animal sacrifice, pilgrimages, festivals, songs, riddles, proverbs and sayings. Malatia dialect pp. 241–274 by Kriler Khantsian.

Bense (or Pense). *See* Movsisian, Sahak

Benveniste, E.

1927   "L'origine de višap arménien." *REA* 7:7–9.

        Variously known as serpent, demon, dragon. Indian and Iranian sources cited. Diabolic element in Armenian folklore.

Bergen, Fanny D.

1898   "Borrowing Trouble." *Journal of American Folklore* 11:55–59.

        Gives story of "My Son Ali" as narrated by Armenian woman. Terminal formula notes a basket coming down from heaven with 12 pomegranates: "Five for me, one for you, Josephine, one for you, Pailoun, one for you Arousiag, one for you, Diran, one for you, Augustine, one for you, Naomi, and one for you, George."

Bezhkeuk-Melikian, L.

1968   "Dagdany." [Dagdans.] *Dekorativnoe Iskusstvo SSSR* 1968(9):48–49. il.

        A collection of amulets and talismans of the Sevan district of Armenia. Mostly geometrical designs.

Billeter, Erika

1966   "Aghthamar: Christian Images in Armenian Anatolia." *Graphics* 22:516–523. il.

        About Church of the Holy Cross built 916–921. Exterior reliefs show plants, animals, and historical items aside from Biblical scenes. Animal symbolism said to be derived frorm Syria. Text in English, German, French.

Bishop, Ellsworth Chaney

1938   *The Origin and Early Development of the Inscribed-Greek Cross in Byzantine and Armenian Architecture.* 143 pp. Thesis, M.A. Columbia University.

        Not seen.

Bishop, Isabella L. Bird

1891   *Journeys in Persia and Kurdistan.* London, John Murray. 2 v. il.

        Some Armenian customs, dress, and superstitions are described in Vol. 1:269–279. Refers to community in Julfa.

Bittner, Maximilian
1909   "Ein armenischen Zauberstreifen." *Anthropos* 4:182–189.
                About some motifs used in Armenian magic, e.g., heavenly bodies,
                planets. Number squares shown for additions from all angles for specific
                numbers from 15; 34; 65; 111; 175; 260; 369; 505, 671; 870; 1105.

Biyagov, Leonid, and Engibarian, Nora
1982   "Pashtamunkayin ojakhner Oshakanits." [Worship Hearths from Oshakan.] *L*
                7:96–98. il.
                Hearths date from 6th–5th centuries B.C. at time when Armenians were
                fire worshipers in the Oshakan area.

Black, George Fraser
1912–13   "The Gypsies of Armenia." *Gypsy Lore Society. Journal*, n.s. 6:327–330.
                Information from the manuscript collection of the late A. T. Sinclair. Rev.
                Geo. C. Reynolds [i.e., Raynolds], missionary in Van, says only few
                Gypsies in Van. They make hair sieves for flour; also make tambourines
                and blacking pigment for eyes. R. M. Cole of Bitlis says they are dancers
                and enchantresses.

Blenkinsopp, E. Leaton
1888   "Armenian Christmas." *Notes and Queries* 7th series, 5:236–237.
                Jan. 6 is nativity; Epiphany 24 days after our Christmas.

Bodenstedt, Friedrich
1865   *Tausend und ein Tag in Orient.* Berlin, R. Decker. 220 pp.
                Description of Armenian wedding, pp. 102–118, includes direct quotes of
                priest's part in ceremony.

Boettiger, Louis A.
1920   *Armenian Legends and Festivals.* Minneapolis, Minn., University of
                Minnesota. 96 pp. (Minn. Univ. Research Publications. Studies in the Social
                Sciences, no. 14.)
                Selective study of Armenian social life from pagan times to later period
                when historical legends and festivals were converted to Christian festivals
                which have contributed to Armenian identity. Originally M.A. thesis,
                Univ. of Minn., 1918.

Boghosian, Efrem
1952   *Nor darvoy done, hin ev nor Hayots kov; Knnagan usumnasirutiun.* [The
                New Year Festival Among Ancient and Recent Armenians; a Critical Study.]
                Vienna, Mkhitarian Dbaran. 100 pp.
                A special feature is presentation of various forms in different regions.
                Also about celebrations by Armenians outside Armenia, e.g., in Tiflis,
                Hungary, Crimea.

1956   *Hampartsman done ev Hay zhoghovurti vijagakhaghe.* [The Ascension Festival and the Armenian Fortune Game.] Vienna, Mkhitarian Dbaran. 216 pp.

Describes preparations and procedures; gives illustrations of songs used in festival. Also describes how festival is observed in 72 areas and villages. Includes music.

Boghosian, H. B.

1942   *Hajeni Enthanur badmutiune ev shrchagay Kozan-Daghi Hay kiughere.* [The General History of Hajin and its Surrounding Armenian Villages of Kozan-Dagh.] Los Angeles, Bozart Press. 857 pp. il., maps.

Social life, family life and customs, pp. 185–229, e.g., weddings, festivals, folk songs; proverbs and sayings, curses, blessings, superstitions. Dialect with some examples, pp. 279–341.

Bolton, H. Carrington

1896   "Armenian Folk-lore." *Journal of American Folk-lore* 9:293–296.

Consists of reviews of *Armenian Popular Songs*, trans. into English, 3rd ed. pub. at Venice, St. Lazar, 1888; *Armenian Proverbs and Songs*, trans. into English by G. Bayan, Venice, St. Lazar, 1889; *Turkish Proverbs*, trans. into English, Venice, St. Lazar, 1880. Suggests European influences.

Bond, Carrie Jacobs

1925   "Armenian Music." *Overland Monthly*, series 2, 83:197–198.

Brief information about pagan songs; when Christianity appeared peasants clung to old songs and folklore. Mentions *ashughs* (minstrels). Music among Armenian orphans administered by the Near East Relief.

Bonet-Maury, G.

1887   "La légende d'Abgar et le Thaddée et les missions chrétienne à Edesse." *Revue de l'histoire des Religions* 16:269–281.

Moses of Khoren claims that Abgar was an Armenian who sent a letter to Jesus to come and cure his sickness. Legend appears in Greek, Syrian, and Armenian.

Borcherdt, Donn

1959   "Armenian Folk Songs and Dances in the Fresno and Los Angeles Areas." *Western Folklore* 18:1–12.

Includes lyrical, dance, and wedding songs; also humorous and sentimental songs, and songs of revolution. Transliterations and translations given in examples. Some music included.

Botsford, Florence Hudson

1921–22   *Folk Songs of Many Lands.* New York, The Woman's Press. 3 v.

In vol. 2:351–367 there are eight Armenian folk songs harmonized; Armenian texts and translations are given.

Bouchor, Maurice
1919   "Coup d'oeil sur le folklore de l'Arménie." *Revue des Traditions Populaires* 34:149–157.
            Gives excerpts and summaries and comments on "The Horde and the Ox"; "The Kurdish Girl"; "The Wise Weaver."

Bourgeois, Henri
1910   "Kani me khosk Hay-poshaneru lezuin vray." [A Few Words about Armenian-Gypsy Language.] *B* 68:265–269.
            Notes some studies made about language of Gypsies in Armenia; gives a word list and a tale in Armenian and Gypsy form.

Bowra, C. M.
1978   *Heroic Poetry*. London, Macmillan. 589 pp. (Reprint of 1952 edition.)
            Important for comparative comments about David of Sassoun and other epics.

Boyajian, Zabelle C.
1916   *Armenian Legends and Poems*. London, J. M. Dent. 195 pp. col. il.
            Covers pagan, golden age, middle and modern periods. Reprinted in New York by Columbia University Press in 1959.

Boyce, Mary
1957   "The Parthian Gōsān and Iranian Minstrel Tradition. *Royal Asiatic Society. Journal* Part 1–2:10–45.
            Includes some information about Armenian *gusans* (minstrels) who were derived from Persian entertainers.

1977   *A Persian Stronghold of Zoroastrianism*. Oxford, Clarendon Press. 289 pp. il.
            There are some customs similar to Armenian ones, e.g., binding engagements; sacrificial feast; fortune game (Armenian *vijag*).

Brambilla, Mario Giovanni
1974–76   "Tipi di casa contadine Armine." *Palladio* 23–25:197–212.
            Floor plans and elevations of peasant houses; also pictures of various decorated tops of columns. Floor plans name the rooms.

Briusov, V.
1948   "The Poetry of Armenia." Trans. by Arra Avakian. *Armenian Review* 1(2):115–129; 1(3):117–129; 1(4):104–114.
            Part of the article about David of Sassoun. Also information on folk songs and notes that they probably derived from minstrels. Does not give original source from which translation was made.

1963   *Sayat-Nova*. Erevan, Izd-vo Armianskoi SSR. 46 pp.
            Includes 12 Sayat-Nova songs in Russian and Armenian, followed by a
            few pages about Sayat-Nova. Some comments about Briusov's
            translation by L. M. Mkrtchian.

1966   *Poeziia Armenii s drevneishikh vremen do nashikh dnei.* [Armenian Poetry
            from Ancient Times to our Days.] Erevan, Izd-vo "Aistan." 511 pp.
            First part of book includes some folk songs and some fortune (*vijag*)
            songs. Includes excerpts from David of Sassoun.

Briusov, V., and Lozinsko, M.
1939   *David Sasunskii.* Moscow, Gos Izd-vo Khodozhestvennaia Literetura. 78 pp.
            A presentation of part of epic David of Sassoun in verse.

Brustian, Ts. G.
1969   "Komitasi steghtsagortsakan skzbunknere." [The Creative Principles of
            Komitas.] *PH* 4:49–60. Russian summary.
            Folk music alone reflected spirit and characteristics of the people. Komitas
            studied folk song melody and the relation of words to the metrical
            structure of music. Polyphony also used. Notes that Komitas collected
            5000 songs.

Brutian, Margarita Aramovna
1971   *Hay zhoghovrdakan erazhshtakan steghtsagortsutyun. I. Geghjakakan Erg.*
            [Armenian Folk Music Creation. I. Peasant Music.] Erevan, "Luys" Hrat.
            274 pp.
            Includes music. First section devoted to musicology with examples of
            musical notation. Second part groups folk songs for work, rituals,
            lamentations, epical and historical themes, jovial songs, lullabies, lyrical
            and émigré songs.

1980   "Komitasi anvan konservatoroayi zhoghovrdakan erazhshtakan
            steghtsagortsutyan kabinete." [The Musical Composition Room for Folk
            Music in the Conservatory Named for Komitas.] *PH* 4:288–290.
            Room organized Oct. 1, 1969 on 100th anniversary of birth of Komitas.
            Purpose: to collect folk music, undertake publication of folk music,
            establish relations with other conservatories.

Bryer, A. A. M.
1960   "Akhthamar and Digenis Akritas." *Antiquity* 34:295–297. il.
            Considers that Digenis describes scenes of King Gagik's palace described
            by contemporary Armenian historian Ardzruni. Some characters in
            Digenis Akritas have Armenian names.

Bulatkin, Iliyan, and Heaton, Mary
1951   "A Rupee Earned: An Armenian Folktale Revealing a Moral on Work."
            Rotarian 79(6)11–12.
            About lazy boy who must work to get inheritance from father.

Buniatov, G.
1893   "Iz poverii predrazsudkov i narodnykh primet Armian Echmiadzinsago
            Uezd." [From the Armenian Beliefs, Prejudices and Folk Omens of the
            Echmiadzin District.] *Sbornik Materialov dlia Opisaniia Mestnostei i Plemen
            Kavkaza* 17(2):174–192.
            About supernatural beings, e.g., fairies, werewolves, demons. Call for
            rain, plagues, oracles for good fortune. Serpents as household protectors,
            attitudes towards animals and persons, etc. Domestic life.

1904   "Armianskiia poslovitsy." [Armenian Proverbs.] *Sbornik Materialov Dlia
            Opisaniia Mestnostei i Plemen Kavkaza* 34:63–90.
            Proverbs number 338 (pp. 63–88) are in Russian transliteration of
            Armenian followed by Russian translation. List of 20 omens (pp. 33–90)
            given only Russian translation.

Burat, Sempat
1935–38   "Lernagani me hushadedre." [Memoirs of a Mountaineer.] *B* 93:36–41; 91–
            100; 205–209; 246–251. 94:106–114. 95:82–89; 300–304. 96:211–215;
            306–316.
            Zeitun area. Special festivals, weddings. Games of Shrovetide, Holy
            Week and Easter. For Palm Sunday olive branches used. Easter eggs
            colored with onion skins. Harvesting, making confections, dances and
            songs. *Madagh* (animal sacrifice).

Burgin, G. B.
1896   "An Armenian wedding." *Chambers's Journal* 13:689–690. Also called vol.
            73, new series and 5th series.
            Place of wedding not specified, but present are a Turk and Kurd. Dance
            by Kurd and Persian. Ritual of dressing groom and going to church.

Burton, Richard, Donat, John, and Koralek, Paul
1958   "Achthamar." *Architectural Review* 123(732):175–181. il.
            Beliefs of the Church of the Holy Cross at Lake Van depict Biblical
            scenes, legendary animals.

C., E.
1876   "Armenian Folk Songs." *Fraser's Magazine*, n.s. 13:283–297.
            Songs relating to various festivals and legends. Examples of songs about
            nature, weddings, bird lays, laments. Notes minstrel contests of songs,
            riddles, repartee. Brief description of family life.

Carnoy, E. Henry, and Nicolaides, Jean
1967   *Les traditions populaires de l'Asie Mineure.* Paris, G. F. Maisonneuve &
         Larose. 369 pp. (Reprint of 1889 edition.)
            Two Armenian narrators are named, though the stories not designated as
            Armenian.

Carrière, A.
1895   "La legende d'Abgar dans l'Histoire d'Arménie de Moise de Khoren." In
         Centenaire de l'Ecole de Langues Orientales Vivantes, 1795–1895. Recueil de
         Memoires. Paris, Impr. Nationale, pp. 357–414.
            Gives summary and commentary on the Abgar legend.

1899   *Les huits sanctuaires l'Arménie payenne d'apres Agathange et Moise de*
         Khoren. Étude critique. Paris, Ernest Laroux. 29 pp. map.
            Armenian King Artashes I, in his conquests in Asia Minor, sent statues of
            Greek gods to Armenia where Armenian gods were worshiped.

Carswell, John, and Dowsett, C. J. F
1972   *Kütahya Tiles and Pottery from the Armenian Cathedral of St. James,*
         Jerusalem. Oxford, Clarendon Press. 2 v. il. (part col.).
            Tiles of interest for designs of ecclesiastical and secular costumes.
            Includes floral designs, and traditional designs from Armenian manuscript
            illustrations. Some copies of Chinese decoration. Date from 16th century,
            some believe 15th century.

Cesaresco. *See* Martinengo-Cesaresco, Evelyn

[Chahan de] Cirbied, [J.]
1820   "Memoire sur le gouvernement et sur la religion des anciens arméniens."
         Société Royale des Antiquaires de France. Mémoires 2:262–311. il.
            Names of gods and goddesses of Armenia; a list of names of each day of
            30-day month and the complementary days of the year, and names of
            hours of day and night.

Chalatianz. *See* Khalatian

Chambers, R.
1869   "Marriage Superstitions and Customs." In his *The Book of Days*, London,
         W. and R. Chambers, v. 1:721–722.
            Describes an Armenian wedding ceremony in a house instead of a church.

Chanikian, Hovseb K.
1895   *Hnutiune Akna.* [Antiquities of Akn.] Tiflis, H. D. Rodiniants. 505 pp.
            First part historical. Second part about customs, special festivals,
            weddings, superstitions, the 6000, fortune telling, evil spirits, *gabk*
            (bewitch); games and entertainments, proverbs and sayings, children's

Chanikian, Hovseb K. *(continued)*
language. Examples of wedding and dance songs. Not seen but taken
from Ghazikian, A. Gh. (1909–12)

Chantre, Ernest
1891   "Superstitions, répandues chez les Tatars de l'Aderbaidjan et recueilles à
Chouche (Arménie)." *Revue des Traditions Populaires* 6:467–469.
Very brief section on Armenian superstitions.

Chanzadjan, Emma
1980   "Kultarlagen in Metsamor im armenischen Hochland." *Des Altertum* 26:34–
40. il.
Metsamor an ancient worship site west of Erevan. Pictures of altars and
artifacts.

Charegh, Aram
1900   "Basen. Zhoghovrdakan erger." [Folk songs of Basen.] *AH* 6:383–390.
Folk songs from Russian section of Basen. There are 94 songs, mostly
dance songs. Basen folk barter dairy products for fruit.

Charuk, Ghazar
1957   *Hushamadean Partsr Hayki: Garinabadum.* [Memorial Book of Upper
Armenia: Garin History.] Beirut, Mshag Printers. 79 pp. il.
Considerable detail about engagement and marriage in Garin (Erzerum),
pp. 352–358. Wedding ceremony, pp. 365–368. Some folk verses in
dialect. Some sayings, pp. 385–391.

Chatterji, Saniti Kamar
1959   "Armenian Hero Legends, and the Epic of David of Sassoun." *Asiatic
Society, Calcutta. Journal* series 4 1:199–220.
Brief history of Armenia, early myths and legends, and David of
Sassoun.

Chaumont, Marie-Louise
1965   "Le culte de la désee Anahita (Anahit) dans la religion des monarques d'Iran et
d'Arménie au l^{er} siècle de notre ère." *Journal Asiatique* 253:167–181.
Most of article about Persia. Among Armenians cult associated with
water. When Armenia accepted Christianity, statues of Anahit destroyed.

Cherez, Minas. *See* Tcheraz, Minas

Cherkezian, G. H.
1981   "Afion Karahisari Haykakan hamaynke." [The Armenian Community of
Afion Karahisar.] *PH* 1:292–299.
Mostly about customs. Strict rule that girl should not see her fiance before
marriage. Anecdote about girl who, in effort to avoid, falls in hole; he

tries to help, she refuses his extended hand, so he informs her family to get her out.

Chituni, [Dikran]

1909   "Sasmants dun." [The Sassoun Clan.] HA 23:111–118, 186–190, 212–216, 274–279.

In parallel columns gives two variants of David of Sassoun in dialect of two villages. Noted to be continued, but was discontinued without explanation. In dialect of Gargar and Spargud.

1911   "Anahid-Arev-Astkhig ev Hay zhoghovrtagan vebe 'Teghtsun-Jam Kohar' " [Anahid-Sun-Astkhig and the Armenian folktale "Teghtsun-Jam Kohar."] *HA* 25:169–172.

Anahid the golden-haired symbol of the sun, golden-haired jewel. Equates Anahid with sun, Astkhig with night.

1911   "Zhoghovrtagan vebe ev deghagan sovorutyunner." [The Folk Epic and Local Customs.] *B* 69:237–238.

A variant of David of Sassoun about clergyman who accompanied Queen Lusik. Custom still remains that someone must always be with bride, usually a close relative, to guide her how she should greet in-laws.

1911   "Zhoghovrtagan veberu hishadz tsiere." [Horses Mentioned in Folktales.] *B* 69:279–282.

Mentions Rostam Zal, David of Sassoun, and St. Sarkis.

1919   *Hampartsman "vijag." Haykakan sovoroytner.* [Ascension Day "Fortune." Armenian Customs.] Constantinople, O. Arzumian. 39 pp.

Describes only the fortune festival observed by young girls and newly married girls. Songs sung are in quatrains.

1930   " 'Sasmants Dun,' Hay zhoghovrtagan tiutsatsnavebin ngarakire." [The Character of the Heroic Folk Epic "Sasmants Dun," i.e., David of Sassoun.] *H* 8(4):52–57.

About David of Sassoun, some variants, origin, national ideals, magnanimity.

1936   "Gomidasi hed." [With Gomidas.] *H* 15(2):80–99.

Chituni collected many folk songs in Van area; recalled tunes but could not transcribe musically, so Komitas helped him. Had meetings in 1907 and 1913. Tells of exile, illness and death of Komitas.

1943   *Sasunagan. Sassounacan, épopée populaire arménienne.* Paris, Araks-Topalian, 1942, i.e., 1943. 1168 pp. port.

Presents seven cycles of the epic, David of Sassoun, on which Chituni worked from 1907 to 1942. Comparing 35 variants, he produced a version in blank verse for the general reader. An English translation of last

Chituni, [Dikran] *(continued)*

       chapter of his work appears in *Journal of Mithraic Studies* 1976(1):107–108, by J. A. Boyle with title "Mher in the Carved Rock."

1949   "L'épopée populaire arménienne." International Congress of Orientalists. 21st, Paris, July 23–31, 1948. *Proceedings* 1949:368–371.

       About David of Sassoun, first recorded by Bishop Servantsian in 1874. Chituni gives his own notes on seven sections of epic. Compare V. Sb. Sahakian's article "Sasna Tsrer" in *L* 1971(4):66–77 concerning Chituni's idea of seven sections.

Chndi, Hachie. *See* Jndi, Hajie

Chobanian, Arshag

1898   "Drevne-Armianskaia literatura." [Ancient Armenian literature.] In *Bratskaia Pomoshch Postradavshim Turtsii Armianam*. 2nd ed. Moscow, I.N. Kushmanov, pp. 474–489. il.

       About heroic tales from Moses of Khoren's *History*.

1902   *Nahabed Kuchagi Divane*. [The Archive of Nahabed Kuchag.] Paris, "Anahid." 133 pp.

       Nahabed Kuchag, a 16th-century writer (d. 1592). His verses considered to be in tradition of minstrelsy. Selections of his love songs, allegorical and hortatory and émigré songs. Includes word list.

1903   *Chants populaires arméniens*. Paris, Libraire Paul Ollendorf. 268 pp. il.

       Some information about Armenian people, history, oral literature. Includes folk poems, songs about love, dance songs and songs for weddings, festivals, lullabies, funerals. Some religious poems and prayers, émigrés, national and miscellaneous subjects.

1906   *Les Trouvères arméniens*. 2nd ed. Paris, Société de France. 297 pp.

       A number of writers from the 13th century onwards who wrote in the minstrel tradition are included. Nahabed Kuchag a leading representative.

1918–29   *La Rosarie d'Arménie*. Paris, Editions Ernest Leroux. 3 v. il.

       Selection of various Armenian works of the Middle Ages. Vol. 2 of special interest since it includes minstrel songs.

1940   *Hayrenneru Purasdane*. [A Garden of Verses.] Paris, H. P. E. Miutian [Armenian General Benevolent Union.] 547 pp.

       A critical study of love songs, émigré songs attributed to the master minstrel Nahabed Kuchag and his followers Hovhannes Bluz, and Frik. Love songs, and some hortatory, allegorical, and religious songs included. The verse form "hayren" is a folk verse form of 15 syllables.

Chrakian, K.
1901   "Mgrdich Emin, 1815–1890." *B* 59:372–377. port.
          Biographical sketch. Emin essentially a linguist and connected with Lazarian Institute in Moscow for many years. In folklore remembered for his 1850 publication *Vebk hnoyn Hayasdani* [Ancient Tales of Armenia].

Chukasizian, B. L.
1964   "Echos de légende épiques iraniennes dans les 'Lettres' de Grigor Magistros." *REA* n.s. 1:321–329.
          Iranian materials have entered Armenian folklore, e.g., Rostam Zal, in David of Sassoun. Also influence of Firdusi.

1984   "Eghia Musheghiane arakagir." [Eghia Musheghian as Fabulist.] *PH* 1:178–195. Russian summary.
          Musheghian (1639–1750?) translated 31 variant Aesop fables from French into Armenian and wrote four fables himself. Considered important as a contact of Armenian with European literary ties. Derived from Musheghian's merchant note book and memory book.

Chulardian, Simon
1880   *Aradzk Azkayin.* [National Proverbs.] Venice, St. Lazar. 183 pp.
          Lists 4516 proverbs, mostly from Constantinople area. Those from other Armenian communities are indicated by a symbol at end of proverb. A dialect word list at end. Abstract of the work appears in *B* (1881) 39:48.

Cirbied. *See* Chahan de Cirbied

Collins, F. B.
1901   " 'David Of Sassoun' National Epos of Armenia." In Arnot, Robert, *Armenian Literature*. Rev. ed. New York, The Colonial Press, pp. 55–79.
          Fragments of three cycles of epic.

1901   "Proverbs and Sayings." In Arnot, Robert, *Armenian Literature*. Rev. ed. New York, The Colonial Press, pp. 3–6.
          Gives 54 proverbs and two tales.

1924   "The Sheep-Brother." *New Armenia* 16:10 –12.
          Armenian folktale, motif of lost shoe. Source of tale not given.

1924   "The Youth Who Would not Tell his Dream." *New Armenia* 16:27–29.
          Armenian folktale, but source not given. Winning bride by performing tasks. Appeared earlier in *Armenia* (1912) 6:82–84.

Conder, Josiah
1827   *Turkey*. London, Printed for James Duncan. 356 pp. (The Modern
            Traveler...v. 14).
                  A descriptive work, but pp. 158–172, about an Armenian wedding, of
                  folklore interest.

Conner, B. S.
1921   "From Ireland to Armenia." *The Near East* 7:15. il.
                  Armenian needle lace; author claims design of first illustration is based on
                  Limerick lace and that the other two are "presumably reticalla."

Conybeare, F. C. (*See also* Marr, N.)
1896   "The Barlaam and Josephat Legend in the Ancient Georgian and Armenian
            Literature." *Folk-lore* 7:101–142.
                  A tale of India, but found its way into Armenian *Monologium* (collection
                  of acts of martyrs, homilies, etc.) and was read in church. Very popular
                  among Armenians in 15th century; Arakel Vartabed put it into Armenian
                  prose-verse.

1901   "Les Sacrifices d'animaux dans les églises chrétiennes." *Revue de l'Histoire
            des Religions* 44:108–114.
                  Includes Armenian ritual of *madagh* (animal sacrifice).

1905   *Rituale Armenorum, Being the Administration of the Sacraments and the
            Breviary Rites of the Armenian Church*. Oxford, Clarendon Press. 536 pp.
                  Of special interest to folklore are sections on animal sacrifice, baptism,
                  marriage. Glossary gives meanings of words not readily available.

1907   "Notes on Some Early Ecclesiastical Practices in Armenia." *Folk-lore* 18:432–
            435.
                  Priests dressed as soldiers; some wore embroidered garments, hides of
                  sable, ermine, wolf, fox worn to invest selves with sanctity of animals
                  from which taken.

Conybeare, F. C., Harris, J. Rendel, and Lewis, Agnes Smith
1913   *The Story of Ahikar from the Aramaic, Syrian, Arabic, Armenian, Ethiopic,
            Old Turkish, Greek, and Slavonic Versions*. 2nd ed., enlarged. Cambridge,
            Cambridge University Press. 234 pp. and 72 pp.
                  Includes Armenian translation, pp. 193–234, and English translation of
                  Armenian version, pp. 24–55, and Armenian version, pp. 56–85.

Coxwell, C. Fillingham
1925   *Siberian and Other Folk Tales*. London, C. W. Daniel Co. 1056 pp.
                  Notes accompany four brief Armenian tales, pp. 1015–1027. Mentions
                  Armenian beliefs of Elisapetpol district. Some comparative information.

Crosby, J. B.
1927   "Modern Witches in Pennsylvania." *Journal of American Folklore* 40:304–309.

> Connects witches with Russian sect of Thondrakians or Paulicians (an evangelical Armenian sect). Much persecution of these sects, so they migrated. Mention of sympathetic magic, evil eye, etc. [NB: Actually the Thondrakian movement started in Armenia. See *The Thondrakian Movement*, by Vrej Nersessian. Allison Park, Pa., Pickwick, 1987. 145 pp.—AMA]

D. H. *See* Dashian, H.

Dabaghian, A.
1967   "Bolsoy Vanetsi khohararnere." [The Constantinople Cooks from Van.] *H* 45(9):40–51.

> Mostly anecdotal about some men from village of Aliur near Van who served as cooks for rich Armenians and Turks in Constantinople. Notes some of the food, with special reference to the famous Van cheese.

Dadalian, Ashot. *See* Ashot, Ashugh

Dadian, A.
1908–10   "Varadayi banavor grakanutyunits." [From the Oral Literature of Varanda.] *AH* 17:37–48; 18:25–32; 19:85–89.

> Includes 226 quatrains of songs, some from Shushi.

Danielian, Ed.
1989   "Hin Hayots ditsabanakan patkeratsummere astghayin erknki masin." [About the Ancient Armenian Representation of the Starry Sky.] *PH* 3:102–113. Russian summary.

> In Armenian mythology the hero arises as a constellation, e.g, Haig, and Ara a star that represents resurrection.

Darakjian, Avedis S.
1960   *Marzvani Hay Avedarnagan Zhoghovurte.* [The Armenian Evangelical Congregation of Marzvan.] Beirut, Dbaran Mshag. 175 pp. il., fold. map.

> Mostly about development of Armenian Evangelical Church, but old Marzvan dialect words, pp. 93–159, followed by local proverbs and sayings, about 480; pp. 160–174.

Darmanian, M.
1958   "The Birthplace of Moses of Khorene." *Armenian Review* 11(2):108–114.

> Gives historical arguments that Khoren, a village of Daron, was the home of the historian. Contradicts A. Malkhasian's belief that Moses was native of Siunik.

Daronian, S. K.

1981   "N. Zariani 'Ara Keghetsike' ev dasakan voghbergutyan avandutyunner." [N.
              Zarian's "Ara the Beautiful" and the Classical Tradition of Tragedy.] *PH*
              4:58–71. Russian summary.
                    A commentary on the tragedy written in 1943–44. Supports the legend of
              Ara's virtue and embodiment of evil in the Assyrian queen, Shamiram.

Dashian, H.

1892   "Bukavinayi ev Transilvanioy Hayots zroytsnere." [Narratives of Bukovina
              and Transylvanian Armenians.] *HA* 6:22–23.
                    A commentary on W. Wlislocki's *Märchen und Sagen*, but it also
              mentions other works I have not been able to locate.

1899   "Khigar ev iur imasdutiunn." [Ahikar and his Wisdom.] *HA* 13:33–38, 74–
              79, 112–116, 129–133, 173–176, 198–201, 236–238, 272–277, 295–299,
              334–338, 372–377.
                    Commentary and critique based on three-volume edition, edited by H. H.
              Baronian, and published in Constantinople, 1884–89. Ahikar had
              reputation as wise man and fabulist. Though not Armenian, very popular
              among the Armenians. Author notes he knew of two women named
              Khigar in 14th and 15th centuries.

1899–1900   "Zhoghovatsoyk aragats Vartanay." [Collection of Vartan's Fables.] *HA*
              13:226–232, 257–263, 311–315, 331–334, 361–370; and 14:7–12, 40–46,
              72–77, 101–105, 151–158.
                    A critique of N. Marr's three volume work about Vartan's fables as well
              as other fables. Gives some selections. In 1900 this was published in
              Vienna, Mkhitarian Dbaran. 198 pp.

Davenport, Martha

1981   "Armenian Embroidery in America." *Needle Arts* 12(4): 16–17. il.
                    Pictures of items worked in Aintab; also includes Marash work.

David of Sassoun. *See index heading:* David of Sassoun, texts

Davtian, K. S.

1967   "Arevi pashtamunki hetkere pronzedaryan Hayasdanum." [Traces of Sun
              Worship in the Bronze Age in Armenia.] *L* 4:77–88.
                    Some genres of Armenian folklore indicate ancient concepts of sun
              worship, e.g., association of birds and lions in connection with the sun.
              Description of sun and moon as sister and brother respectively.

Davtian, Serik

1956   "Haykakan aseghagortsutyan mi hin nmush." [An Old Example of Armenian
              Needlework.] *Banber Madenadarani* 3:41–51. il.
                    An embroidery piece ascribed to 13th century. Describes treelike design
              and notes similar designs in rugs.

1966   *Haykakan Zhanyak.* [Armenian Lace.] Erevan, HSSR, GA Hrat. 48 pp. il. (part col.). Russian and English summaries.

Mostly about needle lace, but also includes some crochet, filet, and embroidery. Mostly work of 19th and 20th centuries.

1972   *Haykakan aseghagortsutyun.* [Armenian Needlework.] Erevan, HSSR, GA Hrat. 92 pp. cli plates (part col.). Russian summary.

Shows embroidery, lace, knitting used for clothing and decoration. Some costumes shown. Historical text includes Cilician Armenia and work of exiles in Crimea, Poland; also some regional styles.

Dayian, Gh.

1936   "Gomidas Vartabed." [Gomidas the Teacher] *B* 94:4–33. port.

Biographical information about Komitas, who collected 3000 folk songs. Lists his lectures, concerts. Gives musical score, arranged for four voices, of the song "Akh Maral Jan" [Akh Dear Maral]. Komitas was also interested in church music.

Demirkhanian, A. R. [Armenian summary gives initials A. H.]

1982   "K probleme simvoliki trekhchastnykh kompozitsii drevnei Armeniia." [On the Problem of the Symbolism of Three-part Composition in Ancient Armenia.] *PH* 4:154–164. il.

Study of forms of three in art in Bronze Age 3000 B.C. Tree of life, horns of moon with cross in between, animal and human forms, plant forms, later used in Christian period.

Deovletian, Sarkis Kh.

1954   *Husher Shabin Karahisaren.* [Memories from Shabin Karahisar.] Paris, "Le Soleil." 230 pp. il.

Weddings, pp. 43–52; minstrels, with some examples of their songs, pp. 53–62; folk medicine with names of some practitioners and their methods.

Der Ghazarian, Eprem

1953   "Marashahay parker." [Customs of Marash Armenians.] *B* 111: 83–86, 125–130.

Vivid descriptions of religious festivals, especially beginning of Lent. Seven feathers stuck in an onion, one pulled each week to indicate passage of time. Special foods prepared for Easter. Pilgrimages to St. Toros ruins; strips of cloth tied to oak branches.

Der-Ghazarosian, H.

1933   "Hay ashughagan kraganutiune." [Armenian Minstrel Literature.] *B* 91:263–266.

Few remnants left; cites 15th century works and few others. Examples of drinking and love songs from various villages.

Der-Ghevondian, Haig
1978   "Osgerchagan zarteri kordzadzutiunn Hayastani mech, 5–12 tarerun."
              [Ornamental Gold Work in Armenia in the 5th–12th centuries.] *HA* 92:107–
              114. il.
                    Some of work shown useful for jewelry designs.

1988   "Haygagan kodinere." [Armenian Waistbands (or Belts).] *B* 146:277–284. il.
              French summary.
                    Functions of belts, materials used. Includes waistbands and belts shown
                    in manuscripts and in bas-reliefs.

1989   "Osgerchutiune Hayastani mech 15–16 tareru entatskin." [Goldsmithing in
              Armenia during the 15th–16th Centuries.] *HA* 103:93–108. il.
                    Shows variety of designs and motifs.

Der Hovhannissian, Harpik
1956   *Armenian Music: A Cosmopolitan Art*. 2 v. 292 pp. Thesis, Ph.D. Florida
              State University.
                    Have seen abstract only in *Dissertation Abstracts* 16:2475. Compares
                    Armenian folk music with other folk music. Folk songs classified and
                    technical aspects examined. Evolution of folk music.

Der Manuelian, L., and Eiland, M. B.
1984   *Weavers, Merchants and Rugs: The Inscribed Rugs of Armenia*. Fort Worth,
              Texas, Kimball Art Museum. 211 pp. col. il.
                    Rugs inscribed in Armenian, 18th–20th centuries. Includes Caucasian
                    types and some prayer rugs.

Der Melkonian, Chaké. (*See also* Der-Melkonian-Minassian)
1953   *Epopée populaire arménienne*. 274 pp. Thesis, Paris.
                    Not seen. About Armenian epic David of Sassoun.

1964   *Contes et legendes arméniennes*. Beirut, Impr. "Mechag." 156 pp. il.
                    Adaptations of legends, myths, and tales. In some instances sources are
                    noted. Three of the items are from David of Sassoun.

Der-Melkonian-Minassian, Chaké
1972   *L'Épopée populaire arménienne David de Sassoun; étude critique*. Montreal,
              Canada, Les Presses de l'Université du Quebec. 219 pp. il.
                    Discovery of epic, various aspects, structure, style, symbolism.

Der Mgrdichian, Kevork
1963   "Gomidas Vartabed." [Gomidas the Teacher.] *H* 41(2):16–18.
                    Author was pupil of Komitas during 1900s. In teaching Komitas gave
                    background and meanings of folk songs. He also gave choral
                    presentations at Echmiadzin.

Der-Mkrtchian, P. M.
1973   "Harsanike Shatakhum." [Wedding at Shatakh.] *L* 9:88–91. Russian summary.
                Selection of bride. Song quoted to accompany shaving and dressing of groom. Church ritual. Entry into groom's house preceded by breaking dish to ward off evil. Food and merriment.

Der Nersessian, Sirarpie
1936   "La légende d'Abgar d'après un rouleau illustré de la Bibliothèque Pierpont Morgan." In *Congrès International des Études Byzantines* 4th, Sept. 1934, Sofia. *Actes*, Sofia, Impr. de la Cour. v. 2:98–106. il.
                Describes amulet and relates legend. Armenians not specifically mentioned.

1965   *Aghtamar, Church of the Holy Cross*. Cambridge, Harvard University Press. 60 pp., 77 plates.
                Church on island in Lake Van. Of special interest are the sculptural reliefs of plants and animals in depiction of Biblical stories. A 10th century church.

Deroyan, G. N.
1983   "Hay geghjuk ergi verlutsatyan Komitasyan metodi masin." [On the Komitasian Method of Analysis of Peasant Songs.] *PH* 4:69–75. Russian summary.
                Consideration should be given to musical elements in addition to historical, geographical, dialect factors. Musical notation given in basic form with several variants.

Deroyan, Mardiros Shvod
1902   "Palui anedzkner ev orhnekner." [Curses and Blessings of Palu.] *B* [60]:479–481.
                Told in the dialect of the Palu district. Aside from blessings and curses includes a few protective words and prayers.

Derzhavin, N.
1906   "Iz oblasti Kavkazkoi etnografii. Iz zhizn Artvinkikh Armian." [Ethnography from the Caucasus Region. Life of Artvin Armenians.] *Sbornik Materialov dlia Opisaniia Mestnostei i Plemen Kavkaza*, 36(2):1–34.
                General information followed by hospitality, wedding and engagement customs, bringing gifts, henna application. Also about births.

Derzhavin, V. V., et al.
1939   *David Sasunskii armianskii narodnye epos*. [David of Sassoun the Armenian Epic.] Erevan, Gosizdvo Armianskaia SSR. xxvi, 384 pp. col. il.
                Four cycles of the unified text in blank verse. There is also a Moscow edition, same date, published by "Khodovzhestvenaia Literatura," xi, 335 pp. il.

Devejian, S. H.
1982   "Eghjerui pashtamunki hetkere hin Hayastanum." [Traces of the Worship of the Deer in Ancient Armenia.] *PH* 2:140–152. Russian summary.
        Bronze statues of deer in Lori district from 3rd century B.C. and evidence in folklore suggest worship of deer.

Devitskii, V.
1904   "Poslovitsy Grecheskiia, Turetskiia, Tatarskiia i Armianskiia sobraniia v Karskoi obl." [Greek, Turkish, Tatar, and Armenian Proverbs Collected in the Kars District.] *Sbornik Materialov dlia Opisaniia Mestnostei i Plemen Kavkaza* 34(3):34–55.
        Armenian proverbs (252) are on pp. 45–55.

Dirr, Adolf
1922   *Kaukasische Märchen.* Jena, Eugen Diedrichs. 294 pp.
        Of the 84 tales, six are Armenian. Has introductory information about tales of the Caucasus. English edition, *Caucasian Folk-tales,* New York, E. P. Dutton, 1925. 306 pp.

Diurian, C.
1905   "Zhoghovrtagan erketsoghutiune Russahayots mech." [Folk Singing among Russian Armenians.] *HA* 19:137–142.
        About work of Magar Egmalian and others on singing of old Armenian songs. Types sung by choral groups. Also notes minstrels who entertained and also introduced songs of social comment.

Downing, Charles
1972   *Armenian Folk-tales and Fables.* London, Oxford University Press. 217 pp. il.
        Includes 28 folktales and and 35 fables. At end of each one gives original source. There are also 171 proverbs selected from A. T. Ghanalanian's *Aratsani.* Erevan, 1960.

Dowsett, C. J. F.
1964   "Ancient Armenian Roller-skates." *Geographical Journal* 130:180–183.
        Tobogganing and rollerskating as pastimes. (Quotes from Strabo).

1973–74 "Some Gypso-Armenian Correspondences." *REA,* n.s. 10:59–81.
        Gypsies from India stayed awhile in Armenia, borrowed from Armenian language. Some became members of the Armenian church. To the credit of Armenians that Gypsies flourished in Armenia. Gypsies did metal and leather work. Also provided dances for special events. Gypsy magic. Some of their sayings and expressions reflected Armenian culture.

Dulaurier, Ed.
1852   "Les chants populaires de l'Arménie." *Revue des Deux Mondes*, n.s. 14:224–255.
            Songs, i.e., tales of mythical and heroic characters of Armenia.

1852   "Études sur les chants historiques et les traditions populaires de l'ancienne Arménie d'après une dissertation de J.-B. Emin." *Journal Asiatique*, ser. 4; 19:5–58.
            Extended version of citation above, summary of a study by Emin, *Vebk hnoyn Hayastani*. Moscow, 1850. Myths and historic songs and traditions embedded in Moses of Khoren's *History of the Armenians*.

Dumézil, Georges
1924   *Le Festin d'immortalité*. Paris, P. Geunthner. 318 pp.
            A comparative Indo-European mythological study; legends connected with ambrosia, pp. 210–218, about the ambrosia cycle among the Armenians. Use of plants Harout and Marout in festivals in which girls seek their fortune.

1926   "Les fleurs Harout-Marout et les anges Haurvatat-Amerrétatat." *REA* 6(2):43–69
            Spring festival based on plants giving health. Comparison with Persian and Indian legends. Also indicates Persian and Parthian influences.

1929   "Le Dit de la Princess Satenik." *REA* 9(1):41–53.
            Satenik legend in Moses of Khoren's *History of the Armenians*. Her various names noted.

1938   "Les légendes de 'Fils d'aveugles' au Caucase et autour de Caucase." *Revue de l'Histoire des Religions* 117:50–74.
            Includes legend of Arshag whose father Diran was blinded by Vasak for the Persians. This led to cycle of tales of Köroghlu among Turks, Armenians, and Persians. Raises question of whether connection with Scythian story of the blind parent.

1938   "Vahagn." *Revue de l'Histoire des Religions* 117:152–170.
            Traditions about Armenian Vahagn corresponding to Indian Vrtrahan; both associated with fire.

Durgarian, K. G.
1963   "Sayat-Novai Hayeren khagheri taghachaputyune." [The Meter of Sayat-Nova's Armenian Ballads.] *PH* 3:67–78. Russian summary.
            Sayat-Nova used various poetic forms; examples given.

Durgarian, K. G. *(continued)*
1971   "Agheksandr Mkhitarian." *PH* 3:183–188. port. Russian summary.
              Life and work of Mkhitarian. On occasion of 125th year of his birth. He
              collected folk and dance songs; also *sharagans* (sacred music) and national
              songs.

Durian. *See* Turian

Dwight, H. G. O.
1856   "Armenian Traditions About Mt. Ararat." *American Oriental Society. Journal*
              5:189–191.
              Tradition that Noah set foot at Arnoiodn and planted willow at Argoori.
              Josephus refers to Nakhichevan, which the Armenians call place of
              descent.

Dzeron, Manoog B.
1984   *Village of Parchanj: General History (1600–1937).* Trans. by Arra S.
              Avakian. Fresno, Calif., Panorama West Books. 280 pp. il.
              Chapter 3 about Armenian customs, mores, folklore, superstitions,
              riddles, charms, oaths, curses, folk songs, games. Translation curtails
              scores of sayings and entirely omits section on witticisms. There is
              information on engagements. weddings, birth, baptism, and fast days.
              Armenian edition *Parchanj kiugh* published in Boston by Baikar Press,
              1938. 280 pp. il.

Dzhanpoladian, M. *See* Janpoladian, M.

Dzhindi, Adzhie. *See* Jndi, Hajie

Dzotsigian, S. M.
1922   *Ararat-Govgas. Masn ergrort. Govgas.* [Ararat-Caucasus. Part two.
              Caucasus.] Paris, G. H. Nerses. 304 pp. il.
              Mostly descriptive geography of some towns. Of special interest customs
              of Armenians in Tiflis, pp. 264–266. Day of the dead celebrated. At
              Christmas the River Kura declared to be the River Jordan, bridge made
              over it, tradesmen appear with banners; water blessed with holy oil;
              children release doves; military shoot cannon. Sick use blessed water for
              healing.

1947   *Aremdahay Ashkhark.* [Western Armenian World.] New York, Leylegian.
              814 pp.
              Mostly descriptive information on various towns and villages. For some
              places it quotes folk songs and lullabies.

Dzovigian, Hovhannes
1939   *Nakhakristoneagan gronk Hayots.* [Pre-Christian Religion of the Armenians.]
        Boston. 31 pp. English summary.
            Brief account of Armenian gods, pagan beliefs, myths, and spirits. A
            table in English lists Armenian gods and equivalents in Greek, Roman,
            Persian.

E. B. *See* Essabal, Paul

Edwards, G. D.
1899   "Items of Armenian folk-lore Collected in Boston." *Journal of American
        Folklore* 12:97–107.
            Includes dreams, superstitions, riddles, games, customs. Notes difficulty
            in collecting; some felt he was trying to ridicule Armenians.

Eghiazarian, A. K.
1986   "Epikakan herosi evolyutsian ev 'Sasna Tsrer' epos." [Hero's Evolution and
        the Epic "Sasna Tsrer."] *PH* 4:106–116. Russian summary.
            To understand the epic of David of Sassoun consideration should be given
            to archaic and medieval conditions. David and other characters reflect high
            moral principles of the people of the Middle Ages.

Egiazarov, S. A.
1898   "Cherty byta Armianskikh krestian." [Features of Armenian Peasant Life.] In
        Bratskaia Pomoshch Postradavshim v Turtsii Armianam. 2nd ed. Moscow,
        pp. 247–252. il.
            About beliefs and practices of special events of the year. Picture shows
            women baking bread.

1898   "Iz tsikle Armianskikh narodnykh skazanii." [From a cycle of Armenian Folk
        Legends.] In *Bratskaia Pomoshch Postradavshim v Turtsii Armianam.* 2nd
        ed. Moscow, pp. 96–105.
            Ascension Day in Armenia and legends connected with it. Gives three
            legends.

Eilers, Wilhelm
1971   "Semiramis." *Akademie der Wissenschaften, Vienna. Philosophische
        Historische Klasse. Sitzungsberichte* 274:11–81. il. (part col.) fold. map.
            Mostly about Semiramis in general, but some attention given to Urartian
            connection, but no mention of Ara.

Emin, Jean-Baptiste [or Mkrtich]
1850   *Vepk hnoyn Hayastani.* [Ancient Tales of Armenia.] Moscow, Vladimiray
        Gotie. 98 pp.
            Presents Armenian myths and tales embedded in Armenian histories. *See*
            Dulaurier, Ed.

Emin, Jean-Baptiste [or Mkrtich] *(continued)*
1864   *Recherches sur le paganisme arménien.* Translated from Russian by A. de
            Stadler. Paris, B. Duprat. 56 pp. Extract from *Revue de l'Orient, de l'Algerie
            et des Colonies*, Oct.–Dec. 1864, but I have not been able to see this issue.
                Names and describes mythical gods of Armenia, their functions and
            attributes; the influences from Persia, Greece. etc. Also notes beliefs in
            good and evil spirits, veneration of sacred trees and fire.

Enikolopov, I. K.
1971   "Gurgan-Khan i Sayat-Nova." [Gurgan-Khan and Sayat-Nova.] *L* 2:108–
            112. Armenian summary.
                In one of his songs Sayat-Nova calls himself Gurgan-Khan. There have
            been conjectures about his identity. Author believes reference is to the
            famous Georgian magistrate and statesman Mirza Gurgan Enigolopov.

Erdmann, Kurt
1935   "Later Caucasian Dragon Carpets." *Apollo* 22(127):21–25. il.
                Carpets described are from 16th–18th centuries. There has been
            discussion of provenance, but author's focus is on artistic content.
            Pictures also indicate museum locations.

Erem, S.
1903–4   "Hay ashughner." [Armenian Minstrels.] *B* 61:362–366, 431–436; 62:81–84.
                K. Akhverdian, a doctor, called in minstrels to bring material to him.
            Includes some information on Sayat-Nova. Songs on various subjects
            with examples.

Eremian, Aram
1921   "Barsgahay ashughner. Ashugh Bagher-Oghlu." [Persian-Armenian
            Minstrels. Bagher-Oghlu.] *HA* 35:286–291.
                Minstrel a native of New Julfa. Examples of songs about contemporary
            events, moral, satirical, and love sones. No biographical information.

1922   "Barsgahay ashughner." [Persian-Armenian Minstrels.] *B* 80:39–41, 73–75,
            108–110.
                Minstrel Der Garabed Ohanian. Songs with moral, historical themes;
            religious and some contemporary themes. Examples given.

1922   "Barsgahay ashughner. Ashugh Hartun Oghli." [Persian-Armenian Minstrels.
            Minstrel Hartun Oghli.] *B* 80:328–333, 357–364.
                Life and environment in which minstrel lived. Some themes of love and
            sojourners. Also hortatory theme. Brief biographical sketch. Article
            commemorates 50th year of his death. Original name Hovhannes
            Harutiunian, born 1789 in Chaharmahal.

1922   "Chaharmahali zhoghovrtagan panahiusutiune." [The Folklore of Chaharmahal.] *HA* 36:30–39, 132–138, 255–268, 382–388, 452–460.

> Folk songs for various occasions, riddles, proverbs and sayings, blessings, oaths, curses, threats, superstitions. Collected from several Armenian villages in Persia. Most of informants were girls, young and old women.

1923   *Chaharmahali Hay Zhoghovrtagan Panahiusutiune.* [The Armenian Folklore of Chaharmahal.] Vienna, Mkhitarian Dbaran. 81 pp.

> Material collected from 13 villages in Persia. Inhabitants descendants of Armenians brought by Shah Abbas in 1606 to Persia. Informants mostly women and young girls. Folk songs of various themes, riddles, proverbs and sayings, spells and superstitions. Includes glossary.

1923–25   "Sbahani Chaharmahal kavare." [The Chaharmahal Province of Isfahan.] *B* 80–82.

> 80:206–210. General description; 80:233–237. Plants, etc. 80:297–301. Domestic life and customs; 80:324–327. Punishments; 80:358–363. Home rituals, and furnishings; 81:6–10. Costume and decoration; 81:36–40. Kinds of food; 81:68–74. More about food and villages; 81:200–204, 233–240. About villages; 81:266–276. About places; 81:297–301. Utensils, etc.; 81:325–335. Weddings, incl. il.; 81:359–361. Funerals; 81:391–394. Festivals; 82:67–70. Festival of lights, Easter, etc.

1924   "Barskahay norakoyn ashughner. Ashugh Allaverdi." [Most Recent Persian-Armenian Minstrels.] *HA* 38:234–244, 312–318, 499–509.

> Allaverdi told and sang tales; close to peasant life. Used mixture of Persian and Armenian tales. [NB: Article was to be continued but not found in later issues.—AMA]

1925   "Barskahay norakoyn ashughner. Ashugh Misgin Mateos." [Most Recent Persian-Armenian Minstrels. Ashugh Misgin Mateos.] *HA* 38:102–111.

> Minstrel was from Chaharmahal area near Isfahan. Samples of songs are given.

1925   *Barskahay norakoyn ashughner.* [Most Recent Persian-Armenian Minstrels.] Vienna, Mkhitarian Dbaran. 120 pp. il.

> Biographical sketches of several minstrels. Some songs included; word list at end. Love and moralistic themes. Minstrels from late 19th century.

1928   "Pshrankner Hay zhoghovrtagan panahiusutiunits." [Fragments from Popular Armenian Folklore.] *HA* 42:536–552.

> Love songs from Marzvan; also lullabies and childhood songs. Some songs from Bayazid about Russo-Turkish war. Folk dance songs from Alashgerd.

Eremian, Aram *(continued)*
1929   *Ashugh Ghul Hovhannes.* [Minstrel Ghul Hovhannes.] Vienna, Mkhitarian
             Dbaran. 94 pp.
                 This minstrel kept the tradition of Persian-Armenian minstrels. Songs
                 grouped by theme, such as love, history, satire and allegory, etc. Songs
                 reflect oppression of early 19th century. Selections of some songs
                 included.

1930   *Ashugh Krikor Dalian (Sheram).* [Minstrel Krikor Dalian (Sheram).] Venice,
             St. Lazar. 64 pp. il. (incl. port.).
                 Biographical sketch, and his high rank among minstrels. Some musicians
                 inspired by his songs and harmonized and vocalized them. This minstrel
                 made his own instrument, performed in various towns. Love and
                 hortatory songs. Short version of this appeared in *B* 1930 (88):331–339,
                 426–436.

1930   *Barsgahay ashughner Ashugh Amir Oghli.* [Persian-Armenian Minstrels.
             Minstrel Amir Oghli.] Venice, St. Lazar. 32 pp.
                 Published on occasion of 100th anniversary of minstrel's death. About his
                 life and work. Some samples of songs given.

1930   *Pshrankner Chughahay ev Huntgahay panahiusutunits.* [Fragments from
             Julfa Armenian and Indian Armenian Folklore.] Vienna, Mkhitarian Dbaran.
             80 pp.
                 These 21 songs are from the 17th and 18th centuries; collected from 1916
                 to 1921 while seeking minstrel songs. When Shah Abbas moved
                 Armenians to New Julfa early in 17th century, some Armenians later
                 moved to India. Includes love and wedding songs which show some
                 influence of Persian language. Word list included. A briefer version
                 appeared in *HA* 1910 (44):346–356, 685–695.

1948   "Iranahay ashughner. Ashugh Pagher Oghli Ghazar (1690–1770)." [Iranian-
             Armenian Minstrels. Minstrel Pagher Oghli Ghazar.] *B* 106:55–67, il.
                 This minstrel of New Julfa sang about economic and political conditions.
                 Some examples given.

1960   "Ashugh Arakel Harutiunian." [Minstrel Arakel Harutiunian.] *B* 118:72–78,
             125–130.
                 About 19th century minstrel. Sang love and satirical songs, and songs of
                 praise, patriotism, mourning and mixed themes. Examples given. Minstrel
                 was 60 years old in 1903.

1964   "Sayeat-Novayi erkeri hadganishnere u arveste." [The Essential
             Characteristics and Art of Sayat-Nova's Songs.] *HA* 78:181–184.
                 About Sayat-Nova, the outstanding Armenian minstrel of the 18th
                 century. His words were in the language of the people and reflected the

environment. His archive includes 66 Armenian songs, 38 Georgian songs, and 117 Azerbaijani songs.

1965   "Andib dagher ashugh Hartun Oghlay." [Unpublished songs of Minstrel Hartun Oghla.] *HA* 79:525–528.

Two songs used at weddings. Minstrel lived from 1760–1840.

Eremian, S.

1912   "Karekin Srvantsdiants." *B* 70:4–11, 50–59.

Biographical information and excerpts from writings. Used a picturesque style, untouched by European influences.

1933   "Vishabe Haygagan korkeru mech." [The Dragon in Armenian Rugs.] *B* 91:181–182.

Armenians worshiped the dragon (or serpent) as a god. The serpent is keeper of the house.

Erevanian, K. S.

1956   *Badmutiun Charshanjaki Hayots.* [History of the Charshanjak Armenians.] Beirut, G. Donigian. 700 pp. il., 2 fold. maps.

Has some folk material, including one of main towns, Perri. Folk life, pp. 223–270. Costume, food, health, family life, special festivals, pp. 473–600. Festivals include weddings, pp. 491–517. Dialect words of which some have extended explanations, pp. 518–575. Sayings, jokes, pp. 579–590. Songs and games, pp. 593–595.

Erevantsian, B.

1930   "A. Aharonian iprev panahavak." [A. Aharonian as a Collector of Folklore.] *H* 8(6):87–96.

Aharonian collected folklore from Surmelu district. Gives some examples of folk verses.

Eriksson, T.-E.

1955   "Die armenische Büchersammlung der Universitäts-Bibliothek zu Helsinki." *Studia Orientalia* 18(2):1–85.

Pages 31–34 note old works about Armenian folklore.

Ernjakian, Nvard

1979   "Lusine Hay zhoghovrdakan havadataliknerum ev sovorytnerum." [The Moon in Armenian Beliefs and Customs.] *L* 2:53–60. Russian summary.

Covers period from late 19th to beginning of 20th centuries. Though there were calendars, the phases of the moon guided planting, etc. New moon considered symbol of strength and growth. Moon and health. In some places moon and sun looked upon as brothers.

Ervandini. *See* Lalayan, Ervand

Erznikian, Grigoris

1898   "Kayan berd ev Kayanoy tsor." [The Fortress and Valley of Kayan.] *AH*
3:316–328

Descriptive, but includes legend of crow that saved life of workers who
were about to eat lunch. Crow sees snake fall in food, tries to warn
workers, falls in food. Workers then understand crow's attempt to warn
about poisoned food; later erect monument for crow. Compare essentially
same legend in Lalayan, E. (1898), p. 48. And before that Servantsian,
K. (1874; reprinted in his *Works*), v. 1, p. 75, only legend involves crane
instead of crow.

1898   "Lornay harsnik." [Lori Wedding.] *AH* 3:329–337.

Describes cradle engagement and regular engagement and wedding. Gives
meaning of *"popuk"* also known as *"nurts,"* artificial tree decorated with
fruits and candles, carried in front of groom to signify changes in life of
groom and bride.

Esaian, S. A.

1962   "Zashchitnoe vooruzhenie v drevnoi Armenii." [Protective Arms in Ancient
Armenia.] *PH* 1:192–201. il. Armenian summary.

Shields, helmets, and coats of mail are described and illustrated. Notes
materials used.

1968   "Amulety sviazannye s kul'tom solntsa iz Armenii." [Amulets Related to the
Sun Cult in Armenia.] *Sovetskaia arkheologiia* 2:255–260. il.

Amulets from area of Sevan, Kirovakan, Dilichan, and Lori in northern
Soviet Armenia, dating from the 6th century B.C. Pictures show several
designs, some on pottery.

E[ssabal], P[aul]

1935   "Gomidas Vartabed." [Gomidas the Teacher.] *HA* 49:430–435.

About life and work of Komitas in folk and other music. Gives
bibliography of published works.

1936   "[Review of] *Sasnay Dsrer*." (Vol.1, Erevan, Bedagan Hrad. 1128 pp.) *HA*
50:408–410.

About the first volume of David of Sassoun epic which contains a number
of versions from the area north of Lake Van.

1944   "Harsanegan takavore." [The Wedding King.] *HA* 58:36–56.

The groom at wedding recognized as king. His virility vulnerable to
demonic forces and evil eye. Protective devices, such as *urts* (or *nurts*)
decorated with red and green threads, flowers, etc. set on a standard. Use
of metaphors to ask for the bride, e.g., to ask for bit of earth from your
hearth; or, to light my light from yours.

1946   *Der Ruf in Reiche der Heimaterde. Der Adler und der Kraniche.* Vienna, Mkhitarist Congregation. 147 pp. col. il.

   Descriptive background of Armenian homeland, spirit of people, hero tales, folk beliefs. Somewhat romantic treatment.

1948   "La religion originaire des armeniens." *International Congress of Orientalists*, 21st, Paris, July 23–31, 1948. *Proceedings*, pp. 163–164.

   Armenian paganism strongly influenced by Persian elements and enriched by Semitic and Asiatic influences.

1961   "The Door and Threshold in Armenian Folklore." *Western Folklore* 20: 265–273 .

   Door must be protected to prevent entry of devils; precautions taken though magical symbols or certain words to maintain the welfare and property of family.

Essabalian, Paul. *See* Essabal, Paul

Ezekian, A. M.
1907   "Azgagrutyune ev Perch Proshian." [Ethnography and Perch Proshian.] *AH* 6:211–213.

   On occasion of Proshian's death and his services to ethnography.

1908   "Sargis Ghazarian Haykuni." *AH* 18:157–159.

   Obituary of Haykuni the folklorist.

1908   "Svastika." [Swastika.] *AH* 17:142–153.

   About origin, various forms, and significance of swastika.

Eznik de Kolb
1959   *De Deo.* Paris, Firman-Dido. 2 v. (*Patrologia orientalis*, v. 28).

   Eznik was a 5th century writer of "Refutation of the sects." This work has some sections on angels, demons, and dragons. Text in French and Armenian.

Faustus of Byzance. *See* Pawstos Buzandasi

Felkin, Robert W.
1887–88 "Ein afrikanisches Märchen." *Zeitschrift für Vergleichende Litteratur-Geschichte und Renaissance-Litteratur.* n.f. 1:442–444.

   Tale of a blind man left behind by his hunting companions. An Armenian translation in *HA* 1890 (4):139–140 with the title "Arasbel m'ar Hays ev Haprige" [A Tale of Armenia and Africa.] Makes comparison with African tale.

Ferrahian, Eunice
1932   *Symphonic Poem. Armenian legend (from Ballad of Raffi).* 44 pp. Thesis,
            Master of Music, University of Southern California.
            Not seen. Can be considered an example of expressing a legend through
            music rather than in writing.

Fetter, [no first name]. *See* Aginian, N., 1894

Feydit, Frédéric
1957   "L'épopée populaire arménienne." *B* 115:27–37, 173–184, 224–231.
            About David of Sassoun first collected by K. Servantsian, and variants by
            others. Epic relates social conditions of times around 10th century.

1964   *David de Sassoun; épopée en vers.* [Paris, Gallimane.] 398 pp.
            Translation of what is known as the unified text of 1939. Introduction by
            Orbeli gives historical background and some comparisons with other
            epics.

1986   *Amulettes de l'Armenié chrétienne.* Venice, St. Lazar. 385 pp.
            Have not seen. Reviewed in *REA* n.s. 21:552–554, J. H. Mahé.

1987   "La démono-mythologie d'après les sources anciennes." *B* 145:316–336.
            Investigates work of Eznik and Moses of Khoren to organize a more exact
            idea of old Armenian mythology; characteristics of deities and their
            activities. Takes into account translation confusions.

Finck, Franz Nikolaus
1907   "Die Grundzüge des Armenisch-zigeunerischen SprachBaus." *Gypsy Lore
            Society. Journal.* n.s. 1:34–60.
            Gypsies in Armenia use Armenian endings of declensions. As an example
            gives a story in Armenian-Gypsy language.

Frasson, Giuseppe
1987   "Aght'amar: contributo all'interpretazione iconografia della cappelle palestina
            d. S. Croce." *B* 145:287–315. il. Armenian summary.
            This 10th century Church of the Holy Cross on island of Aghtamar in
            Lake Van of special interest for its bas-relief decorations representing
            three kinds of life: nature, animal, human. Human control of nature,
            dominion over animals and historically prevailing over enemy powers that
            prevent freedom. Armenian struggle through faith in Christianity. People
            retain individuality.

G., A.
1896   "Mshetsots endanegan geankits mi kani kdzer." [Some Sketches from Mush
            Family Life.] *HA* 10:382–383.
                 Taken from Armenian periodical *Nor Tar* [New Century] no. 187, but no
                 date given. Verses directed by new bride towards her various in-laws.
                 Tone is unfriendly.

1896   "Mshetsots mahn u taghume." [Death and Burial in Mush.] *HA* 10:348–349.
                 An abstract of article from Armenian periodical *Nor Tar* [New Century]
                 no. 162, but no date given. About custom of old women chanting verses
                 to drive away evil spirits and devil. Examples given.

Galstian, G. M.
1966   *Ditsabanakan anunneri ev dardzvatskneri hamarot batsatrakan bararan.* [A
            Short Explanatory Dictionary of Mythological Names and Occurrences.]
            Erevan, "Luys." 153 pp. il.
                 Mostly Greek and Roman names, but includes some Persian and
                 Armenian names.

Galtier, Emile
1905   "Les Fables d'Olympianos." *Cairo. Institut Français d'Archeologie Orientale.
            Bulletin* 4:17–30.
                 Table of 23 fables indicate correspondence to Aesop's fables and Vartan's
                 fables.

Ganalanian, A. T. *See* Ghanalanian, Aram Tigrani

Garegin, Archbishop of Trebizond
1960   "The Ancient Religion of the Armenians." *Armenian Review* 13(2):110–112.
                 Names a few of the deities and gives brief information on their nature and
                 function.

Garnett, Lucy M. J.
1890   *The Women of Turkey and their Folklore.* London, David Nutt. 382 pp.
                 Chapters 6–9 (pp. 194–296) about Armenian women. Description of
                 dwellings, domestic life, birth and baptism, weddings, funerals. Legends
                 and some examples of folktales and songs.

1900   "An Armenian Wedding." *Argosy* 70:347–350.
                 Does not give locale but notes roles of master of ceremonies and best
                 man. Church ceremony. Sheep sacrifice at threshold of house. Children
                 pull off bride's shoes and stockings to get money hidden there.

Garsoian, Nina. *See* Pawstos Buzandasi

Gaspar, Arman
1953   "Digenis Akritas ev Sasuntsi Tavit." [Digenis Akritas and David of Sassoun.]
            H 31(4):13–20.
            Compares the Byzantine epic and David of Sassoun. Remarks that not
            enough comparative studies have been made.

1957   "Digenes Akritas and David of Sassoun." *Armenian Review* 10(1):116–122.
            Byzantine epic found in 1870; compared with David of Sassoun. Both
            belong to about same period and some similarities of locale. Notes more
            study needed.

Gasparian, A. O.
1974   "Meghapahutyune hin ev mijnadaryan Hayastanum." [Bee-keeping in Ancient
            and Medieval Armenia.] *L* 4:93–102. il. Russian summary.
            Notes ancient writers who wrote about bee-keeping. Includes a couple of
            riddles about bees. Illustrations show beehives and wax designs.

Gasparian, Garush
1978   "Zhoghovrdakan bzhshkutyune Hay banahyusutyan ev ditsabanutyan mej."
            [Folk Medicine in Armenian Folklore.] *L* 1:82–87. Russian summary.
            Gives examples from specifications on how ailments were treated.

Gasparian, Samson Gaspari
1961   *Komitas.* Erevan, Haypethrat. 235 pp. il., ports.
            About folk song collector, Komitas; his life, work, and creativity. A list
            of 157 periodical citations and 13 books about him.

1969   "Hay erazhshtutyan hanchare." [The Genius of Armenian Music.] *PH* 4:7–
            14.
            Komitas the patriarch of Armenian classical music who brought out folk
            creations to a high art and professionalism. He declared that the people are
            greatest creators and we should learn from them. He knew not only folk
            songs, but also folk dance music, and was also a musicologist.

Gayayan, H. H.
1976   "Raznovidmosti kover 'drakon feniks,' XIV–XVvv." [Variants of the carpet
            pattern "dragon-Phoenix," 14th–15th centuries.] *L* 5:58–66. il. Armenian
            summary.
            Describes the rug designs and also some similar designs from Armenian
            manuscript miniatures.

1977   "Gorgagortsutyan mej kirarvogh Hayeren pokharyal barer Turkerenum."
            [Armenian terms in the carpet industry which have found their way into
            Turkish.] *L* 8:85–99. Russian summary.
            Explanation of terminology used in rug-making.

1977   "Haykakan gorgagrdzutyune Rumi-Seljukyan Sultanutyunum (VIII-XIVdd)."
            [Armenian Rug Weaving in the Rumi-Seljuk Sultanate (8th–14th centuries).]
            PH 1:168–176. il. Russian summary.
            Asserts that rug motifs depict stylized designs of dragon.

Gazarov, A.

1889   "Armianskikh skazki 'Cherop-Tsar' i 'Nevesta-Vsadnik.' " [Armenian Tales:
            "The Skull Tsar" and "The Bride-Horseman."] *Sbornik Materialov dlia
            Opisaniia Mestnostei i Plemen Kavkaza* 7(2):77–83.
            A couple of tales from village of Karakliss.

Gaziian. *See* Ghaziyan

Gelzer, Heinrich

1896   "Zur armenische Gotteslehre." *Königlich Sächsische Gesellschaft der
            Wissenschaften zu Leipzig. Berichte über die Verhandlungen. Philologish–
            Historische Klasse* 48:99–148.
            Discusses ancient Armenian gods; influences of Iranian, Syrian, and
            Greek beliefs. Armenian translation appears in *B* 1897(55):16–18, 63–70,
            176–180, 353–362, 425–431, 474–479.

Geodakian, G.

1969   "Genii Armianskoi muzyki." [Genius of Armenian Music.] *Erevani
            Hamalsaran* 5:53–58. port. (opposite p. 52).
            About Komitas, his life and work, especially in folk music.

1969   "Komitas i muzikalnoe iskusstvo." [Komitas and Musical Art.] Armenian
            summary.
            Komitas was able to save the more urgent problems of musical art and
            raise the level of 20th century problem solving. His musical principles
            differed from those of 19th century classical music and were closer to
            20th century. Investigations of musical composition. Need to study
            essence of folk music more deeply.

Georgian. *See* Keorkian

Gevorgian, N. Kh.

1984   "Sayat-Novayi khagheri mi kani me patkerneri knabanutyan masin." [The
            Critique of Several Images of Sayat-Nova's Ballads.] *PH* 4:199–207.
            Russian summary.
            Images used: salamander for blood and fire; Klapiton as color of silk
            threads for hair, and other examples from ballads.

Gevorgian, Nikolai
1982   "K voprosi ob ashugskoi poetike 'ilakhi' i 'shakhatai.' " [On the Question of
            Ashugh Poetics "ilakhi" and "shakhatai."] *L* 7:82–92. Armenian summary.
            Concerning two types of poetics used by minstrels. Forms arose in
            Persia.

Gevorgian, S. A.
1980   "Baroyakhratakan mtkere Hay tabanagrerum (XIX dar)." [The Moral
            Advisory Thoughts Inscribed on Armenian Tombstones (19th century).] *PH*
            4:295–299.
            Quotes examples of inscriptions, e.g., transitory life, direct advice on
            conduct of life, etc.

Gevorgian, Sergey
1979   "Pandkhdutyan teman XVIII–XIX dd Hay vimagir banasteghtsutyunneri
            mej." [The Sojourner Theme in Armenian Lithographic Compositions of the
            18th–19th centuries.] *L* 5:58–67. Russian summary.
            Some villagers left home and went to Constantinople to work. Some died
            and their tombstones were engraved with verses noting the sadness of
            their burial away from home.

Gevorgian, T. H.
1967   "Haykakan harsanekan mi tsisakatarutyan masin." [About Armenian Wedding
            Ceremony.] *L* 5:87–92.
            Analysis of practice of *havtruk* (chicken beheading) in wedding. Notes
            various names used in different locations. Practice suggests fertility, bride
            capture. Also relates to ancient bird worship, bird totem. Significance of
            cooked gizzard (wisdom). Even childhood game verses relate to the ritual.

1980   "Loru patma-azgagrakan shrjani banahyusutyune." [The Historic Ethnogra-
            phy of the Lori Region.] *PH* 4:291–295.
            Gives history of collections of folk material of the Lori region. Many
            genres represented.

Gevorgian, Tamara
1984   "[Review of] *Artsakh.*" (Erevan, HSSH. 192 pp. [Hay azgagrutyan ev
            banahyusutyan . . . no. 15]) *L* 7:85–86.
            Original not seen; review does not give author or compiler of the book.
            Artsakh another name for Karabagh in Azerbaijan where many Armenians
            live. Includes 40 folktales, 73 fables; some amusing anecdotes. Some
            songs, dances, traditions, and about 500 proverbs and sayings, 200
            curses, blessings, and threats, and a part of David of Sassoun.

Ghanalanian, Aram Tigrani

1941   *Abovyane ev zhoghovrdakan banahyusutyune.* [Abovian and Folklore.] Erevan, Arfan. 141 pp. port. Russian summary.

Abovian's novel *Verk Hayastani* [Wounds of Armenia] included various genres of folklore. Here are included proverbs and sayings (114) and a few curses and blessings, legends, anecdotes, etc.

1953   "Zhoghovrdakan banahyusutyune hasarakakan mitki tarber hosankneri knanatutyamb." [Folklore in the Estimation of Different Currents of Social Thought.] *Teghekagir* 5:29–48.

In classical Marxism and Leninism are found important thoughts concerning the study and interpretation of folklore which have principles and directive significance socially.

1954   "Zhoghovrdakan banahyusutyan dere H. Baronyani ergitsanki mej." [The role of folklore in H. Baronian's Satire.] *Teghekagir* 3:53–62.

Use of Armenian proverbs and sayings to characterize some persons and Turkish imperialism, political and civic life.

1954   *Zhoghovrdakan banahyusutyan mi kani hartser.* [Some Issues in Folklore.] Erevan, HSSH, GA Hrat. 139 pp.

Folklore as the supernatural view and its specific attributes; the various currents representing the actual political significance. Comments on functions of folklore by Marx, Engels, Lenin, Stalin. Brief attention to origin of Armenian heroic tales, pp. 89–91.

1958   "Haykakan aratsneri hnaguyn gravor skzbnaghbyurnere." [The Most Ancient Written Sources of Armenian Proverbs.] *Banber Matenadarani* 4:25–34.

Birds have been an important source of proverbs; also Greek writers and Armenian historical works. Examples are given.

1959   "Akanavor Hayagete." [The Distinguished Armenologist.] *PH* 4:145–152. Russian summary.

About Manuk Abeghian's career as a linguist and folklorist.

1959   "M. Nalbandyane ev zhoghovrdakan banahyusutyune." [M. Nalbandian and Folklore.] *PH* 1:71–80. Russian summary.

M. Nalbandian, a social democrat of the late 19th century, found much value in Armenian folklore. He used sayings, etc. to illustrate some of his ideas.

1960   *Arhatsan.* [Proverbs.] Erevan, Haykakan SSR, GA Hrat., 396 pp.

Long introduction about proverbs and an explanation of the present compilation, the language, Armenian life and character, etc. Thousands of proverbs arranged by subject. Includes index for motifs, list of sources. Also list of new proverbs, 1951–60.

Ghanalanian, Aram Tigrani *(continued)*

1961   "Zhoghovrdakan avandutyunneri eutyunn u zhanrayin arantsnahatkutyun-
nere." [The Essence and Genre Features of Individual Folk Legends.] *PH*
1:16–35. Russian summary.
    General statements about legends, but the examples are from Armenian
    legends. They reflect national character and spirit and have cultural and
    literary value.

1963   *Manuk Khachaturi Abeghian*. Erevan, HSSH, GA Hrat. 70 pp., port.
    Abeghian's background and teaching. He wrote books and articles on
    Armenian literature, language, and folklore. Took important part in
    compilation of variants of David of Sassoun under title *Sasna Tsrer*. R.A.
    Babajanian's bibliography of works by and about Abeghian are
    included—206 items.

1963   "Sayat-Novan Haykakan avandut'yunnerum." [Sayat-Nova in Armenian
    Traditions.] *PH* 3:79–90. Russian summary.
    Various stories told about the minstrel Sayat-Nova, e.g., after he became
    a priest he heard of a minstrel contest in Tiflis. He went there in secular
    clothing and enjoyed merriment. Many contradictions in tellings which
    mostly arose 50 years after his death.

1963   *Sayat-Novayi steghtsagortutyan zhoghovrdakan akunknere*. [The Folk
    Sources of Sayat-Nova's Work.] Erevan, HSSH, GA Hrat, 81 pp.
    The minstrel Sayat-Nova used proverbs, tales, and traditions in his songs.
    Examples given are designated by numbers assigned in the 1959 edition
    of his songs edited by M. S. Hasratian.

1963   "Vastakavor Hayakete." [The Worthy Armenologist.] *PH* 2:57–70. port.
    Russian summary.
    About K. A. Melik-Ohanjanian on the occasion of his 70th birthday.
    About his work in Armenian folklore.

1965   *Armianskie narodnye skazki*. [Armenian Folktales.] Erevan, Izd-vo
    "Aiastan." 398 pp.
    There are 85 tales translated into Russian by various Armenians. Source
    of each tale given. Introductory essay discusses types of tales and kinds
    of characters.

1965   "Hay zhoghovrdakan hekiatnere." [The Armenian Folktales.] *PH* 3:35–48.
    Russian summary.
    Divides folktales as (1) fantastic and wonder tales and (2) realistic tales.
    Titles given for each type.

1966   "Hay banahyusutyan mets erakhtavare." [The Great Benefactor in Armenian Folklore.] *PH* 1:17–32.

        About Karekin Servantsian on the 125th anniversary of his birth. His biography, work, and publications.

1966   "Manuk Abeghiani keankn u gitakan gortsuneutyune." [The Life and Work of Manuk Abeghian.] In Abeghian's *Erker* [Works]. Erevan, HSSR, GA Hrat. Vol. 1:vii –xxiv.

        Gives Abeghian's parentage, education, teaching, studies abroad, his many literary works and folklore studies.

1967   "Akademikos Hovsep Orbelu Hayagitakan gortsuneutyune." [The Work in Armenology by Academician Hovsep Orbeli.] *PH* 1:15–28.

        On the occasion of Orbeli's 80th birthday. He published on Armenian antiquities, worked with N. Marr. Also involved with publications on Armenian folklore.

1968   "Zhoghovrdakan avandutyunneri zhanrayin arandznahatkutyunneri masin." [About the Genre Individuality of Folk Legends.] *Banber Erevani Hamalsarani* 2:73–88. Russian summary.

        The place of legends in oral prose, individuality of legends, and different kinds of legends.

1970   "Sovetahay banagitutyune hisunatarum." [Fifty Years of Armenian Folklore.] *PH* 3:19–32. Russian summary.

        Chronological survey of principal contributions, projects, and publications.

1975   "Hayrenakan paterazmi tarineri Hay banahyusutyune." [Armenian Folklore During the Years of the Patriotic War.] *PH* 2:43–50.

        The war period in 1942 inspired various genres of folklore, folk songs, dances, tales, curses, anecdotes. Examples are given.

1979   *Armianskie predaniia.* [Armenian Traditions.] Erevan, Izd-vo Armianskoi SSR. 353 pp. English summary.

        First published in Armenian in 1969 with the title *Avandapatum*; I have not seen that edition. This is a revised Russian translation. First part about the genre in general. Second part gives texts (930), including variants and notes on sources from which obtained. Grouped by subjects: physical features, land, plants, animals, etc.

1979   "Chartarapetutyan ev kari arvestagortsutyan artatsolume Hay banahyusutyan mej." [The Reflection of Architecture and Masonry in Armenian Folklore.] *PH* 3:62–79.

        Quotes from various folklore items from Moses of Khoren, minstrel songs, and folk songs that describe structures and engravings.

Ghanalanian, Aram Tigrani *(continued)*
1980   "V. Saroyani steghtsagortsutyan azgayin-banahyusakan armatnere." [The
             Ethnic-Folkloristic Roots in William Saroyan's Work.] *PH* 3:43–57. Russian
             summary.
                      In talks William Saroyan gave in Erevan he introduced ideas based on
                      Armenian proverbs. Evidence in some of his writings that there is basic
                      folk knowledge in his work.

1982   "Zhoghovrdakan banarvesti artatsolume Sayat-Novayi ergerum." [The
             Reflection of Folklore in the Songs of Sayat-Nova.] *PH* 1:17–27. Russian
             summary.
                      Sayat-Nova's intimate knowledge of Armenian dialect of Tiflis; the
                      proverbs and sayings appear in his songs. Familiarity with heroes and
                      heroines of Persian folklore also enriched his songs.

1985   *Drvagner Hay banagitutyan patmutyan.* [Works in the History of Armenian
             Folklore.] Erevan, HSSH, GA Hrat. 292 pp.
                      Essays about Khachatur Abovian, Michael Nalbandian, Karekin
                      Servantsian, Manuk Abeghian, Komitas, N. Marr, K. Melik-Ohanjanian.
                      Also an essay about Ghanalanian by S. Harutyunian. Includes extensive
                      folklore bibliography (pp. 211–282) arranged chronologically, 1830–
                      1982, and has subject list.

Gharibian, A. S.
1958   *Hayereni norahayt barbarneri mi nor khump.* [A New Group of Newly Found
             Armenian Dialects.] Erevan, HSSH, GA Hrat. 193 pp. Russian summary .
                      Dialects of Aramoy, Kapusi, Edessa. Includes grammar and word list for
                      each group with examples of anecdotes for each. Word lists are in
                      Standard Armenian followed by dialect.

Ghazar-Charek [no first name given]
1957   *Hushamadian Partsr Haiki; Garinabadum.* [Memorial of Upper Armenia;
             History of Garin.] Beirut, Mshag. 791 pp. il., fold. map.
                      Mostly historical, but pp. 338–391 relate to folklore: the character and
                      customs of the people of Garin (Erzerum); food and drink. Engagements
                      and weddings (pp. 352–358). The Garin dialect with examples of songs,
                      including children's songs (pp. 788–790).

Ghazarian, J. A.
1967   "Baroyakan mi kani skzbunkner 'Sasuntsi Davit' eposum" [A Few Moral
             Principles in the Epic "David of Sassoun."] *L* 2:51–62.
                      Presents values such as patriotism, feeling of freedom, and
                      humanitarianism, respect for women, love of family, etc. Gives
                      supporting quotations.

1976   *Baroyakan skzbunknere 'Sasuntsi Davit' eposum.* [The Moral Principles of the Epic "David of Sassoun."] Erevan, "Hayastan," Hrat. 175 pp.
          The work ethic, love of man, happiness and freedom. Supporting examples quoted from epic.

Ghazikian, A. Gh.
1909–12   *Haygagan nor madenakidutiun ev hanrakidaran geanki.* [Modern Armenian Publishing and Encyclopedia of Life.] Vols. 1–2 in 1 vol. Venice, St. Lazar.
          Covers the alphabetic list of authors, A–N. Original intent to complete, but no explanation of why discontinued. The work is a bibliography that gives contents of works by authors, and sometimes summaries. Includes works of folklorists.

Ghaziyan, A. [This name appears with single initial A., also with A. S., and with first name Alvard. I think they are all the same person.—AMA]
1974   "Lernayin Gharabaghi banahyusutyune 1970–1973tt grarumneri himan vra." [About the Folklore of Mountainous Karabagh in the years 1970–73 based on transcriptions.] *PH* 4:235–241.
          Survey of various genres of folklore. Narrators still used opening and closing formulas, but different from earlier forms. More realistic tales than wonder tales, and more variants of comic tales. Music material not plentiful.

1974   "Yirmenskii geroichnii epos 'Sasna Tsirer.' " [Armenian Heroic Epic "Sasna Tsirer."] *Narodna Tvorchist ta Etnografiia* 6:64–71. ports.
          Has portraits of M. Abeghian and I. Orbeli in celebration of 100th anniversary of publication of David of Sassoun, and some later variants. Comments on epic and the unified text of 1939.

1977   "Hnaguyn mi sovoruyti ardzaganknere Hay banahyusutyan mej." [Echoes of a Most Ancient Custom in Armenian Folklore.] *PH* 2:275–280.
          About tales in which an old father is banished by sons. Examples of several short tales and variants are given. Information from various Eastern Armenian provinces and Vaspuragan.

1978   "Gharabaghi zvarchakhos Pul Pughin." [The Gharabagh Jester Pul Pughin.] *L* 9:60–69.
          A local humorous character with sharp wit. Examples of how he dispenses justice. Somewhat like the Hoja.

1980   " 'Sasna Tsrer' zhoghovrdakan norahayd patumneri gitakan hratarakutyune." [The Scholarly Edition of Newly Discovered Versions of the Popular Epic "Sasna-Tsrer."] *PH* 3:286–288.
          This is about volume 3 of the epic David of Sassoun in 14 sections in the language of Moks, Shadakh, and Mush. Recorded on modern machine.

Ghaziyan, A. *(continued)*
1983   "Hay zhoghovrdakan snahavatakan zruytsneri dasakarkman hartsi shurj."
            [About the Classification of Armenian Superstitious Folk Sayings.] *L* 8:77–
            85. Russian summary.
                Classifications relate to spirits, saints and holy places, holy plants and
                animals, transformations, angels of death and future life, divination.
                Gives examples of beliefs within these classes.

1985   "Hayrenakan mets paterazme Hay zhoghovrdakan ergerum." [The Great
            Patriotic War in Armenian Folk Songs.] *L* 4:13–21.
                The war in 1940s inspired folk songs based on earlier folk tunes. Themes
                are patriotism, love, anti-Hitler. Family-oriented songs about departure,
                news, letter songs.

1989   *Hay zhoghovrdakan razmi ev zinvori erger.* [Armenian Folk Songs about War
            and Soldiers.] Erevan, Haykakan HSSH, GA Hrat. 390 pp.
                Includes 287 songs and music for 16 songs. Notes indicate where song
                first published, or whether it is in archives.

Ghltchian, Arsen
1912–13   "Hay hin iravunke." [Ancient Armenian Law.] *AH* 22:1–60; 23:68–113;
            24:5–50.
                About adoption, marriage, status of husband. Sources of customary law,
                family organization, marriage rights, monogamy and polygamy, child
                marriage.

Ghzhrikian, D.
1962   "Vardiknere mijnadaryan Rumanakan zhoghovrdakan ergerum." [The Vardiks
            in Medieval Rumanian Popular Songs.] *PH* 4:83–94. Russian summary.
                The Armenian Vardik family important in Rumania in 16th century
                according to documents. Important in business community. Members of
                family subject of heroic ballads. Family ballad in Rumanian and
                Armenian.

Gilliat-Smith, Bernard
1913–14   "The Dialect of the Drindaris." *Gypsy Lore Society. Journal,* n.s. 7:260–298.
                Of Armenian folklore interest p. 297 which has a long footnote: Drindari
                Gypsies were called to make music for Armenian marriage feasts and
                other rejoicings. They learned some Armenian and used a Gypsy as
                majordomo.

Gippert, Jost
1987   "Old Armenian and Caucasian Calendar Systems." *Annual of Armenian
            Linguistics* 8:63–72
                Gives old Armenian calendar months with Georgian equivalents. Persian
                calendar based on festival names. Six Armenian month names based on
                Persian.

Girard, M. D.
1902   " 'Les Madag' ou Sacrifices arménien." *Revue de l'Orient Chrétien* 7:410–
            422.
            Author's personal observations on preparation of animal for sacrifice in
            Caesarea and Marzovan.

Goian, Georg
1952   *2000 let armianskogo teatra.* [Two Thousand Years of the Armenian Theater.]
            Moscow, Gosudarstvennoe Izd-vo Iskusstvo. 2 v. il. (part col.), maps.
            Plan for five volumes, but only first two available, not certain if others
            ever published. History and development of theater from 59 B.C. to 10th
            century. Illustrations from old Armenian manuscripts show minstrel
            figures.

1954   *Two Thousand Years of the Armenian Theater.* New York, The Armenian
            National Council of America. 48 pp. il.
            A digest of the author's Russian work. The digest is by Veronica
            Arvanian and Lillian G. Murad. Theater started from pagan ceremonials
            related to gods, funerary rites, bacchanals. Use of masks, development of
            tragedy and comedy. Folk theater used animal masks. Rev. Charles A.
            Vartanian gives information on development in modern times, dramatists
            and actors.

Gokian, S.
1945–46   "Haygagan harsaniki hntevrobagan timakidze." [The Indo-European Profile
            of the Armenian Wedding.] *H* 23(6):55–71; 24(1):83–97; 24(2):86–96;
            24(3):90–92; 24(4):94–105.
            Notes similarities: capture, purchase, asking for hand of bride. Also notes
            special Armenian wedding customs and superstitions, and also special
            concern for bride and tenderness toward her. First installment begins title
            with single word "Hay."

Gombos, Karoly
1981   "Old Armenian Dragon Rugs." *Armenian Review* 34:358–360.
            Dragon in Armenian rugs not derived from China but from Armenian
            folklore. Notes the Armenian Hercules, Vahakn as the dragon killer in
            Armenian myths. Paper was presented at Symposium on Armenian Rugs,
            Washington, D.C., Oct. 15, 1980.

Gomidas. *See* Komitas

Goodspeed, Edgar J.
1906   "Tertag and Sarkis: An Armenian Folktale." Translated from the Ethiopic.
            American Antiquarian and Oriental Journal 28:133–140.
            Curious tale about origin of Armenian church and Armenian alphabet. Part
            of it matches Armenian history, but names are wrong. Alphabet letters are
            incomplete. Translator gives notes about historical facts.

Gopesa, L.
1887–88   "Armenische Hochzeit." *Ethnologische Mitteilungen aus Ungarn* 1:176–177.
            Description of wedding including church service.

Goyan. *See* Goian

Gray, Louis H.
1926   "Les Mètres paiens d'Arménie." *REA* 6:159–167.
            Gives Armenian text, then the transliteration, then French translation from
            Moses of Khoren and Gregoire le maître (9th century) metrical study,
            especially of Vahakn's song.

Grayian, Mesrob. *See* Karayan, Mesrop

Gregoire, Henri
1932   "Les sources historiques et littéraires de Digénis Akritas." *Congres
            International d'Études Byzantines*. 3rd, 1910. *Actes*. Athens, Impr. Hestia.
            pp. 281–294.
            Some have opinion that the Byzantine epic has some relationship to the
            Armenian epic David of Sassoun. Includes some Armenian place names.

Greppin, John A. C.
1978   *Classical and Middle Armenian Bird Names: A Linguistic, Taxonomic, and
            Mythogical Study*. Dellmar, N. Y., Caravan Books. xxi, 290 pp. il.
            Text in order of scientific names of birds followed by names in Armenian,
            Greek, Iranian, Sanskrit, English. Thematic index, e.g., names of
            bellicose birds.

1985   "Some Further Comments on Armenian Bird Names." *Annual of Armenian
            Linguistics* 6:45–50.
            Frankelin, raven, and small birds caught in nets. Does not mention
            folklore, but article is important for birds that do appear in Armenian
            folklore, e.g., raven.

1987   "Some Early Botanical Loan Words Shared by Armenian and Semitic."
            Annual of Armenian Linguistics 8:73–82.
            There are 16 words, some of which are important in Armenian cookery.

Grigorian, Grigor
1951   *Hay zhoghovrdakan banahyusutyun*. [Armenian Folklore.] Erevan, HSSR,
            GA Hrat. 595 pp.
            A chrestomathy that presents various genres of folklore: myths, hero
            tales, legends, anecdotes, various kinds of songs, fables, proverbs,
            abridged version of David of Sassoun. Includes excerpts from writings of
            Karl Marx, Engels, Lenin, Stalin.

1954 "Nerkin harstaharichneri dem Hay zhoghovordi mghats sotsialakan paykari artatsolume 'Sassna Tsrer' eposum." [The Reflection of the Armenian People's Social Struggle Against Oppressors from Within in the Epic "Sasna Tsrer."] *Teghekakir* 8:29–49.

In the epic "David of Sassoun," aside from foreign oppression, there is the internal struggle against lords. They are considered dragons who ruled over water rights and demanded girls in exchange. Dragon personages opposed by heroes representing social class struggle.

1956 *Hatentir Hay zhoghovrdakan banahyusutyan.* [Selection of Armenian Folklore.] Erevan, Haypethrat. 390 pp.

Various genres of Armenian folklore, including David of Sassoun (pp. 67–159), but no explanation of what variant. Some folktales, mostly realistic. Various folk songs, proverbs and sayings (463), pp. 322–327. A few fables. One section devoted to Soviet songs, ballads, and part of "Lenin Pasha" (pp. 359–366).

1958 " 'Sasuntsi Davit' eposi zhoghovrdaynutyan probleme." [The Problem of the Folk Spirit of the Epic David of Sassoun.] *PH* 2:97–113.

The epic really expresses folk spirit of Armenians. Historically represents growth of people through struggle against oppression.

1960 *Hay zhoghovrdakan herosakan epose.* [The Heroic Armenian Epic.] Erevan, HSSH, GA Hrat. 783, [i.e.] 683 pp. Russian summary.

A comprehensive study of the Armenian epic, David of Sassoun: its history, special ideas of independence, war and peace, work, friendship of peoples. Study of some of characters in the epic.

1960 "Sovetahay patmakan-vepakan ergeri zhanrayin hatkanishnere." [The Genre Features of Armenian Historical Epic Songs of the Soviet Period.] *PH* 3:27–38. Russian summary.

About real people, some living at time of writing; no gods or religion. Realism as in "Lenin Pasha."

1965 *Sovetahay vipergern u patmakan ergayin banahyusutyune.* [Soviet Armenian Epic Songs and Historical Song Folklore.] Erevan, HSSR, Hrat. 251 pp.

Survey of folklore of Soviet history, especially praise of Lenin and his accomplishments, historical events, e.g., Battle of Stalingrad, military songs. In style of epic songs; some examples give original and adaptation.

1967 *Hay zhoghovrdakan banahyusutyan.* [Armenian Folklore.] Erevan, "Luys" Hrat. 493 pp.

Folklore and its ties to literature and other disciplines. Developmental stages through songs, legends, medieval and capitalistic folklore. Includes various genres of folklore, and David of Sassoun. About 100 pages devoted to Lenin and the revolution.

Grigorian, Grigor *(continued)*
1969   *Lenine ev Hoktembere Hay banahyusutyan mej.* [Lenin and October in
              Armenian Folklore.] Erevan, "Hayastan" Hrat. 72 pp.
                   Mostly about epic "Lenin Pasha" (1934) by Garo who learned it from
                   Sepoy, a carder, 1921–24. Excerpts in verse tell of Lenin's heroic
                   qualities, his great intelligence, good attributes. Also includes "Lenin
                   Hekiat" [Tale] about mother's dream of threat to his life. Also "Lenin
                   Khanate" in which Lenin plans to avenge death of his father and brother.

1973   "Sasna Davit ev Mher." [David of Sassoun and Mher.] *Banber Erevani
              Hamalsarani* 2:171–194.
                   Version of David of Sassoun collected in village of Ghaznafor as told by
                   Gevorg M. Petrosian who heard it from paternal uncle. But no text exists
                   of uncle's version.

1974   *Hay banahyusutyan krestomati.* [Armenian Folklore Chrestomathy.] 2nd ed.
              Erevan, Erevani Hamalsarani Hrat. 533 pp.
                   Long introductory survey (pp. 3–165) about folklore. Wide selection of
                   various genres, including David of Sassoun. Some folktales, legends,
                   fables, anecdotes. Proverbs and sayings (547) pp. 325–348 are classified;
                   riddles (103) pp. 353–358. Songs arranged by subjects, pp. 359–453 and
                   folk drama, pp. 463–466, using song and mimicry. Soviet folklore, pp.
                   473–532 includes songs and dances in praise of Lenin and Bolsheviks.

1974   "Hay eposagitutyan patmutyunits." [From the History of Armenian Epic
              Studies.] *PH* 2:31–46. Russian summary.
                   The epic David of Sassoun belongs to history of 9th–10th centuries, but
                   not noted by historians of the period. Written evidence in 16th century
                   Portuguese. K. Servantsian first transcribed epic in 1874. By 1936 there
                   were 50 variants. Cites nationwide spirit of work and ideals represented.

1986   *Hat zhoghovrdakan vipergnere ev patmakan ergayin banahyusutune.*
              [Armenian Epic Folk Songs and Historic Folklore in Songs.] Erevan, HSSH,
              GA Hrat. 417 pp.
                   Songs about Armenian legendary and historical figures. Of particular
                   interest the modern Soviet period that includes epic "Lenin Pasha," pp.
                   305–312. Notice at end gives Lenin as great savior of people.

1987   "Azgagraget Sargis Kamalian." [Ethnographer Sargis Kamalian.] *PH* 2:86–
              95. Russian summary.
                   Little attention has been given to Kamalian; aside from ethnography he
                   collected folklore that has not been published but is in the archives.

Grigorian, R. H.

1970 *Hay zhoghovrdakan ororotsayin ev mankakan erger.* [Armenian Folk Lullabies and Children's Songs.] Erevan, HSSH, GA Hrat. 466 pp. Russian and English summaries.

> There are 766 numbered songs, but counting variants the number goes up to 1000. Sections include cradle songs, lullabies, songs of praise, game songs, songs of waking and bathing. Notes indicate place and informant. Word list, subject list, and list of first lines.

Grigorian, Rouben

1952 "Armenian Music—Past and Present." *Armenian Review* 5(2):59–66.

> Includes pre-Christian period, minstrels, the Goghtn singers. Christian period introduced church hymns known as *sharagans*. Komitas did much work on folk songs.

Grigorian, Roza

1986 "Zhoghovrdakan eposi Gegharkuniki asatsoghnere." [The Folk Epic Narrators of Gegharkunik.] *L* 2:47–50.

> Seven versions of David of Sassoun collected from settlement of Gegharkunik in the Lake Sevan basin. Narrators are migrants (since 1828) from western Armenia and some Armenians from Persia. They preserve language of their areas.

Grigorian, Sh. S.

1971 *Hayots hin gusanakan ergere.* [Old Minstrel Songs of Armenia.] Erevan, HSSH, GA Hrat. 236 pp.

> First part discusses historical evidence about the old minstrels of Armenia and their songs. Definitions of various songs. Second part about metrical problems of medieval poetry and gives examples of minstrel songs.

Grigorian-Spandarian, M. M.

1971 *Lernayin Gharabaghi banahyusutyune.* [The Folklore of Mountainous Gharabagh.] Erevan, HSSH, GA Hrat. 476 pp. port.

> Material collected between 1920 and 1960 in the Karabagh dialect. Included are 1804 quatrains of songs used by girls for *vijag* (fortune festival or game). Rest of book includes 43 tales; legends and traditions; 31 anecdotes; 243 riddles; 13 tongue-twisters; 24 humorous stories; 26 blessings; 53 curses; 62 mockeries. Notes and word list, and names of informants.

Grigorov, N.

1892 "Selo Tatev." [The Village of Tatev.] *Sbornik Materialov dlia Opisaniia Mestnostei i Plemen Kavkaza* 13(1):59–125.

> Dwellings, furnishings and clothing; weddings; pilgrimages; entertainments. Notes 71 superstitions. A tale "The Pampered," a legend of Alexander of Macedon. Some riddles (20), and proverbs (30).

Gronow, Pekko
1975   "Ethnic Music and Soviet Record Industry." *Ethnomusicology* 19:91–99.
              Notes availability of records in ethnic areas, including Armenia.
              Recordings in 33 and 78 rpm for folk music. Statistics are for 1959.
              Notes catalogs if available.

Grousset, René
1947   "Le Paganisme arménien." In his *Histoire de l'Arménie, des origines à 1071.*
              Paris, Peyot. pp. 117–120.
              Brief information on Armenian paganism. An Armenian translation
              appears in *H* 28(4):25–27. 1950. Translated by Sarkis Yerganian.

Gulakyan. *See* Gullakian

Gulbenkian, Eduard
1984   "The Attitude to War in 'The Epic of Sassoun.' " *Folklore* 95:105–112.
              The epic David of Sassoun shows fairness in battle. Wars were
              defensive—Armenians not aggressive. David embodies childlike belief
              that right will always prevail over might. Probably explains why
              Armenians were not empire builders.

1989   "Measures of Length in Medieval Armenian Texts." *HA* 103:81–92.
              Metric equivalents are given to the various measurements in the texts.

Gulbenkian, Roberto, and Berbérian, H.
1971   "La Légende de David de Sassoun d'aprés deux Voyageurs portugais du
              XVIe siécle." *REA*, n.s. 8:175–188.
              Gives account of travelers Antonio Tenreiro (1523 & 1539) and Mestre
              Afonso (1565) in which reference is made to the Armenian epic David of
              Sassoun.

Gullakian, Suzanna [Later appears with initials S. A.; I think same person.—AMA]
1976   "Armianskie skazki na stranitsakh Russkikh dorevoliutsonnykh izdanii."
              [Armenian Tales Published in Prerevolutionary Russia.] *L* 9:46–55.
              Armenian summary.
              Mentions tales published by August von Haxthausen in 1857 in his
              "Zakavkazskii krai." Also notes that various teachers and students
              collected 120 tales from Elisapetpol and Erevan and published them in 44
              issues of *Sbornik Materialov dlia Opisaniia Mestnostei i Plemen Kavkaza*,
              1881–1915. Also some in *Etnograficheskoe Obozrenie*. Caught Russian
              attention.

Gullakian, Suzanna [here as S. A.]

1979   "O personazhakh Armianskikh volshebnykh skazok." [On the Personages of Armenian Magic Tales.] *Banber Erevani Hamalsarani* 1:49–62. Armenian summary.

         Persons or motifs in tales are grouped as historical, religious-mythological, fantastic. Propp and Aarne-Thompson's *Types of the Folktale* mentioned.

1979   "Personazhi Armianskikh volshebnykh skazok po ikh soslovnoi prinadlezhnosti i professional'nym zaniatiam." [Characters in the Armenian Fairy Tales According to their Social and Professional Occupations.] *PH* 4:172–187. Armenian summary.

         For the period 1860–1905, 570 tales were examined. Classes in tales: kings highest, beggars lowest. Occupational classes: hunters, fishermen, blacksmiths, carpenters, shepherds. Number of characters as to position, e.g., 371 kings, and 175 daughters of kings.

Gurahian, Jennifer

1990   "In the Mind's Eye: Collective Memory and Armenian Village Ethnographies." *Armenian Review* 43(1):19–29.

         Based on bibliography prepared by Sarkis Karayan: "History of Armenian Communities in Turkey." *Armenian Review* (1980) 33(1):89–96.

Gusev, V. Y.

1961   "Folklore Research in the USSR." *Soviet Review* 2(1):51–58.

         No specific reference to Armenia, but a guide to scope of research which might apply to Armenia. Notes need to study the epics and the peoples of the USSR. Methodology for research.

H., Gh. *See* Hovnanian, Gh.

Hachian. *See* Hajian

Hagopian. *See* Hakobian

Haig, Vahe

1959   *Kharpert ev anor voskeghen tashte.* [Kharpert and her Golden Plain.] New York. 1500 pp. il., maps.

         Title pages and introduction in Armenian, English, French. Folklore material scattered: 374 proverbs and sayings, pp. 69, 86, 291, 1393–97. Brief treatment of manners and customs, dress, marriage, births, festivals, pp. 675–689; songs, dances, children's rhymes, pp. 1304–1321; provincial expressions classed as parts of body, pp. 1375–1380. Between pp. 1389–1391 are 65 riddles, 64 blessings, 55 curses, 24 threats, 21 oaths.

Haigaz, Aram
1957   *Shabin Karahisar u ir herosamarde.* [Shabin Karahisar and her Heroic
            Struggle.] New York. 459 pp. il. fold. map.
                 Brief scattered folklore information, pp. 39–44, on pilgrimages. Shrove-
                 tide skit, p. 57: two youths dress as bride and groom; latter dies, wife
                 weeps, he revives; said to symbolize winter and spring. Some festivals,
                 pp. 58–66.

Haigazn, Edouard
1895   "Traditions et superstitions de l'Arménie." *Revue des Traditions Populaires*
            10:296–297.
                 Narrates a couple of traditions: "Hermit in the Town" and "Bridge of the
                 Non-humans."

Hajian, M.
1907   *Hin avantagan hekiatner Khodorochnoy.* [Old Mythical Tales of Khodorchi.]
            Vienna, I Vans Bashdban Asdvadzadzno. 87 pp.
                 Compilation of tales remembered that were told in village Khodorchi in
                 Erzerum area. There are 20 tales in dialect, and footnotes explain dialect
                 words.

Hakobian, Ed.
1972   *Komitasi hemaykin dag.* [Under the Charm of Komitas.] Beirut, Shirag
            Hrad. 191 pp. il.
                 A collection of essays by various persons about special musical events
                 and programs that featured Komitas. Includes some music.

Hakobian, G. A.
1962   "Nerses Shnorhalu antip haneluknere." [The Unpublished Riddles of Nerses
            Shnorhali.] *PH* 4:105–114. Russian summary.
                 Medieval writer had published only 120 riddles, but about 200 not
                 published. Of these, few derived from Biblical subjects in classical
                 Armenian, but rest in quatrain form and many relate to nature. Some
                 examples are given.

Hakobian, G. V.
1988   "Mkrtutean tsesi het kapvats azgaktsakan terminere Hayerenum." [Armenian
            Relationship Terminology Connected with the Rite of Baptism.] *PH* 3:144–
            150. Russian summary.
                 Use of baptism terminology from the 5th to 15th centuries which involve
                 slight changes in designating the child and sponsors.

Hakobian, Grigor
1965   *Srbagortsvats havatalikner.* [Sanctified Beliefs.] Erevan, "Hayastan." 81 pp.
                 Discusses elements or features that have been venerated or sanctified:
                 earth (the soil), water, bread, the sun, fire, the flag, the right hand that

leads the left, the club or scepter, stone gods, hair worship. Significance of the above.

Hakobian, N.

1976   " 'Sasna Tsrer' eposi ergitsakan makanunnere." [The Satirical Nicknames in the Epic "Sasna Tsrer."] *Banber Erevani Hamalsarani* 3:127–133. Russian summary.

Title would be more accurate without the word satirical. About the nicknames of the principal characters in the epic; names belonging to the heroic and brave are dignified; names of enemies are derogatory.

Hakobian, N. K., and Sahakian, A.

1978   "Haykakan zhoghovrdakan hekiatneri zhanrayin tarberakman hartsi shurj." [About the Question of Genre Variations in Armenian Folktales.] *Banber Erevani Hamalsarani* 1:127–138. Russian summary.

Discussion of 57 fantastic and realistic Armenian folktales of 19th century and beginning of 20th century. Realistic tales use motifs familiar to village life. The fantastic or wonder tales about heroic persons and events.

Hakobian, P. H.

1969   "Sayat-Novayi Haghbati vankum linelu hartsi shurje." [On the Question of whether Sayat-Nova stayed at the Haghbat Monastery.] *PH* 3:209–225.

Belief that Sayat-Nova spent 25 years at Haghbat Monastery not correct. Place is in ruins; no steps taken to repair it since 1778: still deserted in 1780 and there were Lesgian raids up to 1792. Also suggests that Sayat-Nova died in 1801, not 1795.

Halahčjan, Hovhannes

1978   "L'Architecture civile dell'Armena medioevale." *Simposio Internationale di Arte Armena.* 1st, Bergamo, 28–30 June 1975. *Atti* pp. 213–225. il.

The illustrations show some internal scenes of domestic architecture.

Hamamchian, E.

1897   "Banants giughi kurgannere." [Burial Mounds of the Village of Banants.] *AH* 2:307–315.

Results of archeological work in the village. Superstitions derive from some of items found in mounds.

Hambroer, Joh.

1953–54   "Iranean darrer Hay zhoghovrtagan havadkin mech." [Iranian Elements in Armenian Folk Beliefs.] *HA* 67:196–205; 68:544–561.

Article written in German for *HA*, and translated by E. Boghosian. Have not been able to find German original. Discusses Armenian *krogh* (the writer) and Iranian equivalent *srosh*, and Armenian *ergnayin akaghaghe* (heavenly cockerel) and Iranian *barotarsh* (the one who sees).

Hannesian Brothers
1960–63   *Tsaynakryal Shirag erkaran.* [Vocal Shirag Songbook.] Beirut, Dbaran
            Shirag. 2 v. with music.
                   Vol. 1 , pp. 75–122, minstrel songs; pp. 123–154, folk songs; pp. 195–
                   204, dance songs. Vol. 2, pp. 89–132, minstrel songs; pp. 133–171, folk
                   songs; pp. 219–226, dance music. Most of these have been harmonized.

Harfouche, Jamal Karam
1965   *Infant Health in Lebanon, Customs and Taboos.* Beirut, Khayats. 121 pp.
            col. il.
                   Survey based on Armenian, Maronite, and Sunni communities. Breast
                   feeding, maternal diets during and after pregnancy; menstrual taboos; evil
                   eye effect on mother and child. Illustrations show charms to use against
                   evil eye.

Harris, J. Rendel
1904   "Notes from Armenia, in Illustration of The Golden Bough." *Folklore*
            15:427–446.
                   Notes some Armenian practices and customs: rain charms, Vartavar (Feast
                   of the Transfiguration); Candlemas; foundation sacrifice; offering first
                   fruits; holy trees; childbirth customs.

Harutiunian, Is[ahak]
1898   "Sanahin." *AH* 3:273–315. il.
                   History of Sanahin: the village, relics, manuscripts, and monastery.

1903   "Gosha vank, kam Nor Getik." [Gosh Monastery, or New Getik.] *AH* 10:5–
            36. il.
                   History and description, and some information about Mkhitar Gosh and
                   his law book.

Harutyunian. *See also* Aroutyounian and Arutiunian

Harutyunian, A. A.
1968   "Hay kaghakayin zhoghovrdakan ergaruest erazhshtakan ojakan himnakan
            tipere." [Fundamental Types of Armenian Town Folk Musical Art.] *L* 6:70–
            81. Includes music.
                   From last half of 19th century to start of the 20th century, folklorelike
                   music of various types introduced in towns.

Harutyunian, N. Kh.
1969   "Batsman khosk." [Opening Remarks.] *PH* 4:3–6. port. opposite p. 3.
                   On the occasion of the 100th anniversary of birth of Komitas, the
                   Armenian folk-song collector who introduced Armenian folk songs to the
                   world and saved them.

Harutyunian, S. B. *See* Arutiunian, S. B., for articles with Russian titles.

Harutyunian, S. B. (sometimes appears as Sargis)
1959   "Zhoghovrdakan hanelukneri mi kani arantsnahatkutyunneri masin." [About
          Some Unique Characteristics of Folk Riddles.] *PH* 1:163–174. Russian
          summary.
              Historic development of types of riddles. Gives examples of some riddles
              and some of formulas used.

1960   *Hay zhoghovrdakan hanelukner.* [Armenian Folk Riddles.] Erevan, HSSR,
          GA Hrat. 169 pp. Russian summary, pp. 157–168.
              Study of an old genre of Armenian folklore. Not a list of riddles, but
              presentation of many problems relating to the folk material and spiritual
              life. Considers characteristics of types of riddles, their form, artistry,
              metrics. Examples given. Riddle contests.

1965   *Hay zhoghovrdakan hanelukner.* [Armenian Folk Riddles.] Erevan, HSSH,
          GA Hrat. 389 pp. Russian and German summaries.
              Introductory essay about riddles; footnotes show contact with several
              foreign writers, including Archer Taylor. There are over 2000 riddles plus
              variants. Arranged by subject. When known, locale of each riddle is
              given. There are notes and various indexes and symbols used in riddles.

1965   "Mets Hayagete." [The Great Armenologist.] *PH* 1:137–152. port. Russian
          summary.
              About Manuk Abeghian on the occasion of 100th year of his birth. His
              life work as linguist and folklorist.

1968   "Garegin Hovsepiane orpes banaget." [Garegin Hovsepian as a Folklorist.]
          PH 1:147–154. port.
              Hovsepian had view that folklore reveals much about history of a people,
              their occupations, beliefs, and superstitions. He was active in collecting
              and publishing Persian epic Rostam Zal that reflects an Armenian
              environment.

1969   "Vastakashat banagete." [The Eminent Folklorist.] *PH* 1:155–162. port.
              Biographical sketch and summary of work of Aram Ghanalanian who
              prepared brief versions of 1000 folktales for a future concordance.

1970   *Manuk Abeghian, kianke u gortse.* [Manuk Abeghian, his Life and Work.]
          Erevan, HSSH, GA Hrat. 667 pp.
              First part about Abeghian's life. Large part (pp. 191–641) gives summary
              of his principal works; some commentary included. Abeghian principally
              a teacher and linguist. Under Soviet period he worked on spelling reform.
              Has a bibliography (216) roughly classified, many articles in journals not
              easily available.

Harutyunian, S. B. *(continued)*

1971   "Karapet Melik-Ohanjanian (1893–1970)." *Erevani Hamalsarani* 10:56–61. Russian summary.

           Biographical sketch. Wrote historical works and was interested in Persian and Armenian folklore, including Soviet period. In 1914 attended Berlin University, studied Sanskrit. Returned to Armenia in 1920.

1975   " 'Karos Khach' vipergi mi mijnadaryan patum." [A Medieval Version of the Tale "Karos Khach."] *L* 9:87–93. Russian summary.

           Tale dates from 14th to 16th centuries. Seven variants printed between 1874 and 1972. Tale about wonder-working cross relating to Arab-Armenian relations. Abeghian discusses it in vol. 1 of his works.

1981   "Vishapamarte 'Sasna Tsrer' um." [The Dragon Fight in "Sasna Tsrer."] *L* 11: 65–85. Russian summary.

           About David of Sassoun. Relates that the fight comes from very ancient tradition of Indo-European, east against west, but with an Armenian slant.

1983   "Aram Ghanalanian." *L* 7:98–99. port.

           Obituary of Armenian folklorist, 1909–1983.

1983   "Hay vipagitutyan mets erakhtavore." [The Great Benefactor of Armenian Folklore.] *PH* 2–3:65–73. port. Russian summary.

           About K. Melik-Ohanjanian. His interest in folklore developed in early 1930s when he went about villages where Western Armenians had settled and he collected several variants of David of Sassoun.

1985   "Aram Ghanalanian." In Ghanalanian, Aram: *Drvagner Hay banagitutyan patmutyan*. Erevan, HSSH, GA Hrat, 1985, pp. 189–211.

           About Ghanalanian's works in various genres of folklore. Also his continuation of folklore work in the tradition of his teacher M. Abeghian.

1985   "Mahvan patkeratsumnere Haykakan anetsknerum." [The Depiction of Death in Armenian Curses.] *L* 12:53–65. Russian summary.

           Most common form is *krogh* (the writer) in combination with other words, meaning "may the writer take you away," *krogh* being the recorder of man's life. Examples of various expressions are given.

1989   "Aram Ghanalanian." *PH* 3:12–17. port.

           A summary of Aram Ghanalanian's life and writings. Based on a long article that appeared in Ghanalanian's *Drvagner Hay banagitutyan patmutyan*, 1985, pp. 189–211.

1989   "Mi drvag Hay araspelabanutyunits." [An Excerpt From Armenian Mythology.] *PH* 1:157–166. Russian summary.

           On basis of comparative materials, reconstructs function of dogs in ritual mythological representation in ancient Armenia. Dogs take away souls of the dead, but also bring down or resurrect heroes; protect people with life's blessing, bread. Dogs represented as mediators between heaven, earth, and underworld.

Harutyunian, S. B., and Bartikian, H. M.

1975   " 'Sasna Tsreri' ardzagaknere 'Sharaf-Nameum.' " [Relections of "David of Sassoun" in "Sharaf-Name."] *PH* 2:90–104. Russian summary.

Some elements of David of Sassoun appear in the Kurdish epic Sharaf-Name.

Harutyunian, S. B., and Sahakian, Arusyak

1973   "Sasna Tsrer." [Daredevils of Sassoun.] *L* 7:55–84. port. 8:49–74. Russian summary.

On occasion of transcription of David of Sassoun by Karekin Servantsian 100 years ago. A version of epic given here was transcribed in 1972 as told in Mush dialect by Abaju Sato. In blank verse, 2109 lines.

Harutyunian, V. A.

1976   *Hay groghnere ev banahyusutyune entdem kroni.* [Armenian Writers and Folklore Against Religion.] Erevan, "Hayastan" Hrat. 680 pp.

Folklore material, mostly anti-clerical anecdotes; also some proverbs and sayings, and verses by minstrels. Quotations from Marx, Engels, Lenin, and some Armenian writers featuring anti-clerical characters or mockery of clerics. Book intended for lecturers, agitators, and students engaged in propaganda.

Hasratian, M. S.

1969   "Orn e Movses Khorenatsu tsnntavayre." [Which is the Birthplace of Moses of Khoren?] *L* 12:81–90. Russian summary.

Author thinks that Korni-Tsor in the district of Korissi is the birthplace.

Hasratian, Morus. *See* Sayat-Nova (1963) *Hayeren*, etc.

Hatsuni, Vartan

1910   "Ertmunk tivats ev akhdits." [Oaths Against Demons and Diseases.] *B* 68:369–379, 421–434, 478–487. il.

Though called oaths, these are more like exorcisms and papers with special inscriptions. Comments on symbolism of some numbers and letters.

1910   "Hay ev odar ertmank." [Armenian and Foreign Oaths.] *B* 68:257–265, 321–334.

Customary oaths, oaths in court, religious oaths, contractual and reconciliation oaths. Some comparisons with Greek and Jewish oaths.

Hatsuni, Vartan *(continued)*

1910   "Mer nakhnik inchpes g'ertnuin." [How our Ancestors took Oaths.] *B* 68:49–61, 107–120.

        Discusses regular and irregular oaths, occasions when taken, those who take oaths, e.g., others and Christians; places where oaths are taken; holy items, e.g., Bible, cross, etc. Forms of oaths—worldly, religious, written; sealed oaths, intercessory oaths. Perjury, false oaths, incorrect oaths.

1910   "Zhamhar ev zankag." [Timekeeper and Bell.] *B* 68:193–203

        Describes wooden device that timekeeper clapped together to announce time to attend church services. Based on Armenian sources. Bell introduced later.

1912   *Jasher ev khnjoyk hin Hayasdani mech.* [Meals and Feasts in Ancient Armenia.] Venice, St. Lazar. 503 pp.

        Not a cookbook, but about food and its place in Armenian life. Storerooms, granaries, kinds of things stored, utensils are described. Invitations and significance of bread and salt. Use of animal sacrifice (*madagh*) shared with people. Meals for repose of soul, Easter, baptism. Fasts and defiled foods. Information from over 100 sources. Review in *B* 1913 (71):335, signed H. Avker.

1923   *Badmutiun hin Hay Darazin.* [History of Ancient Armenian Costume.] Venice, St. Lazar. 470 pp. il.

        Covers period from Urartian times through 17th century. Sources are coins, sculptures, manuscript illustrations, and descriptive works. Costumes used for special events: baptism, weddings, mourning. Military and clerical garb discussed. Mostly about costume of important personages. Review in *HA* 1925 (38):411–416, by A. Madigian.

1932   *Ertmank hin Hayots mech.* [Oaths Among Ancient Armenians.] 2nd ed. Venice, St. Lazar. 271 pp.

        A study of oaths, not a list. Oaths in general, occasions, places, and witnesses, times, forms (written and otherwise), errors. Comparison of Armenian oaths with foreign oaths. Also considers what some consider exorcisms.

1936   *Hayuhin badmutian archev.* [The Armenian Woman in History.] Venice, St. Lazar. 471 pp. il.

        Study based on written works, hence the women of higher rank. Peasants were not written about. Various aspects of life of women: domestic life, marriage, including description of wedding, motherhood, and activities in various spheres; her social life, benevolence, courage and suffering, mourning; her place in foreign palaces. Illustrations show costumes.

Haxthausen, August von
1854   *Transcaucasia. Sketches of the Nations and Races Between the Black Sea and
            the Caspian*. London, Chapman and Hall. xxiii, 448 pp. il., fold. map.
            There are 17 Armenian tales and legends on pp. 353–377. Other parts of
            book of interest since some customs are described. Author met the
            Armenian writer Khachadour Abovian from whom he learned about home
            life of Armenians. (Translated by J. E. Taylor from the manuscript of the
            author's "Transkaukasia" previous to its appearance in the original
            language.)

1856   *Transkaukasia*. Leipzig, Brokhaus. 2 v. in 1.
            Vol. 1, pp. 318–339, has 17 Armenian tales and legends. Various parts of
            same volume give information about some Armenian customs and folk
            life. Author met Khachadour Abovian, the Armenian writer, from whom
            he derived his information.

"Hay Guin" Society. Publication Committee.
1974?   *The Costume of Armenian Women*. Teheran, Published and Produced by
            International Communications. 32 pp. 42 col. plates.
            Descriptive text in Armenian and English. Most colored plates
            accompanied by pictures from historical sources from which costumes
            were copied. Costumes date from pre-Christian era to 19th century.
            Models wearing costumes not named.

Haykuni, Sargis
1901   "Davit ev Mher." [David and Mher.] In *Eminian Azgagrakan Zhoghovatsu*
            2:19–50.
            Told by Vardan of Mogk. Page 50 gives information about the narrator of
            this part of epic David of Sassoun.

1901   "Sanasar ev Baghdasar." [Sanasar and Baghdasar.] *Eminian Azgagrakan
            Zhoghovatsu* 2:3–17.
            This part of David of Sassoun is told in the dialect of Moks as told by
            Sakho. On pp. 15–17 some information about Sakho's family and life in
            the area.

1901   "Zhoghovrdakan vep ev hekiat." [Folk Epics and Tales.] *Eminian Azgagrakan
            Zhoghovatsu* 2:1–447.
            Two David of Sassoun sections have been given in the preceding two
            citations. On the rest of the pages are Kurdish epics or tales that contain
            Armenian elements (pp. 51–104) and 42 Armenian folktales (pp. 117–
            447).

Haykuni, Sargis *(continued)*
1902   "Zhoghovrdakan hekiatner." [Folktales.] *Eminian Azgagrakan Zhoghovatsu*
                4:1–462.
                    There are 48 tales; give narrators and dialects in which told. Supplement
                    includes two variants of David and Mher from David of Sassoun epic, pp.
                    369–398 in Shadakh dialect, and pp. 399–462, the Ararat branch.

1904   "Hay Krdakan veper." [Armenian-Kurdish Tales.] *Eminian Azgagrakan
                Zhoghovatsu* 5:3–304.
                    Includes 28 tales; narrators and dialects noted. Supplement of 12 pp.
                    gives 13 Kurdish songs with musical notations by Komitas.

1906   "Zhoghovrdakan erg, arats, asats, haneluk orhnank, anetsk, ev aylin." [Folk
                Songs, Proverbs, Sayings, Riddles, Oaths, Blessings, Curses, etc.] *Eminian
                Azgagrakan Zhoghovatsu* 6:1–419.
                    Songs with various themes; total of 3036 proverbs and sayings, many
                    riddles, blessings, oaths, etc. Notes places or dialects from which
                    derived.

1907   "Zhoghovrdakan arakner." [Folk Fables.] *AH* 16:214–215.
                    A bibliographical comment about a book by E. Lalayan about Haykuni's
                    book of fables.

Hayots Azgagrakan Enkerutiun. [Armenian Ethnographic Society.] [Information.]
1906   [Constitution.] *AH* 14:185.

1907   [Various Activities and Publications.] *AH* 15:214–217.

1907   [Supplement. Plan to Collect for the Society's Museum information on
                dwellings, costumes, food and drink, family life, etc.] *AH* 16:1–26.

1908   [Various activities.] *AH* 17:161–168.

Hayrabedian, Vahan
1932   "Nmushner Kghi kavari panahiusutenen." [Examples of Folklore from the
                Kghi District.] *H* 10(8):93–96.
                    A few folk songs; footnotes explain dialect words.

Hayruni, A. N.
1990   "Raffin ev zhoghovrdakan banahyusutyune." [Raffi and Folklore.] *Banber
                Erevani Hamalsarani* 3:108–113. Russian summary.
                    Raffi, the 19th century Armenian novelist, used folklore in combination
                    with history in his novels to convey the national spirit and psychology of
                    Armenian characters.

Hay zhoghovrdakan hekiatner. [Armenian Folktales.]

This title is in several volumes and editors vary. Only volumes I have seen are listed here. This publication project will probably extend to 20 volumes. All published in Erevan by HSSH, GA Hrat. *See also* Nazinian, A., 1959–85.

1959   Vol. 1. 669 pp. port. of E. Lalayan.

There are 48 tales from Ararat province (from its districts Ashtarak, Oshakan, Parpi) and the supplement has 11 variants. Dialect word list and notes for each tale. Most were collected by E. Lalayan in 1914–15 and appeared in his book *Margaritner* [Pearls], but unable to find that book.

1959   Vol. 2. 657 pp. port. of Tigran Navasardiants.

There are 56 tales from Ararat province. Some appeared in the collection published by Navasardiants in 1882–1903. Also from E. Lalayan's *Margaritner.* Dialect word list; also notes that give narrator and place.

1962   Vol. 3. 671 pp. port. of S. Haykuni.

There are 48 tales plus 10 in supplement from Ararat province. There is a dialect word list, and notes give place and narrator of tale. Tales were collected in 1890s and 1901–1902. A motif index covers vols. 1–3.

1963   Vol. 4. 550 pp. port. of Aleksandr Mkhitari Mkhitariants.

There are 56 tales from Shirak province and 13 tales in supplement. Word list and names of places and motifs. Notes give names of collectors and places.

1984   Vol. 12. 650 pp.

There are 78 tales from the Taron area; recorded 1915–16 from informants who were exiles from Mush, Turkey. Tales collected under direction of E. Lalayan. Notes name narrators and transcription date. Includes word list.

1985   Vol. 13. 613 pp.

There are 66 tales collected from Taron-Mush areas in 1915–16 under direction of E. Lalayan. Notes give names and dates of narrators, and places. Includes a word list, and a motif index for vols. 9–13.

Hazarabedian, Margit Abeghian

1986   "A Bibliography of Armenian Folklore." *Armenian Review* 39(3):32–54.

A classified list of 294 items includes: general works, epics and myths; humor and jokes; proverbs and sayings; fables; songs and dances; folktales; legends: beliefs; curses and blessings; folk drama; music; crafts and costumes. Most of the citations on these topics are in western languages, but include some Russian and Armenian items.

Herald, Leon Surabian

1927   "Memories." *Dial* 82:188–191.

Describes an Armenian wedding in the United States.

Hermann, Alfred, and Schwird, Martin
1951		*Die Prinzessin von Samarkand; Märchen aus Azerbaidschan und Armenien.*
		Cologne, Greven Verlag. 148 pp.
			Of the 13 tales only four are Armenian, the fourth being a fable of
			medieval times retold from H. Tumanian's verse version. Some of the
			tales interpreted by Alfred Hermann.

Hintlian, G.
1981		"Armenian Lace-stones: The Khachkar." *American Fabrics and Fashions* no.
		121:48–49. il.
			The decorative elements on cross-stones look like lace and served as
			religious symbols. Had secular connection when made for military
			victories or building of a bridge. Also made when a church building was
			completed.

Hnaser, K.
1928–29	"Hay kraganatiune dabanakareru vrav." [Armenian Inscriptions on
		Tombstones.] *B* 85:208–215, 264–269, 369–395; 86:17–22, 43–46, 149–
		151, 229–232.
			Inscriptions from 51 tombstones in Constantinople from 15th century to
			1865. Subjects vary from brief statements to moral comments.

Hogrogian, Rachel
1971		*The Armenian Cookbook.* New York, Atheneum. 152 pp.
			Recipes are clearly stated and authentic. Some suggested menus.

Hoogasian, Susie. *See also* Villa, Susie Hoogasian

Hoogasian, Susie, and Gardner, Emelyn E.
1944		"Armenian Folktales from Detroit." *Journal of American Folklore* 57:161–
		180.
			Nine tales collected 1940–42; names of narrators and tale types given.

Hovagimian, Hovagim
1967		*Batmutiun Haygagan Pontosi.* [History of Armenian Pontus.] Beirut,
		"Mushag." 951 pp. il.
			Considerable part about Trebizond. Dialect, family life, customs, pp.
			840–849 and includes 340 proverbs. Weddings, pp. 850–855. Games for
			children, pp. 855–865. Hamshe village life, pp. 866–908, and dialect,
			pp. 931–938. Various genres collected by S. Haykuni, pp. 917–930. A
			disorganized arrangement.

Hovannisian, Vartiter Kotcholosian
1972   *Tsitogh Tashti Garnoy*. [Tsitogh in the Plain of Garin.] Beirut, Dbaran
          Hamaskayin. 364 pp. il.
              Historical and ethnographic study of the village Tsitogh in Erzerum area.
              Village life described, pp. 29–67, and several village songs, with music,
              pp. 362–364.

Hovhaness, Alan
1963   *12 Armenian Folk Songs; piano, op. 43*. New York, C. F. Peters Co. 11 pp.
          score.
              Based on Armenian village songs, except one designated as a plow song.

Hovhannesian, Krikor
1965   *Badmakirk Sivri-Hisari Hayots*. [History Book of Sivri-Hisar Armenians.]
          Beirut, Dbaran Mshag. 687 pp. il., map.
              Dialect word list, pp. 459–479, followed by expressions to call animals,
              expressions for pain and grief, reduplicated words, proverbs and sayings,
              threats, oaths, curses. Female role, costume and adornment, pp. 481–
              493. Customs, pilgrimages, weddings, pp. 497–533.

Hovhannesian, V.
1928   "Sepastioy karasun mangants gdage." [The Testament of the 40 Youths of
          Sebastia.] *B* 85:99–108.
              Cites many commentaries about legend; gives names of persons; says
              Armenian, though not all names sound Armenian.

Hovhannessian, Hratchia
1963   *Sayat-Nova, 1712–1962*. Erevan, Haypethrat. 36 pp. Cover portraits by R.
          Rukhkian.
              On 250th anniversary of minstrel's birth. Biographical sketch.
              Introductory remarks in Armenian and English. A few of Sayat-Nova's
              songs in English, French, German, Italian, Polish.

Hovhannisian, N. G.
1990   "Sayat-Novayi Hayeren khagheri hunchyunakan hamakargi arandzna-
          hatkutyunnere." [The Special Characteristics of the Phonetic System of Sayat-
          Nova's Armenian Ballads.] *L* 9:48–56. Russian and English summaries.
              The dialect of Tiflis in 18th century—a mixture of eastern and western
              Armenian. Arose among Armenians who fled from Persia after Shah
              Abbas had moved Armenians to Persia in 17th century.

Hovhannisian, S.
1968   " 'Sasna Tsreri' Hay entanekan iravunki patmutyan karevor hushartsan."
          ["Sasna Tsrer" an Important Monument to History of Armenian Family
          Rights.] *Banber Erevani Hamalsarani* 3:96–109.
              David of Sassoun a valuable source of family rule and practice. Betrothal
              and marriage of juridical importance. Secular character of marriage was

Hovhannisian, S. *(continued)*
>>inherent in pagan Armenia. Religious meaning given when Christianity adopted.

1976   *Amusna-entanekan iravunke vagh avantakan Hayastanum (IV–IX dd).* [Marriage-family law in early feudal Armenia (4th–9th centuries).] Erevan, HSSH, GA Hrat. 440 pp.
>>Emphasis on law, not rituals of marriage. Chapter on engagement notes significance of *nishan*, the engagement involving giving of ring. Sources of marriage law, foreign influences, ending of marriage. Personal and property rights. Family forms, functions and relationships.

Hovnanian, Gh.
1888–90   "Hedazodutiunk nakhnyats ramgorenin vray." [Investigations on Early Popular Language.] *HA* 2:155–158; 4:249–255.
>>This title is part of a series, but here is noted only part ascribed to Catholicos Nerses the Graceful. Gives 26 riddles, but also calls them fables. The 1890 part is about various fables.

1891   "Mer aragats Hntgaganats hed haraperutiunn." [The Relationship of our Fables with India's.] *HA* 5:175–178; 210–214, 295–300, 329–333.
>>Indian origin of some Armenian fables. More research of manuscripts needed. Some examples given.

Hovsepian, Aleksis
1953–58   "Hamarod deghakrutiun Arapkeri ev desutiun anor parkerun ev aradznerum." [Brief Information about Arabkir and a View of its Customs and Sayings.] *B* 111:182–188; 113:233–237; 114:170–174; 115:72–78, 130–134, 160–165, 213–217, 258–261; 116:190–196, 258–264.
>>About bread, foods, storage methods. Also about engagements, weddings, festivals, followed by dialect word list.

Hovsepian, Garegin
1892–93   *Pshrankner zhoghovrdakan banahiusutiants.* [Fragments from Folklore.] Tiflis, Tip. M. Sharadze. 139 pp.
>>Folk songs (14) from various sources; includes four fables; some legends about Tamerlane and St. George. Life in Aparan, pp. 47–82, where some Armenians migrated from various Turkish towns at time of Russo-Turkish war (1828–29). Village life described. Some riddles, curses, blessings, and songs.

1901   "Rostam Zal." *AH* 7–8:205–254.
>>Transcription of an epic, told in dialect of Moks. Some recognize this as Persian, some Armenian. Includes glossary of 500 words.

1904 "Rostam Zal." *AH* 12:5–39.
     Rostam Zal said to have some Armenian connection; this is a study based
     on an Armenian version in dialect of Moks. Compares tale with Shah
     Name. This is not the text itself.

1907 "Katoghikosakan hugharkavorutiun ev taghumn." [The Funeral and Burial of
     Catholicoses.] *AH* 16:205–209.
     Describes procedures and rites.

1910 "Katoghikosakan entrutyun ev s. otsumn." [The Selection of Catholicoses
     and the Holy Anointment.] *AH* 19:189–200.
     Descriptive presentation of election of Catholicoses and rituals connected
     with anointment.

Huet, G.
1918 "Les contes populaires d'Arménie." *La Voix de l'Arménie* 1:254–259.
     Selections of some folktales from French and German compilations.
     Notes similar tales in other countries.

Hulunian, Harutiun, and Hajian, Madteos
1964 *Hushamadean Khodorchuri.* [Memorial Book of Khodorchur.] Vienna,
     Mkhitarian Dbaran. 560 pp. il., map.
     Area near Erzerum. Of folklore interest, pp. 100–113 about engagements
     and weddings; funeral customs and pilgrimages, pp. 114–119; seasonal
     customs, pp. 120–142; dwellings and division of work, pp. 143–154;
     superstitions, pp. 155–157; folk medicine, pp. 158–159; proverbs (55),
     pp. 160–161; riddles (32), pp. 161–162.

Iakobson, R.
1982 "Drevnearmianskii Vakhagn v svete sravnitel'noi mifologii." [The Ancient
     Armenian Vahagn in the Light of Comparative Mythology.] *PH* 4:80–83.
     Armenian summary.
     Vahagn is equated with the Slavic mythological personages that originated
     in the same Iranian source Svarak and his son Svarozhish (sun) and on
     the other side equates Rarakh or Rarashik, the demoniacal bird.

Iazikova, O.
1904 "Armianskie poslovitsy i pogovorki." [Armenian Proverbs and Sayings.]
     Sbornik Materialov dlia Opisaniia Mestnostei i Plemen Kavkaza 34(3):56–62.
     There are 100 proverbs and sayings, but no specific area noted.

Ierevanly, Akbar
1958 *Ermeni-Azerbaichan shifahi khalg edebiiat elageleri.* [Armenian-Azerbaijan
     Folklore Ties.] Erevan, Haypethrat. 269 pp.
     History and criticism of both folk literatures and comparisons. Excerpts
     included. Considerable space to *ashughs* (minstrels), pp. 124–187.
     Bibliography of Armenian citations given in Russian and Armenian.

Ioannisian, A. I.
1968   *Armianskie skazki.* [Armenian Tales.] Moscow, Izdatel'stvo
            Khudozhestvennia Literatura. 192 pp. il.
                There are 28 tales from the Ararat hills. Epilogue by A. M. Nazinian (pp.
                186–189) gives notes about Armenian folklorists and kinds of tales
                represented in collection. The translations into Russian are by various
                Armenians.

Ioannissian [also spelled Joannissiany], Abgar [or Avgar]
1871   "Armenische Sprichwörter." *Das Ausland* 44:403–405.
                There are 106 proverbs translated into German; no place of origin.

1871   "Armianskie poslovitsy." [Armenian Proverbs.] *Sbornik Svedenii o Kavkaze*
            1:329–333.
                Includes 98 proverbs. In an opposite column 40 equivalents of Georgian
                proverbs "Gruzinskie poslovitsy" are given by N. G. Borzenovyn in
                Russian.

Ionedes, H. K.
1956–57   "Lace VII. Needle made laces. Bebilla." *Embroidery*, n.s. 7(4):114–116. il.
                Bebilla, the floral and fruit designs for edgings on gauze or other fabrics
                made with the same stitch as Armenian needle lace.

Ipekian, G.
1913   "Kavor." [Godfather, or Sponsor.] *AH* 24:90–110.
                Importance of godfather in Armenian wedding ritual. Sometimes called
                cross-brother.

Isahakian, A.
1904   "Pshrankner zhoghovrdakan banahiusutiunits." [Fragments from Folklore.]
            AH 12:104–108.
                A few lines of songs or rhymes in dialects of Kharpert, Basen, Mush,
                Van and Shirak.

1922   *Sasmay Mher.* [Mher of Sassoun.] Vienna, Mkhitarian Dbaran. 54 pp.
                This is author's use of the character Mher of the epic David of Sassoun to
                construct a poetic rendition of Mher's story.

Isahakian, M.
1898–99   "Shiraki zhoghovrdakan erger." [Folk Songs of Shirak.] *AH* 4:161–176;
            5:200–212.
                Folk songs in quatrains, grouped under subjects of songs.

Israelian, H. R.
1967   "Arevi pashtamunki hetkere bronzedaryan Hayastanum." [Remnants of Sun
            Worship in Armenian Bronze Age.] *L* 4:77–88. il.
            Some drawings of objects and on animal forms show evidence of sun
            worship.

1980   "Erkvoryakneri pashtamunki hetkere hin Hayastanum." [Traces of the Twin
            Cult in Ancient Armenia.] *PH* 3:216–228. il. Russian summary.
            Rock carvings in ancient Armenia from 2nd to 1st century B.C. show
            figures of twins in mountain area of Gegham. Twin figures and
            ornaments appear in tomb decorations, 11th to 10th centuries B.C.

Iuzbashev, Tigran
1892   "Armianskaia skazka." [An Armenian Tale.] *Sbornik Materialov dlia
            Opisaniia Mestnostei i Plemen Kavkaza* 13(2):323–329.
            One tale about the Seven Brothers.

Izraelov, G.
1889   "Legenda i skazka." [Legend and a Tale.] *Sbornik Materialov dlia Opisaniia
            Mestnostei i Plemen Kavkaza* 7(2):86–89.
            From Armenian folk literature the legend is: "The Jew and the
            Silversmith"; the tale is "Three Youths."

Jablonski, Ramona
1979   *Traditional Designs of Armenia and the Near East to Color*. Owings Mills,
            Maryland, Stemmer House Pub. 56 pp. il.
            Armenian designs are derived from ancient Armenian illustrated
            manuscripts.

Janigian. *See* Chanikian

Janpoladian, M. G.
1969   "Armianskii narodnyi epos v obrabotke Tumaniana." [Tumanian's Treatment
            of the Armenian Epic.] *Banber Erevani Hamalsarani* 2:48–61. Armenian
            summary.
            About how Tumanian put together his version of David of Sassoun. Used
            several variants and tried to keep spirit of the work. Adapations made to
            enhance the literary quality. Examples are given in Russian only.

1969   *Tumaniane ev zhoghovrdakan epose*. [Tumanian and the Folk Epic.] Erevan,
            Hamalsarani Hrat. 197 pp.
            About Tumanian's version of David of Sassoun. He adapted words
            suitable for young people; removed violent parts. Used rhymed verse
            form. Some comparisons in Armenian and others in Russian and
            Armenian. Reviewed in *Banber Erevani Hamalsarani* 1969(3):242–244,
            by A. Ghanalanian.

Jaowari. *See* Jauari

Jauari, N. H.
1965   "Komitase ev Krdakan erarzhshtutyune." [Komitas and Kurdish Music.] *PH*
             4:188–192.
             Notes persons who have given attention to Kurdish folklore: K. Abovian
             among the first; Raffi's comments in his novel *Gaidzer* [Sparks]. Komitas
             gave professional attention to development of Kurdish music and
             transcribed some of it. [NB: Komitas wrote his thesis on Kurdish music,
             but thesis not available. *See* Begian, H., 1964.—AMA.]

Jedlicka, J.
1961   "Betrachtungen über das armenische und georgische Volkslied." *HA*
             75:1007–1019.
             Gives brief examples of Armenian texts, study of rhythms, but no
             Georgian texts. Georgian songs epic and dramatic; Armenians use bird
             themes, fatherland, dialogues.

Jenanyan, H. S.
1898   *Harutune, or Lights and Shadows of the Orient.* Toronto, William Briggs.
             301 pp. il.
             An evangelical book, but includes a bit about family and school life.
             Pictures are of special interest (some photos, some drawings) which show
             costume, household activities, tradesmen, school scenes, including mode
             of punishment (*falaka*), mode of transport of children in *mahfe* on animal.
             Also tournament *jerid*.

Jivani, Ashugh
1922   *Ashugh Gharibi hekiate (erkerove miasin).* [The Tale of Minstrel Gharib,
             (Together with his Songs).] Constantinople, M. Der Sahagian. 110 pp.
             Has many elements of a folktale, but many conversations are in verse.
             Depicts minstrel contest in coffee house, riddles in song, use of Ardashes
             and girdle motif, alternate singing of love song, quest to cure father's
             blindness, etc. Somewhat contrived.

Jizmejian, Manug K.
1955   *Kharpert ev ir zavagnere.* [Kharpert and her Children.] Fresno, Calif. 740 pp.
             il.
             Section about folklore and customs, pp. 667–728, written by Dzeron,
             partly from his book *Parchanj.* Family life, weddings, festivals,
             superstitions, admonitions, sayings, riddles. Also two tales.

Jndi, Hajie

1965   *Hay ev Kurd zhoghovrdneri barekamutyan artatsulumnere banahyusutyan mej.* [Reflections of Armenian and Kurdish Peoples' Friendship in Folklore.] Erevan, HSSR, GA Hrat, 157 pp. incl. music. Russian summary.

        Similarities of Kurds and mountain Armenians in dress, customs, tales. Some dance songs bilingual in some stanzas. Armenian folklorists have done much to collect Kurdish tales. Soviet Kurds have some songs in praise of Lenin. Komitas vocalized 13 Kurdish songs.

Joannissian. *See* Ioannissian

Jones, W. R

1973   "The Wandering Jew in Medieval Armenia and England: The Origin and Transit of the Legend." *Armenian Review* 26(2):64–69.

        Armenian connection noted or hinted in early chronicles. Suggests that probably the pre-Latin Armenians may have been vehicle of transmission during the Crusades.

1975   "The Legend and Letter of Abgar, 'King of Armenia.' " *Armenian Review* 28(1):39–44.

        A legend used by Moses of Khoren. Probably a third-century forgery.

Julardian. *See* Chulardian

K., A.

1929   "Areve Hay zhoghovrtagan havadkin mech." [The Sun in the Faith of Armenian Folk.] *HA* 43:634–650.

        Sun considered as an eye. Sun goes to mother at night. Sun as a live object.

Kaimakamian, Ferdinand

1965   "The Pagan Era of Armenian Church Music." *Armenian Review* 18(1):20–33.

        Gusan or Goghtan songs; dance songs; dance of gods; murmuring songs of professional mourners. Some passed into church music, some into customs of Armenian people.

Kajberuni. *See* Ter-Hovhannisian, Gabriel

Kalantar, A.

1898   "Katnayin ardiunkner." [Dairy Products.] AH 4:276–292.

        Various products derived from mllk in Armenian and Caucasian areas: butter, buttermilk, yogurt (*madzun*) and various cheeses.

Kalashev, Aleksandr
1889   "Anekdoty Shamakhinskikh Armian." [Anecdotes of Shamakh Armenians.]
        Sbornik Materialov dlia Opisaniia Mestnostei i Plemen Kavkaza 7(2):129–
        135.
                Five numbskull anecdotes from the village of Kerkendzh, south of
                Shamakh.

Kalashev, Nikolai
1887   "Armianskie skazki." [Armenian Tales.] *Sbornik Materialov dlia Opisaniia
        Mestnostei i Plemen Kavkaza* 7(2):141–231.
                There are 12 tales from the Shamakh district. When names are used they
                are Moslem. Traditional formula is used in eight tales with the Russian
                "zhil byl."

Kalbouss, George
1977   "On 'Armenian Riddles' and their Offspring 'Radio Erevan.' " *Slavic and
        East European Journal*, series 2, 21:447–449.
                Really Russian, with pseudo-Armenian accent. Anti-ethnic Russian
                humor aimed at home life and politics of pre-1917 middle class. Radio
                Erevan anecdotes anti-Georgian, Tatars, Chinese, Jews, blacks. Claims
                Armenian riddles originated in middle class before 1917.

Kalemkiar, Gr.
1896   "Eine Armenische Fabel." *Ethnologische Mitteilungen aus Ungarn* 5:154.
                Does not give name of fable. Something about price of precious stone. In
                Armenian transliteration, followed by German translation. Taken from a
                man in Krakow.

Kalfaian, Aris
1982   *Chomaklou; the History of an Armenian Village*. Translated by Krikor
        Asadourian. New York, Chomaklou Compatriotic Society. xlii, 200 pp. il.
                Chomaklou is near Caesarea. Of folklore interest, pp. 3–29: some
                historical information and descriptions; notes that name derived from
                Persian word for scepter. Patriarchal organization of family life, brief
                comments about customs and beliefs.

Kalfayan, Mireille
1975   *Armenian or American Heroes: The Universality of an Archetype*. 112 pp.
        M.A. thesis, University of Alberta, 1975.
                Not seen. Compares David of Sassoun and Pecos Bill.

Kalusdian, Kr. H.
1934   *Marash, gam Kermanig ev heros Zeytun*. [Marash, or Kermanic and Heroic
        Zeytun.] New York, Gochnag. 944 pp. il., fold. maps.
                Primarily historical, but pp. 307–425 relate to family and social life.
                Topics include food, dress, weddings, festival days. Gives dialect verses
                with standard Armenian. Lists proverbs, curses, insults, blessings,

endearments, greetings, superstitions, and several stories and conversations in dialect. Word list, pp. 411–425. Marash minstrels, pp. 535–567.

Kamalyan, S.
1925–26   "God in the Guise of a Mendicant: An Armenian Folktale." *New Armenia* 17:75–77, 88–90; 18:8–10. port.
Has some elements of a folktale, but some of the language is quite literary.

Kanewski, Clement
1840   "Überreste des Heidentums bei den Armenien." *Das Ausland* 13:321–323.
Remnants of paganism among Armenians despite introduction of Christianity, e.g., Anahid and feast of Vartavar.

Kaprienlian, M. S.
1908–9   "Agnats kavaraparpare." [The Dialect of Agn District.] *HA* 22:181–186, 201–206, 207–212, 248–252, 279–288, 315–319, 344–350; 23:54–61, 91–96, 120–124, 155–159, 190–192, 221–224, 252–256, 267–273, 376–379.
Dialect conversations of two women. Proverbs and sayings (256); greetings, blessings (250); lullabies (15). Also some wedding and folk songs. Explanation of grammar and special words.

Karagyulian, E. G.
1969   "H. Harutyunyani 'Manyak' zhoghovatsui ergeri hamarot verlutsutyune." [Brief Analysis of H. Harutyunyan's "Manyak" Collection of Folk Songs.] *L* 8:76–83. Russian summary.
A musical analysis of harmonic pattern of songs: dance, lyrics, work, rituals and custom. Musical notations given as examples.

Karakhanian, G. H.
1974   "Orsi desaranner XIII dari patkerakandaknerum." [Hunting Scenes in 13th Century Reliefs.] *L* 1974:70–85. il. Russian summary.
Art motifs of interest even though hunting was sport of upper classes.

Karamanlian, A.
1931   "Ervant Lalayan." *HA* 45:294–301.
Biographical sketch of Lalayan the folklorist and a list of his writings.

1931   "Zhoghovrtagan havadke Ezniki kov." [Folk Belief in Eznik.] *HA* 45:232–246, 423–432, 489–518, 637–657.
Eznik, a fifth century writer, noted that the Armenians believed in devils that brought illness, bad dreams, sorcerers. NB: In last installment title changes to "Hrashdagner u sadananer Hay zhoghovrtagan havadkin mech." [Angels and Devils in Armenian Folk Belief.]

Kara-Murza, Hovsep
1901   "Tsragir tnaynagortsutyan veraberyal nyuter havakelu." [Plan to Collect
              Subjects Relating to Cottage Industry.] *AH* 12(Suppl.):3–32.
              Guide to obtaining necessary information about various aspects of cottage
              industry.

Karapetian, E. T.
1956   "K 60-letiiu Armianskogo etnograficheskogo periodcheskogo izdanii
              'Azgagrakan Andes.' " [Sixty Years of the Armenian Ethnographic Periodical
              "Azgagrakan Handes."] *Sovetskaia Etnografiia* 2:111–114.
              Brief summary of work done in folklore before the periodical started in
              1896 and since then, especially the area studies by E. Lalayan, et al.

1965   "Ob odnom personazhe Armianskoi svad'by." [About a Certain Personage in
              the Armenian Wedding.] *PH* 2:211–216.
              About the Armenian *kavor* and his role; serves as godfather or sponsor of
              groom and has important duties as representative of the groom's family.

Karapetian, Emma
1978   *Ozhide Hayots mej.* [The Dowry Among Armenians.] Erevan, HSSH, GA
              Hrat. 110 pp. [Harvard catalog says 118 pp.] col. plates.
              Historical-ethnographic study. Basic structure of dowry, development of
              the practice. Parts of dowry: clothing and ornaments, extension to
              utensils, silver. Gifts of relatives part of dowry. Variations under different
              social conditions; various areas studied. Rules and legal aspects of dowry.

Karapetian, G. O.
1967   *Armianskii fol'klor.* [Armenian Folklore.] Moscow, "Nauka." 223 pp.
              Proverbs and sayings (1634) pp. 13–71; riddles (289) pp. 75–105; jests
              (12) pp. 111–120; tales (22) pp. 123–190. Excerpt from David of
              Sassoun, pp. 203–219.

1973   *Armianskie poslovitsy i pogovorki.* [Armenian Proverbs ard Sayings.]
              Moscow, "Nauka." 263 pp.
              There are 832 proverbs and sayings in Armenian followed by Russian
              translation and Russian equivalents. At end there are 25 one or two line
              anecdotes. Indexes only in Russian.

1975   *Zabavnye i nazidatel'nye istorii Armianskogo naroda.* [Amusing and Edifying
              Tales of the Armenian People.] Moscow, "Nauka." 158 pp.
              Translations of certain sections by various Armenians. Includes fables,
              anecdotes about the Karabagh jester Pyl-Pugi, and some other amusing
              characters.

1979   *Armianskii fol'klor.* [Armenian Folklore.] Moscow, "Nauka." 373 pp.
              Amusing stories of Pyl-Pugi, the Karabagh jester (164) pp. 25–99;
              anecdotes (110) pp. 100–150; anecdotes about clergy (19) pp. 151–159;

momentary anecdotes (53) pp. 160–169; riddles (180) pp. 170–200; proverbs and sayings (869) pp. 209–304. Sources indicated for above. Thematic and motif index, and glossary.

Karayan, Mesrop

1965   *Palu.* Antelias [Lebanon], Gatoghigosutean Hayots Medz Dann. 767 pp. il. map, fold. map.

Historical and descriptive information of town of Palu and its environs. Of folklore interest: costume, pp. 147–155; marriage, pp. 287–310; birth and death, pp. 311–318; festivals, pp. 319–382. Proverbs and sayings are scattered throughout the text.

Karayan, Sarkis

1980   "History of Armenian Communities in Turkey." *Armenian Review* 33(1):89–96.

Lists almost 100 titles; most contain ethnographic and folklore material.

Karst, Josef

1948   *Mythologie Armeno-Caucasienne et Hetito-Asiatique.* Strassbourg, P. H. Heitz. 400 pp.

Names Armenian deities, meanings of names, their attributes and their equivalents in other countries, pp. 1–59; mythology of David of Sassoun and giant Tork, pp. 61–69. Armenian calendar, sun, planets, seasons, hours of day and night, pp. 69–89.

Kasbar. *See* Gaspar

Kasparian, Alice Odian

1968   *Badmakirk Anguriey ev Sdanozi Hayots.* [The History of the Armenians of Angora and Stanos.] Beirut, Doniguian Press. 247 pp. and 72 pp., il., map and fold. map.

English section of 72 pp. at end has historical and family life information, etc. Includes name list.

1983   *Armenian Needlelace and Embroidery.* McLean, Virginia, EPM Publications. 127 pp. il. (some col.).

Includes information on history of lace making as well as instructions on how to make the lace. Colored illustrations of embroidery on towels, ornaments, etc.

Katsakhian, Karapet

1985   *Zhoghovrdagititiune Hay parberakannerum.* [Anthropology in Armenian Periodicals.] Erevan, Azgagrutean Petakan Tankaran. 2 parts.

Part I, 253 pp., is a complete table of contents of periodical *Azgagrakan Handes*, 1896–1916. Introduction by Artashes Nazinian. Summary of Armenian ethnography and folklore development on pp. 10–13.   Part II,

Katsakhian, Karapet *(continued)*
>66 pp., is a complete table of contents of periodical *Eminian Azgagrakan Zhoghovatsu,* 1901–1913.

Kay-Shuttleworth, Rachel B.
1955–56   "Lace II. Needlemade Lace. How did Lace Begin?" *Embroidery*, n.s., 6(1):86–88. il. "Lace VI." *Embroidery*, n.s. 7(3):34–36.
>"Lace II" notes that lace derived from Arabs and was made for insertion only, yet it shows illustrations from Maynard's article on Armenian lace! "Lace VI" notes Arab lace, also laces of England, Palestine, Cyprus, and shows picture of Armenian lace, but this not named.

Kazanjian, Hovh.
1898   "Evdogiots Hayots kavaraparpare." [The Dialect of Tokat Armenians.] *HA* 12:97–105, 146–147, 174–175, 208–210, 298–306.
>Mostly about dialect, and includes word list. Three anecdotes in dialect: 1. An old man thief pretends poverty, gets shelter for night, and runs off with gold, slippers, and mule. 2. Man running away from death. 3. Lazy bride who suggests in-laws take turns at work.

Keleshian, Misak
1949   *Sis-madian.* [Sis–Book.] Beirut, Dbaran "Hay Jemarani." 771 pp. il., map.
>History of Sis, capital of Cilicia. Of folklore interest: games and recreation, pp. 397–401; home remedies for humans and animals, pp. 401–410; anecdotes about particular persons, pp. 432–441; children's language, p. 458; superstitions, pp. 460–461; riddles, p. 461; minstrels, pp. 463–469; weddings, pp. 511–513; foods, pp. 513–518; festivals, pp. 518–530; dress, pp. 530–533.

Keolian, Ardashes H.
1913   *The Oriental Cook Book.* New York, Sully & Kleinteich. 349 pp. port.
>Probably the first Armenian cookbook published in English in the United States. Meaning of "Oriental" in title is different from today's usage. Author an Armenian from Constantinople so he uses many Turkish names for recipes.

Keorkian, Garo
1963   *Nor Knar.* [New Lyre.] 3rd ed. Beirut. 612 pp. il.
>Most of songs are with music. Arrangement of songs mixed; some folk songs included. Illustrations are of musicians and poets. An earlier edition appeared in 1954 in Beirut, but no publisher named.

Kermanikian, Mesrob
1964   "Immortal Troubadour." *Ararat* 5(3):39–41.
>Brief biographical sketch of Sayat-Nova, the 18th century Armenian minstrel.

Kéténedjian, Hermine

1918   *Les pratiques obstétricales au Arménie (superstition, magic, sorcellerie et fétichisme.)* 46 pp. Thesis in medicine, Paris.

Topics include treatment of sterility, hygiene of pregnancy, sex prediction, childbirth, the newborn, difficulties of childbirth.

Kevorkian, Karnig

1970   *Chnkushabadum; knnagan badmutiun Hayots Chnkushi.* [The Story of Chunkush; Critical History of the Armenians of Chunkush.] Jerusalem, St. James Press. Second imprint: Drexel Hill, Pa., Groong Publishing Company. Vol. 1 (625 pp.) il., maps.

A second volume was planned, but the author died. Of folklore interest, pp. 225–386; 413–471. Various songs with some music. Tales, anecdotes, curses, blessings, proverbs (646). Domestic life, secular and religious festivals, superstitions, including some accounts of spirits.

Kevorkian, Komitas. *See* Komitas

Khachatrian, P. M.

1969   *Hay mijnadaryan patmakan oghber.* [Medieval Armenian Historical Laments.] Erevan, HSSH, GA Hrat. 341 pp.

Covers the period 14th–17th centuries. Although about specially written laments for persons and events, the introduction notes the early practice of calling special mourners; some wore special clothing, disheveled their hair, used murmuring or shrieking voices.

Khachatrian, Robert

1987   "Gora Ararat v Russkikh srednevekovykh istochnikakh." [Mt. Ararat in Russian Medieval Sources.] *L* 9:44–51. Armenian summary.

Many references to Ararat in Russian annals, dictionaries, church and political writings, and observations of travelers. Mt. Ararat looked upon as symbol of Armenia.

Khachatrian, T. S.

1975   *Drevniaia kul'tura Shiraka.* [Ancient Culture of Shirak.] Erevan, Izd-vo Erevanskogo Universitata. 276 pp. il.

Although about the archeology of the Shirak area, 3rd to 1st century B.C., the interest is in the designs shown in the pottery.

Khachatrian, Zh. D.

1985   "Anahit ditsuhu pashtamunkn u patkeragrututiune Hayastanum ev nra aghersnere Hellenistakan ashkhari het." [The Cult and Iconography of the Goddess Anahit in Armenia and its Mutual Supplications in the Hellenic World.] *PH* 1:123–134. il. Russian summary.

The goddess Anahit in Armenia bore the function of great mother, most honored. With coming of Christianity her function transferred to Virgin Mary. Anahit pictured with child presented idea of fertility.

Khachatrian, Zh. K.

1968   "Javakhki parere ev nrants hurahatkutiunnere." [The Dances of Javakhk and their Unique Characteristics.] *L* 3:70–83. Includes music.

Dances for men, women, unmarried persons, children, and mixed groups. Describes how to do the steps. Includes music.

1975   "Traditsionnye svadebnye pliask Armian." [Traditional Armenian Wedding Dances.] *Sovetskaia Etnografiia* 2:87–93. il.

Describes dances, and one illustration shows a line dance, another a circle dance.

Khachatriants, Ia. Kh.

1933   *Armianskie skazki*. [Armenian Tales.] 2nd. ed. Moscow, "Akademia." 368 pp. il.

Includes 40 tales, mostly folktales from works by Armenian collectors. There are four tales by authors who have based their stories on folktales. Comparative notes by N. P. Andreev.

Khachaturian, V. A.

1977   "Simvolika tsveta y odnom Armianskom arkhitekturnom pamiatnike XIV veka." [Color Symbolism in an Armenian Architectual Monument of the 14th century.] *PH* 2:191–198. il. Armenian summary.

About St. Thaddeus church in Iran. Lower stones dark, upper ones light. On the cupola colors alternate, but top all white and signifies light of sky. Lower dark and light stones signify struggle between darkness and light, a continuation of struggle.

Khachigian, Nerses

1936   "Kiughis 'oror'nere." [Lullabies of my Village.] *H* 14(12):40.

Nine lullabies are from village of Khurnavi in Divrig area. One is to be sung when child awakes.

Khachikian, H. I.

1963   "Sayat-Novayi geghagitakan hayatskneri bnutagrman shurje." [About the Characterization of Sayat-Nova's Aesthetic Views.] *PH* 3:455–52. Russian summary.

Sayat-Nova created not for artists but for people to understand life. He did not rely on past poetic forms. Influenced minstrels who came after him.

Khachikian, Ia.

1969   "Tumanian nashei muziki." [The Tumanian of our Music.] *Sovetskaia Muzika* 10:80–84. port.

On 100th anniversary of birth of Komitas, the Armenian folk song collector. Brief biography. Compares achievement with well-known Armenian poet H. Tumanian.

Khalatian, Bagrat

1901   *Irani herosnere Hay zhoghovrti mech.* [Iranian Heroes Among the Armenians.] Paris, "Panaser." 79 pp.

About heroic tales and their characteristics; emphasis on Iranian tales and their use by Armenians. Some similarities, but notes that Armenian spirit retained. Includes tales the author recorded in 1899–1900 in small villages in Erevan area.

1902   "Die armenische Heldensage." *Zeitschrift des Vereins für Volkskunde* 12:138–144, 264–271, 391–402. il.

About David of Sassoun. Gives some historical background, also some quotations from epic.

1903   *Hay zhoghovrtagan tiutsaznagan vebe hanterts knnataduteamp.* [The Armenian Heroic Epic Together with Criticism.] Vienna, Mkhitarian Dbaran. 67 pp. il.

About David of Sassoun, the area of the epic. Structure of the epic, comments on characters and historical basis. Includes some musical notation. This was originally published in *HA* (1902) 16:132–136, 173–177, 252–256, 330–333, 349–354. Portrait of teller, but no music.

1904   "Hin Hayats zhoghovrtagan vebere ev Movses Kkorenatsi." [Ancient Armenian Tales and Moses of Khoren.] *HA* 18:14–18, 102–105, 146–149, 204–206.

Discusses the heroic folktales or legends of ancient Armenia as presented by Moses of Khoren. Emphasis on Haig.

1906   "Hay azgagrutiune." [Armenian Ethnography.] *AH* 14:175–182.

Important bibliographical essay about rise of folklore literature. Cites Grimm and Russian Afanasev and contributors to the journal. Also some notes on Kurdish folklore.

Khalatian, Grigor

1887   "David von Sassoun; armenische Volksepos." In his *Märchen und Sagen.* Leipzig, W. Friedrich, pp. 81–132.

Prose version in German, but does not give source. Research disclosed that it is translation of first version published by K. Servantsian in 1874.

1887   *Tsragir Hay azgagrutean ev azgayin iravabanakan sovorutiunneri.* [Plan for Armenian Ethnography and Ethnic Judicial Customs.] Moscow, O. O. Herbeg. 115 pp.

States there should be better organized study of ethnography and folklore. Plan arranged in 10 subject groups (372 paragraphs); notes what the collector should inquire about; detail emphasized. Second part relates to judicial customs in Armenian communities, structure and organization, domestic rights, crime.

Khalatian, Grigor *(continued)*

1887   *Märchen und Sagen.* Leipzig, W. Friedrich. xxxvii, 147 pp.
            Introduction about folktales and some comparative information. Includes
            six tales; David of Sassoun (pp. 81–132); proverbs (pp. 133–147).

1896   *Armianskii epos v istorii Armenii Moiseia Khorenskogo.* [The Armenian Epic
            in Moses of Khoren.] Moscow, Tip. Varvary Gatsyk. 2 parts in 1.
            First part about research done on the topic of heroic tales. Second part
            comparisons of works by others on subjects in work of Moses of
            Khoren. Quotations are given.

1898   "David Sasunskii." *In Bratskaia Pomoshch postradavshim Turtsii Armianam,*
            2nd ed. Moscow, Kushnarev. pp. 67–81.
            Does not give source, but I discovered that it is from K. Servantsian's
            version first published in 1874. But here first two sections are left out
            because not directly related to David.

1898   "Dva Armenista." [Two Armenologists.] In *Bratskaia Pomoshch Postradav-*
            shim v Turtsii Armianam. 2nd ed. Moscow, Kushnarev, pp. 179–191. ports.
            About N. O. Emin, i.e., Mkrtich Emin, pp. 179–185; and K. P. Patkanov
            pp. 186–191. Emin taught many years at the Lazarian Institute of Oriental
            Languages and was interested in Armenian ethnology and folklore. He left
            legacy of 10,000 rubles, the income of which was used for publication of
            Eminian Azgagrakan Zhoghovatsu (Eminian Ethnographic Collection)
            1901–1913. Patkanov was a linguist, a pupil of Emin.

1898   "O nekotorykh liubimikh motivakh Armianskikh skazok." [About Some
            Favorite Folk Motifs of Armenian Tales.] In *Bratskaia Pomoshch*
            Postradavshim v Turtsii Armianam. 2nd ed. Moscow, Kushnarev, pp. 570–
            578.
            Motifs included are *vishap* (dragon), demon, golden nightingale, water of
            life, apple of immortality, speech reversal.

1908   "Endhanur azgagrakan hodvatsner. 2. Koylturi patmutyun." [General
            Ethnographic Articles. 2. History of Culture.] *Eminian Azgagrakan*
            Zhoghovatsu 7:1–224.
            Khalatian has edited the volume which includes articles from various
            sources and some translations from foreign languages that relate to
            ethnography, including folklore.

1971   "Grigor Khalatiani andip namaknere Garegin Srvandztyantsin." [The
            Unpublished letters of Grigor Khalatian to G. Servantsian.] *PH* 1:111–130.
            Six letters, 1884–87, comment about work of Servantsian, meaning of
            some expressions, and some questions about David of Sassoun. Stresses
            need to collect folktales to compare with European tales.

1974   "Grigor Khalatyani namaknere Sargis Haykunum." [Grigor Khalatyan's Letters to Sargis Haykuni.] *PH* 2:239–256. Russian summary.

Fifteen letters mostly concerned with Khalatian's editorship of *Eminian Azgagrakan Zhoghovatsu*; Haykuni one of contributors. Of interest for history of Armenian folklore publications. V. Vardanian compiled the letters.

Khalpakhchian, H. Kh.

1961   *Hayastani arteakan karutsvatsknere*. [The Modern Structures of Armenia.] Erevan, HSSR, GA Hrat. 90 pp. il.

Excavations reveal wine presses, oil presses, water mills. Outside views as well as some floor plans.

Khandanian, Arshalouys

1978   "Le theme de la sirène-oiseau dans l'enluminure des manuscrits arméniens." In *Simposia Internazionale di Arte Armena*. 1st, Bergamo, 28–30 June, 1975. *Atti*, pp. 377–394. il.

Armenian manuscripts of 12th–13th centuries examined for bird-siren motif. Bodies represent birds, heads are human. Classified according to headdress: hats, crowns, crowns with foliage, etc. Birds in Armenian tales discussed.

Kharatian, Z. V.

1981   "Traditional Demonological Notions of the Armenians." *Soviet Anthropology and Archeology* 20(2):28–55.

Translation of article in *Sovetskaia Etnografiia* 1980 (2):103–116. Data from family life of 19th and early 20th centuries. About spirits associated with the house and housekeeping, family rituals. Riches of the house— i.e., guardian spirit of the house usually a serpent. Evil spirit, *shvod*, of house usually a cat that represents February which operates latter part of month and leaves March 1.

Khatchadourian, Arpine

1979   *David of Sassoun: An Introduction to the Study of the Armenian Epic*. M.A. thesis, University of Wisconsin, 1979.

Not seen.

Khatchatrianz, I.

1946   *Armenian Folk Tales*. Translated from Russian by N. W. Orloff. Philadelphia, Colonial House. 141 pp. il.

Sixteen tales. Introduction notes some internal evidence that tales came from Turkish, Persian, and Russian Armenians. Tales selected from Khachatriants, Ia. Kh. (1933) [note variant spelling of name].

Khdshian, Nshan K.
1890–95   "Azkayin zhoghovrtagan aradsner, Drabizoni geanken kaghuadz." [National
            Folk Proverbs, Collected from Trebizond Life.] *HA* 4:163–164, 289; 5:116,
            300–301; 6:24, 183–184, 382–383; 7:358–359; 9:13.
            A total of 705 proverbs and sayings from Trebizond.

Kherdian, David
1982   *Pigs Never See the Stars: Proverbs From the Armenian.* Aurora, Ore., Twin
            River Press. 46 pp. il. Limited ed.
            There are 184 proverbs, but sources not given.

Khostikian, M.
1916   "Azgagrakan nyuter Ezniki 'Aghts aghandats' ergi mej." [Ethnographic
            Subjects in Eznik's "Refutation of Sects."] *AH* 26:137–147.
            About Satan, demons, *vishaps* (dragons) astrology, fate, folk medicine.

Khrimian, M.
1907   "Kondak." [Pastoral Letter.] *AH* 16:7–8.
            Greetings of the Armenian Catholicos to the Armenian Ethnographic
            Society.

Khtshian. *See* Khdshian

Kiwrtian. *See* Kurdian

Kloos, Helmut
1974   *Gardens of Armenian-Americans in Fresno, California: Food and Medicinal
            Plants.* 198 pp. il. M.A. thesis, California State University, Fresno.
            Gives population background of Fresno, 1900–1970, and also some
            history of Armenians and their immigration. Studied 100 Armenian-
            Americans and 120 non-Armenians. Names plants grown for food and
            medicinal uses. Main focus on a few Armenian gardens, with photos.

Knobloch, J.
1984   "Le langage des femmes en Indo-Européan d'après les isoglosses
            arméniennes, grecques et albanaises." *REA*, n.s. 18:317–325.
            Certain word usages differ for men and women. For example, some parts
            of body named differently. To avoid word magic, women devised words
            for taboo language.

Kobler, John
1943   "They Ordered *Kouzou kzartma.*" *Saturday Evening Post* 215(30):11, 42, 45.
            col. il.
            About George Mardikian and traditional Armenian food served at his
            restaurant, Omar Khayyam. Grape leaves (stuffed), lamb, pilav are
            illustrated.

Kocharian, Suren

1942   *David Sasunskii; Armianskii narodnyi epos.* Erevan, Armgiz. 79 pp.
         A summarized text based on translation by V. Derzhavin, et al.

196?   *David Sasunskii geroicheski narodnyi epos.* [Sound recording.] 2 discs.
         Based on V. Derzhavin's translation. Notes by I. Orbeli on container.
         A 33 1/3 rpm. recording. Matrix ho. 031505–031508. I have not heard
         this, but it is well to know that it exists. It is noted in the *National Union
         Catalog*, 1973–77, vol. 102, p. 168.

Kochoyan, A.

1963   "Sayat-Novayi Hayeren khagheri parayin kazme." [The Vocabulary of Sayat-
         Nova's Armenian Ballads.] *PH* 1: 259–261.
         Of the 2060 words used by Sayat-Nova, 1274 are Armenian; the rest are
         Arabic, Persian, Azeri, Georgian, etc. Notes frequency of certain words.
         Based on Sayat-Nova's *Hayeren, Vratseren, ev Adrbejaneren Khagher
         zhoghovatsu*, ed. by M. Hasratian, 1959.

Komitas, Vardapet

19?   *Hay keghchug erker.* [Armenian Rustic Songs.] Paris.
         I have seen only numbers 13–32. There are 10 songs in each group (nos.
         13–22 and 23–32). Texts of songs in Armenian. Music is harmonized.

1928   *Chors menerk.* [Four Solos.] Paris, Editions Maurice Senart. 12 pp.
         Four melodies with piano accompaniment. Songs have Armenian texts
         with transliteration and translation by Archag Tchobanian (Arshag
         Chobanian).

1933   *Sirerkner ev barerkner ergser khmpi hamar.* [Love Songs and Dances for
         Group of Both Sexes.] Paris. 12 pp.
         Ten songs, translated into French by Arshag Chobanian. Collected and
         harmonized bv V. Sarkisian (Sarxian). Armenian text in transliteration.
         Sarkisian heard these songs from Komitas and noted them from memory.

1938   *La Lyre arménienne.* [Hay knar.] Paris, Max Eschig. 45 pp.
         Collection of 12 songs transcribed and harmonized. Songs give Armenian
         texts and are also translated into French.

1950   *Chants of the Liturgy of the Armenian Apostolic Orthodox Church.* New
         York, Delphic Press. 95 pp.
         Harmonized, with words in English and Armenian. Not folk music, but
         some claim that liturgical music based on folk elements.

Komitas, Vardapet *(continued)*
1958   "Komitasi antip namaknere." [The Unpublished Letters of Komitas.] *PH*
                1:215–267. Russian summary.
                Letters to Armenian writer Arshag Chobanian. Some views on music and
                church matters. Notes some musical terminology. On p. 255 amusing
                comment: during visit to Shirijian family in Geneva, encountered parrot
                that whistled folk song "Im chinari yarn" that Komitas had collected.
                Preface comments about letters by M. H. Muradian.

1965–69   *Ergeri zhoghovatsu khmberkner.* [Collection of Choral Songs.] Erevan,
                Hayasdan. 3 vols.
                I have seen only vols. 2 and 3. In these two volumes there are 99 songs
                with musical scores and Armenian texts. The songs are based on folk
                songs and include some variants.

1976   "Plowing song of Lori as sung in the village of Vardablur." *Armenian Review*
                29(2):136–166.
                Includes musical notation. Gives the song, text and structure. Also gives
                tempo, time, meter, style and spirit, and glossary of interjections.
                Translated by Anahid Der Manuelian Keshishian. Original Armenian in
                Navasard Yearbook of 1914, edited by Daniel Varoujan and H. Siroun.

Komitas, Vardapet, and Abeghian, Manuk
1904   *Hazar u mi khagh* [A Thousand and One Songs.] Vagharshapet, Tparan
                Mayr Atoroy S. Ejmiaysin. 72 pp.
                Only 50 songs selected from the original compilation which I have not
                been able to see.

Komitas Centennial Committee
1970   *The Music of Komitas.* Hempstead, N.Y.
                An album of two 12", 33 1/3 rpm stereo discs. Soloists are Armenian. A
                review appears in *Ararat* (Winter 1974) 15(1):29–31. Reviewed by John
                M. Sarian who notes that the recording includes songs, dances, and
                divine liturgy. A booklet accompanies recording about Armenian folk
                music and the work of Komitas. I have not heard the recording.

Korvin-Kresinski, Cyrill von
1977   "Vorchristliche Matriarchalische. Einflüss in der Gestaltung ältester koptischer
                und armenische Kreuze." *Symbolon* (ser. 2) 3:37–73. il.
                Comments on Armenian crosses and figures, pp. 52–54.

Kostandian, E.
1970   "G. Srvandztyantsi lusavorakan gortsuneutyune." [The Enlightening Work of
                G. Servantsian.] *PH* 1:187–196.
                Emphasis on educational work; his survey of Armenian areas. It was
                during survey that he found the epic David of Sassoun and transcribed it.

1970   "Garegin Servandztyants." *Banber Erevani Hamalsarani* 1:127–137. Russian summary.

         Biographical information on Servantsian, founder of Armenian folklore. He observed village life and activities. Also some mention of his political activities.

Kostanian, K.

1906   "Proyk ev tuayr." [Dowry and Marriage Settlement.] *AH* 13:131–138.

         About girl's dowry and groom's gift to the bride.

1906–7   "Davit *Vardapet* Alavka orti." [David the Teacher, son of Alavka.] *AH* 14:105–112; 15:62–67.

         Alavka refers to place (David [1112–1137]) and his canons that relate especially to mice that may defile food. Also some rules about women and their behavior. Against magic.

Koushagian, Torkom

1988   *Saints & Feasts of the Armenian Church.* Abridged edition. Translated and edited by Haigazoun Melkonian. New York, St. Vartan Press. 62 pp.

         Some of church festivals derived from pagan festivals, such as *Vartavar*. Unfortunately no chronological list of dates given.

Koushakdjian, Mardiros, and Madourian, Boghos

1970   *Hushamadean Musa Leran.* [Memorial Book of Musa Ler.] Beirut, Dbaran Atlaz [Atlas Press]. 877 pp. il.

         Locale is that of Franz Werfel's book *The Forty Days of Musa Dagh*. Of folklore interest, pp. 163–188 and pp. 219–254. Customs, beliefs, superstitions, weddings, festivals, songs and dances. There are 377 proverbs; some good wishes, curses, and oaths.

Kouymjian, Dickran

1978   "The Problem of the Zoomorphic Figure in the Iconography of Armenian Pentecost: A Preliminary Report." In *Simposia Internationale di Arte Armena.* 1st, Bergamo, 28–30 June, 1975. *Atti* pp. 403–413. il. Venice, St. Lazar.

         A 13th century miniature painting shows animal head together with human head on human figure. This appears in other manuscripts of the 17th century. Figure represents pagans from distant land; date of entry probably from time when Mongols invaded Armenia; prevailed later in association with Tiridates, while still pagan, changed to boar.

Krappe, Alexander H.

1949   "The Indian Origin of an Armenian Folk Tale." *Armenian Review* 2(1):110–113.

         Refers to folktale "Otzezar" that appeared in A. von Haxthausen's *Transcaucasia*. Man marries a girl; Indian fakir says she is a transformed snake. Same theme appears in Greece and China.

Krayian, Mesrob. *See* Karayan, Mesrop

Krikorian, Khachadur
1940   "Ashugh Hagope." [Minstrel Hagop.] *H* 18(11):110–115.
                Minstrel Hagop born Hagop Yekinian in village of Rashli between 1865
                and 1870. Worked at cutting wood and grass. Became blind at age 15.
                Sang songs of love and peace, and national songs.

Kudian, Mischa
1969   *Three Apples Fell From Heaven.* London, Rupert Hart–Davis. 128 pp. il.
                A collection of Armenian folk and fairy tales. Of these 18 tales, several
                based on retellings by H. Tumanian.

1970   *The Saga of Sassoun, the Armenian Folk Epic.* London, Kaye & Ward. 175
                pp. il.
                The four cycles of the epic are retold in prose, based on a number of
                variants.

1983   *More Apples Fell From Heaven.* London, Mashtots Press. 82 pp.
                A selection of Armenian folk and fairy tales. Half the 16 tales are repeats
                of those that appeared in his earlier book (see 1969 above).

Kurdian, H.
1930   "Haygagan vishab korkere arasbel en?" [Are the Armenian Dragon Rugs a
                Myth?] *B* 88:413–420.
                A reply to seven points in article by Arthur Upham Pope about dragon
                rugs. Kurdian replied to Pope in English, but does not note when or
                where the English article was published.

1930–31   "Haygagan vishab korkeru arasbele." [The Myth of the Armenian Dragon
                Rugs.] *B* 88:377–386; 89:115–124.
                This is a commentary on Arthur Upham Pope's article, and also a
                translation of Pope's article (see Pope, 1925). Kurdian notes that Pope
                has limited knowledge of Armenian dragon rugs.

1931   "Ashugh Sefer." [Minstrel Sefer.] *B* 89:537–540.
                Sefer an overlooked minstrel of the 17th century. From an Echmiadzin
                manuscript Kurdian quotes three ballads. Evidence of familiarity with
                Bible.

1931   "Vishabe Haygagan korkerun mech (naev piunig ev ardziv)" [The Dragon in
                Armenian Rugs (also the Phoenix and the Eagle).] *B* 89:259–264, 300–304,
                417–425, 473–478. il.
                Description of dragon, also phoenix and eagle in Armenian rugs, with
                illustrations. Later reprinted as a book; Venice, St. Lazar, 1932. 43 pp.
                But book also includes information on worm *kirmiz.*

1932   "Ortan (garmir) gam kirmiz." [The Red Worm or *Kirmiz*.] *B* 90:62–68, 157–163.
        About use of red derived from the *kirmiz* worm. The red color is used in Armenian rugs.

1935   "Nakhamichnatarean Hay dagher." [Pre-Medieval Armenian Songs.] *H* 13(5):40–47.
        Singers of Goghtn. Period from 5th–13th centuries creative in many ways. Notes six songs found in 1681 manuscript, four of which not religious; fifth song a lullaby, a rarity in early times.

1940   "Corrections to Arthur Upham Pope's 'The Myth of the Armenian Dragon Asiatic Carpets.' " *Royal Asiatic Society. Journal*, Part I:65–67.
        Points out some historical errors by Pope. *See* Pope, 1925.

1947   *Korke Hayots mod.* [The Rug Among Armenians.] Venice, St. Lazar, Mkhitarian Dbaran. 160 pp. il.
        Armenian rug-making since ancient times; use of natural dyes and craft of making rugs. Uses of rugs by various classes. Traditions from and superstitions about rugs. Quotes from Melik-Shahnazarian's article in *HA* 1928 (42):475–478 about tradition in Karabagh to use rug to predict sex of child.

1948   "A Historical Glimpse of the Art of Rug Weaving in Armenia." *Armenian Review* 1(4):22–30. il.
        Cites works that note Armenian rug-making, e.g., Marco Polo.

1952–53 "Armenian Cartoonist Alexander Saroukhan." *Armenian Review* 5(4):88–90. port.
        Aside from information about Saroukhan, Kurdian gives some background information. Armenian manuscripts do not depict humorous drawings, though human-headed birds look curious. He does not recall Armenian cartoonists in Constantinople or Tiflis. In U.S. he knows Constantin Aladjalov, an Armenian Kurdian knows personally, but Aladjalov does not identify himself as Armenian. (NB: Kurdian had an extensive library, including Armenian manuscripts, so his observations not casual.—AMA)

Kusikian, I.
1948   "Fol'kloristika v Sovetskoi Armenii." [Folkloristics in Soviet Armenia] *Sovetskaia Etnografiia* 1:238–240.
        Notes some of folklore work, e.g., publication of part of David of Sassoun in 1936 and 1944; "Lenin in Armenian Folklore," in 1936. Also mentions some of M. Abeghian's work.

Kyulbenkian, G.
1964   "Meknabanutyun 'Sanasar ev Baghdasar' dyutsaznerkutyan i luys Siumera
            Hay barbari." [An Interpretation of the Epic "Sanasar and Baghdasar" in the
            light of Sumero-Armenian Dialect.] *PH* 1:73–90. Russian summary.
                A selection and explanation of 53 words or phrases from Sanasar and
                Baghdasar portion of David of Sassoun.

L., G.
1898   "Armianskie poslovitsy i pogovorki." [Armenian Proverbs and Sayings.] In
            Bratskaia Pomoshch Postradavishim v Turtsii Armianam. 2nd ed. Moscow,
            Kushnerev. p. 579.
                A list of 37 Armenian proverbs and sayings. In Russian.

L., Th.
1876   "Chansons populaires de l'Arménie." *Revue Britannique*, n.s. 2:291–318.
                Songs have appeal to heart of all classes. Bird themes, e.g., the crane.
                Also flower themes; Ara and Semiramis. Songs are from the Van area.

Labubna [no first name]
1868   *Divinakir tbri Edesioy tukht Apkaru.* [Register of the Scribe of Edessa; the
            Letter of Apkar.] Venice, St. Lazar. 71 pp.
                About the legend of Apkar's letter to Jesus Christ.

Lalayan, Ervand [Name sometimes appears as Lalayean, Lalayian, Lalayants, or Lalayantz;
            first name also as Ervant]
1894   "Dajgakhos hromagan Hayer." [Turkish-Speaking Catholic Armenians.] *HA*
            8:313–315.
                In 1829 Catholic Armenians migrated to Vel, a village of Ardahan. The
                Beg of Ardahan fired those who spoke Armenian. Armenian Catholics
                and Georgians never intermarried. Armenian customs retained and family
                terminology kept.

1894   "Surp Sarkis." [St. Sarkis.] *HA* 8:350–353.
                Describes the St. Sarkis festival in dialect of Akhalkalak. Presented in
                conversational style. St. Sarkis was the patron saint of the festival known
                as *vijag* (fortune).

1895   "Hamarot tesutiun Hay azgagrutean." [Brief View of Armenian Ethnogra-
            phy.] *AH* 1:7–26.
                Very little ethnographic material has survived. Few today aware of need to
                save what fragments exist, and some even try to uproot. Gives as example
                the Goghtan songs: historical sources, places, genres, dialects, style and
                spirit.

1895   "Hratarakchits." [From the Publisher.] *AH* 1:5–6.
           About the journal *AH* (Ethnographic Review) to supply need for national
           identity. Ethnography is mirror of people. Dialects enrich language and
           literature. Ethnography section at end shows what others have done, and
           what we should pursue. (NB: I should note here that the first volume
           bears date 1895, yet 1896 is declared historically as first date of issue. I
           have accepted date 1895.—AMA)

1895   "Légendes et superstitions de l'Arménie." [Later series called "Traditions et
           superstitions de l'Arménie."] *Revue des Traditions Populaires* 10:1–6, 119–
           120, 193–197.
           About fairies, guardian angels, various spirits. Gives some short tales as
           examples.

1895   "Tsragir amusnutean ev harsaniki sovoroytneri masin niuter havakelu." [Plan
           for the Collection of Materials on Marriage and Weddings.] *AH* 1, suppl:127–
           130.
           A list of 26 questions to ask informant.

1895–97   "Javakhk." *AH* 1:117–378; 2:245–294. il.
           About the province of Javakhk. The pages of volume 1 give history and
           geography of villages; population, including Gypsies. Dwellings,
           clothing, family customs and life, illness, death, burial, birth and early
           childhood, beliefs, etc. Pages in volume 2 about special festivals, and old
           manuscripts in churches.

1896   "Les anciens chants historiques et les traditions populaires de l'Arménie."
           Revue des Traditions Populaires 11:1–12, 129–138, 337–351.
           Gives sources, origin and dates of singers, attempt of clergy to have
           people forget old songs, but fragments remain. Notes genres, dramatic
           arts, musical instruments. Some examples of songs. Heroic characters.
           Under this title a shorter version appeared in *Société d'Anthropologie.
           Bulletin*, ser. 4, v. 6:500–510 (1895).

1897   "Kendanakan vep." [Animal Tales.] *AH* 2:345–362.
           Includes 16 tales featuring fox. Nothing to indicate source of tales; they
           seem like fables.

1897   "Kh. Abovian." *AH* 2:316–320. port.
           Biographical sketch of Abovian. Year of birth not certain—1804 or 1805.
           His novel *Wounds of Armenia* (translated title) includes folklore.

1897   "Varanda." *AH* 2:5–244.
           Lalayan as editor presents works by various persons about the province of
           Varanda—its history, geography, economy, education, marriage, birth
           and baptism, family life, health, death, future life, beliefs.

Lalayan, Ervand *(continued)*
1898   "Sisian." *AH* 3:105–272. il.
              About area of Sisian, the various villages, their history, geography,
              customs, family life, costume. Information on marriages includes costs.
              Includes information on births, burials, special festivals; 110 folk songs.
              Also has two legends about Alexander the Great.

1898   "Tsatskalezuner." [Secret Languages.] *AH* 4:159.
              Examples given on how syllables are added to words or between
              syllables. Some call it bird language. (NB: My mother and her sisters,
              who grew up in Kharpert, Turkey, spoke bird language fluently.—AMA)

1898   "Varanda. Nshanavor toner." [Special Festivals of Varanda.] *AH* 3:338–349.
              Villagers give little attention to New Year, make visits to neighbors. At
              Christmas a special loaf baked with piece of money enclosed for good
              fortune. Children go to neighbors to collect gifts.

1898   "Zangezur." *AH* 4:7–116. il., map.
              Gives historical and geographical information about area of Zangezur and
              some of its special localities and monasteries. Considerable space given to
              weddings; some information on family life, folk medicine, birth and
              baptism, death and burial, special festivals. Compare crow legend,
              footnote, p. 48, with crow legend in a different location (see Erznikian,
              Grigoris, 1898).

1899   "Perch Proshian." *AH* 5:407–408. port.
              On 40th anniversary of Proshian's work in literature and ethnography in
              his novels.

1899–1901   "Gantsaki Gavar." [Province of Gantsak.] *HA* 5:213–360; 6:231–382; 7–
              8:255–270. il.
              Volume 5 gives historical and geographical information, flora and fauna,
              information on some towns and villages of area and German and other
              communities. Volume 6 about costumes, marriage, birth and baptism,
              family life, food and drink, health, death, beliefs, special festivals,
              fortune songs. Volume 7–8 about Molokans, their customs, and family
              life.

1901–4   "Borchalui Gavar." [Province of Borchalu.] *AH* 7–8:271–437; 9:197–262;
              10:113–268; 11:33–128. il.
              Volumes 7–8 about geography, flora and fauna; volume 9, mixed
              population, dwellings, costume, birth and baptism, marriage; volume 10,
              family organization, food and drink, health and folk medicine, death and
              burial, laments, special festivals; volume 11, oral literature, various folk
              songs, riddles, village nicknames, proverbs and sayings, oaths,
              blessings, curses.

1902 "Ara Geghetsik." [Ara the Beautiful.] *AH* 9:144–159.
   Armenian legend told by Sahak Safarian, aged 100, of Erzerum. Told in mixed dialects since Safarian had been to many places. Lalayan transcribed as told, then converted it to literary form.

1903 "Aghaksandr Makedonos." [Alexander of Macedonia.] *AH* 10:305–309.
   Some Alexander the Great anecdotes and legends told to Lalayan by *Ashugh* (Minstrel) Arakel and several old folks.

1903 "Davit Anhaght." [David the Invincible.] *AH* 10:310–313.
   David considered very brilliant 5th century philosopher so many stories told about him. This one told by 90-year-old Okhnants Papa.

1904 "Nakhijevan Gavar." [Province of Nakhijevan.] *AH* 11:291–334. il.
   History, geography, politics of Goghtn area of the province. The area is mentioned by Moses of Khoren in his *History*.

1904 "Ordubadi kam varin Agulisi ostikanakan shrjan, ev kam Goghtn." [Ordubad or lower Agulis Constabulary area or Goghtn.] *AH* 12:109–174. il.
   About dwellings, costume, family customs, birth and baptism, death and burial, and special festivals.

1904 "Sharur-Daralagyazi Gavar." [Province of Sharur-Daralagyaz.] *AH* 12:235–293. il., map.
   Descriptive and historical material about Daralagyaz, also known as Vayots Tsor. Includes legend of the place Vayots Tsor where two priests were killed. Photo shows women working in dry river bed to induce rain.

1904 "Stepan Zelinski." *AH* 12:306. (Article signed Ervanduni.)
   Zelinski of Armenian parentage, baptized as Solomon, but father renamed him in another baptism. Zelinski contributed to Armenian papers; best known for research on Caucasus and Transcaucasus.

1904 "Vanskii vilaiet." [The Vilayet of Van.] *Sbornik Materialov dlia Opisaniia Mestnostei i Plemen Kavkaza* 44:1–84.
   Information about inhabitants, description of houses, costumes for men, women, and children. Some outlines of costumes are given. Also information on ornaments, family life, weddings.

1904 "Zangezuri Gavar (Kapan kam Ghapan)." [Province of Zangezur (Kapan or Ghapan).] *AH* 12:175–202.
   History of area and various *Melik* families and some of the legends connected with them. *Melik* from Arabic *malik*, meaning lord or prince.

1906 "Dagh-Murad Shah." *AH* 14:100–104.
   A king's son, born with closed fist, which later opens, and he gains great strength.

Lalayan, Ervand *(continued)*

1906   "Hovsep Kara-Murza." *AH* 14:183.
           Kara-Murza was a Caucasus specialist who spent five years to collect
           information on rug making in Caucasus. He had a plan to write an
           extensive book on the subject, but died.

1906   "Khosrov Tagavor." [King Khosrov.] *AH* 14:86–99.
           An epic tale told by Ter-Murat, a priest.

1906   "Rostam Zal." *AH* 14:69–85.
           A Persian tale, but some consider it has Armenian connections.
           Transcribed in dialect of *Nor* Bayazet (New Bayazet).

1906   "Sasna Tsrer." [Daredevils of Sassoun.] *AH* 13:39–82.
           A version of David of Sassoun. Text in prose. Told by Arakel Shekoyan
           in dialect of *Nor* Bayazet (New Bayazet).

1906   "Vayots Tsor. Azgagrutiun." [Ethnography of Vayots Tsor.] *AH* 13:139–
           166; 14:133–155. il.
           Volume 13 about customs. Marriage customs and the saying "Observe the
           mother, marry the girl." Parental choice, but more recently boy may send
           apple to girl; if she approves, she sticks cloves in apple and sends it back
           to boy. Wedding described. Volume 14 gives details about birth and
           baptism, suggested names; folk medicine, protection from evil eye.
           Examples of songs when child first walks. Death and burial.

1906–7   "Nakhijevani ostikanakan shrjan, kam Nakhijevan." [The Constabulary of
           Nakhijevan, or Nakhijevan.] *AH* 13:199–226; 15:131–163. il.
           Description of area and villages, activities, churches and inscriptions.

1906–13   "Nor Bayazeti Gavar, kam Gegharkunig." [Province of New Bayazet or
           Gegharkunig.] *AH* 13:167–197; 14:5–37; 15:165–206; 16:9–65; 17:86–125;
           18:109–156; 19:5–34; 20:33–60; 22:101–112; 23:125–148; 24:51–60.
           Volume 13 gives general information, geography, flora; vols. 14–15
           excavations and tombs; vol. 16 family customs; vol. 17 beliefs; vols. 18,
           19, 20, 22, 23, and 24 descriptions of various villages of area.

1908   "Sevan." *AH* 17:53–85.
           About the island in Lake Sevan; the monastery, its history, relics,
           manuscripts, furnishings.

1910   "Aparani banahyusutyunits" [From the Folklore of Aparan.] *AH* 19:151–159.
           A tale narrated by a farmer in 1909. In winter he visited various villages
           and told tales. This tale is about Hunter Manuk.

1910 "Javakhki banahiusutyunits." [From the Folklore of Javakhk.] *AH* 19:158–163.

   A tale "Miso" collected in 1888 told by an illiterate old man. Told in dialect of Akhalkalak. About Miso, the saddler, and his adventures.

1910 "Nor Bayazeti Gavari banahyusutyunits." [From the Folklore of New Bayazet.] *AH* 19:115–150.

   Three folktales: 1. "The Zangezur Tale," pp. 115–135; 2. "Gislaraj," pp. 135–144; 3. "Lalazar," pp. 144–150.

1910 "Peghumner Nor-Bayazeti Gavarum." [Excavations in the Province of New Bayazet.] *AH* 19:59–84.

   Excavations of various tombs in 1908.

1910 "Vaspurakan." *AH* 20:116–212.

   Folklore collected from Van, Tosp, Vayots Tsor. Descriptive information about some villages. Marriages and weddings with examples of related songs. Also information on birth and baptism, family life, death.

1910–11 "Sasna Tun." [The House of Sassoun.] *AH* 20:61–101; 21:101–126.

   A version of David of Sassoun told in Van dialect, by Manuk Sarksian.

1910–12 "Vaspurakani nshanavor vanker." [Well-known Monasteries of Vaspurakan.] *AH* 20:197–212; 21:37–100; 22:85–100.

   Names monasteries and gives descriptive information of each.

1911 "Agheksandri ksen." [They Tell of Alexander.] *AH* 23:161–165.

   A legendary tale of Alexander the Great, told in the dialect of Van.

1911 "Ostana tun ev Tlal Davit." [The House of Ostan and Tlal Davit.] *AH* 21:127–149.

   Two variant names of David of Sassoun. Transcribed in 1910, told in the dialect of Van.

1911 "Rostam Zal." *AH* 21:150–160.

   Some think that this Persian tale has an Armenian connection. Told in the dialect of Van.

1912–13 "Vaspurakani banahyusutyunits." [From the Folklore of Vaspurakan.] *AH* 22:117–197; 23:149–196; 24:117–180; 25:109–164.

   A total of 29 folktales, some in dialect of Shatakh.

1913 "Tnaynagortsutyune Vaspurakanum Shatakhi shalagortsutyune." [Cottage Industry in Vaspurakan Shatakh's Shawl Industry.] *AH* 25:189–215.

   About various aspects of making shawls—from washing wool, carding, dyeing, spinning, weaving.

Lalayan, Ervand *(continued)*

1913   "Vaspurakani Asorinere." [The Assyrians of Vaspurakan.] *AH* 24:181–232.
              Gives distribution in population in Turkey, Iran, Russia. Ethnological
              information, language and literature, occupations, dwellings, furnishings,
              costume and decoration, marriage and weddings (including cradle
              marriages), childhood, funerals. All kinds of sects included, such as
              Jacobites, Maronites, etc.

1913   "Vaspurakani banavor grakanutyunits." [From the Oral Literature of
              Vaspurakan.] *AH* 24:117–180.
              Lists seven folktales and narrator of each. No collection date given.

1913–16   "Vaspurakan Havatk." [Vaspurakan Beliefs.] *AH* 25:21–60; 26:195–210.
              Worship of mountains, rocks, water, plants and animals, fire, sun,
              spirits.

1916   "Mush-Taron." *AH* 26:149–194.
              In September 1915 some Armenians fled from the Mush-Taron of Turkey
              and crossed the border. The Armenian Ethnographic Society collected 874
              tales and many songs from the refugees. Includes information on
              customs, weddings, songs used in rituals, death and burial.

1916   "Vayots Tsor. Nshanavor vanker." [Well-known Monasteries of Vayots
              Tsor.] *AH* 26:5–84.
              Names monasteries and describes them.

1983   *Javakhk*. Erevan, HSSH, GA Hrat. 455 pp. il., port.
              First volume of Lalayan's works. Covers history and descriptive
              information of the province of Javakhk and some of the villages.
              Dwellings and dress, pp. 130–138. Family life, pp. 138–166 and pp.
              176–191, includes weddings. Birth and baptisms, pp. 166–176. Folk
              medicine, death and burial, pp. 191–212. Beliefs and superstitions, pp.
              212–259. Fasts, pilgrimages and special festivals, pp. 259–291. Fortune
              songs (177), pp. 302–328. Secret language, p. 328. Prayers for various
              purposes, pp. 331–351. Love and dance songs for various occasions, pp.
              352–389. Traditions, pp. 390–409. In-law anecdotes and verses, pp.
              409–411. Supplement, pp. 415–440, about Erzerum Armenians who
              migrated to Russian territory after the 1828–29 Russo-Turkish war.

1988   *Artsakh*. Erevan, HSSH, GA Hrat. 505 pp. il., fold. map.
              Second volume of Lalayan's works. Today *Artsakh* is known as
              Karabagh (Karabakh; Gharabagh). In this volume, the areas under study
              are Varanda and Gantsak. Historical and descriptive information for both
              areas. Of folklore interest for Varanda: Marriage and weddings, pp. 97–
              120. Birth and baptism, pp. 120–125. Family life, pp. 126–142. Folk
              medicine, death and burial, pp. 142–152. Beliefs about nature, myths,

saints, magic, superstitions, pp. 153–193. Special festivals, pp. 191–
202. For Gantsak: Marriage and weddings, pp. 339–361. Birth, baptism
and care of children, pp. 361–376. Family life and food, pp. 376–400.
Health and death, pp. 401–415. Beliefs about nature, spirits, saints,
sorcery, superstitions, pp. 415–444. Special festivals, pp. 444–451.
Fortune songs (170), pp. 451–471. Molokan community, pp. 474–487.

Lalayan, Ervand, and Aznavurian, H.
1898   "Javakhk. Banavor grakanutyun." [Oral Literature of Javakhk.] *AH* 3:91–
            104.
            Fortune songs: 91 collected by Lalayan; 86 by Aznavurian.

Lalayan, Ervand, and Hamamchian, E.
1897   "Kurganner." [Burial Mounds.] *AH* 2:307–315.
            Excavations at Gharabulagh village, pp. 307–308, by Lalayan, and at
            Banants village by Hamamchian, pp. 308–315. Notes about burials and
            the artifacts found. Hamamchian reports superstition of villagers about
            some items found and taken home. They bring bad luck so destroy them.

Lang, Andrew
1950   *Olive Fairy Book*. New York, David McKay. 236 pp.
            The Armenian tales are: "The Golden Headed Fish," pp. 66–75; "The
            Clever Weaver," pp. 115–118; "The Story of Zoulvisia," pp. 222–236.

Lankau, Joh. M.
1897   "Armenische Sprichwörter." *Deutsche Rundschau für Geographie und
            Statistik* 19:266–268.
            A few Armenian proverbs and sayings with explanations.

La Pierre, Richard Tracy
1930   *The Armenian Colony in Fresno County, California: A Study in Social
            Psychology*. Ph.D. thesis, Stanford University, 1930. 641 pp.
            Has considerable information on Armenian customs scattered through the
            text.

Lavrov, L. I.
1979   "K istorii severokavkazkogo fol'klora (do XIX v)." [On the Folklore History
            of the Northern Caucasus (pre-19th century).] *Sovetskaia Etnografiia* 1:29–
            41.
            Includes the North Caucasus legend of Princess Satenig and Ardashes
            from Moses of Khoren's *History*.

Lease, Emory B.
1919   "The Number Three, Mysterious, Mystic, Magic." *Classical Philology* 14:56–
             71.
                      Macedonian, Thracian, and Phrygian oaths in triads. No Armenians
                      noted, but some historians believe Armenians came from Thrace to
                      Phrygia, so may be of interest historically.

Lehmann-Haupt, C. F.
1910   *Die historische Semiramis und ihre Zeit.* Tübingen, C. B. Mohr. 76 pp. il.
                      Of interest to Armenians because it is believed Semiramis founded Van,
                      and loved the Armenian Ara. Other legends about her.

Leo. *See* Babakhanian, Arakel

Lernian, R.
1924   "Gomidas Vartabedi inknagensakrutune." [The Autobiography of Gomidas
             Vartabed.] *H* 2(7):83–87.
                      Author tells of meeting Komitas in Tiflis in 1908 when Komitas gave his
                      autobiography for translation. Illness delayed Lernian; Komitas also ill, so
                      matter dropped, but later renewed. Brief sketch of career and list of
                      publications.

Levin, Isidor
1977   "Armenier." In *Enzyklopädie des Märchen*, Berlin; New York, Walter de
             Gruyter. Vol. 1:794–806.
                      General history of Armenian folklore from early historical works to the
                      present. Names some of the leading folklorists.

1982   *Armenische Märchen.* Düsseldorf-Köln, Eugen Diedrichs Verlag, 286 pp. 2
             maps.
                      Collection includes 25 tales. Notes give sources and tale type numbers.
                      Gives brief history of Armenia, and names of some collectors. A review
                      of the book in English in *Annual of Armenian Linguistics* 7:110–112, by
                      Roland Bielmeier.

Levonian, G.
1903–06   "Ashughneri masin; patmakan-knnakan hayeatsk." [About Minstrels;
             Historical-Critical View.] *AH* 10:39–93; 11:129–l96; 12:84–94; 13:87–111.
             il.
                      History and significance of minstrels in Greece, Rome, Arabia, Persia,
                      Turkey, Armenia, and the West. Lists 391 Armenian minstrels in 1000
                      years. The art and life of a minstrel. On p. 60 (vol. 10) begins discussion
                      about *tvyal* (enumerated) songs about which there has been much
                      controversy. Minstrel in relation to audience. Form and meter of songs.
                      Secret language, including examples. Musical contests. Pictures of
                      instruments with names.

Lipinski, Edward
1971   "El's Abode, Mythological Traditions Related to Mount Hermon and to the
            Mountains of Armenia." *Orientalia Lovaniensia Periodica* 2:13–69.
            Mythological traditions of Armenia, including landing place of Noah's
            Ark, pp. 41–50.

Lisitsian, Srbui
1958–72   *Starinnye pliaski i teatral'nye predstavleniia Armianskogo naroda.* [Old
            Dances and Theatrical Presentations of the Armenian People.] Erevan, Izd-vo
            Akad. Nauk, Armianskoi SSR. 2 v. il. (part col.)
            Vol. 1 has 612 pp. and 130 plates, part colored. Vol. 2 has 500 pp. and
            113 plates, part colored. Text is in Russian, but each volume has section
            of dance songs, with music, and words are given in Armenian and
            Russian. Dance steps shown, and there are pictures of costumes.
            Festivals are considered as theater.

Lisitsian, Stepan
1907   *Hayreni araspelnerits ev veperits patvatskner Hayots patmutiunits.*
            [Explanations of Armenian History from Native Myths and Tales.] Tiflis,
            "Hermes." 80 pp. il., maps.
            Nine tales of Armenian heroes; intended for parish schools. Also a short
            supplement about Noah's Ark.

1925–26   "K izucheniiu Armianskikh krest'ianskikh zhilishch." [Contributions to the
            Studies of Armenian Peasant Dwellings.] *Akademiia Nauk SSSR. Kavkazkii
            Istoriko-Arkheologicheskii Institut, Tiflis. Izvestia* 3:97–108; 4:55–70. il.
            Illustrations include floor plans and cross-section elevations of dwellings.

1969   *Zangezuri Hayere.* [The Armenians of Zangezur.] Erevan, HSSH, GA Hrat,
            383 pp. port., 130 plates (part col.), folded chart.
            Published long after author's death. Material based on pre-Soviet times.
            Some history and descriptive material, but mostly about customs,
            costumes, festivals, worship of mountains, moon, sun (regarded as
            feminine; moon masculine). Photos have no dates or names of
            photographers. Review by K. Melik-Pashayan in *PH* 1970 (1):261–263.

Löbel, Theophil
1897   *Hochzeitsbräuche in der Türkei.* Amsterdam, J. H. de Bussy. 298 pp.
            About Armenian marriage and wedding, pp. 85–119. Notes customs in
            Constantinople and also mentions some Anatolian towns. Importance of
            parental role. Quotes priest's words and prayer used during ceremony.

Luzbetak, Louis J.
1951   *Marriage and the Family in Caucasia, a Contribution to the Study of North Caucasian Ethnology and Customary Law.* Vienna, Mödling, St. Gabriel's Mission Press. 272 pp.
         Includes some Armenian information about marriage customs of olden days that still persist in recent times.

M., A. *See* Alishan, Ghevont

M., Kh. *See* Alishan, Ghevont

M., M.
1913   "Azgagrakan nyuter Pavstos Byuzandatsvo Hayots patmutyan mej." [Ethnographic Subjects in the History of Armenians by Faustus of Byzantium.] *AH* 25:5 20.
         Notes pagan remnants of various folk practices.

Macler, Frédéric
1902   "Choix de fables, etc." *See* Mkhitar Gosh, 1902, "Choix de fables, etc."

1903–4   "Contes arméniens" I–IV. *Revue des Traditions Populaires* 18:506–516; 19:29–30, 184–196, 357–358.
         Part I: "Histoire des trois femmes"; Macler heard the tale in various parts of Turkey, but he is sure of Armenian origin but told in Turkish by Armenians. Parts II–IV are various tales from K. Servantsian, *Hamov-Hodov.*

1905   *Contes arméniens.* Paris, Ernest Leroux. 194 pp.
         Gives biographical sketch of Karekin Servantsian and translations of 21 tales from *Hamov-Hodov.*

1911   *Contes et légendes de l'Arménie.* Paris, Ernest Leroux. xv, 196 pp.
         Includes 34 tales and legends taken from various Armenian collectors. Notes his sources.

1913   "A Very Strange Story." *Armenia* 7:45–46. port.
         Tale about a pagan who marries Christian girl and later becomes converted. Taken from citation above (1911), pp. 91–95.

1922   "Une forme arménienne du thème des 'amants malheureux.' " *REA* 2:91–116.
         Traces various literary accounts of unfortunate lovers, then gives a resumé of Mam and Zin, a story recognized by some as Armeno-Kurdish.

1927   "En marge de l'église arménienne." In his *Trois conférances sur l'Arménie faites à l'Université de Strasbourg*. Paris, Paul Geuthner. pp. 48–91.

About gods in Armenian folklore during paganism; Persian influences, and later Biblical elements. Includes example tales: "Le conte des dormeurs" and "Le poisson à tête d'or."

1928–33 *Contes, légendes et épopées populaires d'Arménie*. Paris, Paul Geuthner. 2 v.

The first volume consists of 23 tales and second volume has seven legends. These have been translated and adapted from the Armenian. They are taken from various sources which Macler cites.

1929   *Les dews arméniens; Parsifal; Iconographie demonologique*. Paris, Ernest Leroux. 122 pp. il.

Discusses demons (dews) in Biblical accounts and in Armenian folklore and iconography. Illustrations are from old manuscripts showing demons in various forms, human and animal, and in combined forms.

1930   "L'enfant exposé—la lettre substituée. Étude de folklore comparé." *L'Ethnographie*, n.s. 21–22:52–70.

Study of comparative folklore. Two Armenian tales of fate compared with tales from various parts of the world.

1932   "Folklore arménien." *L'Ethnographie*, n.s. 25:140.

Brief comment that Armenian folklore offers much for investigation in various genres. Well for scholars to present facts about Armenians in their investigations. Here is a mine that holds some surprises. Notes special need to study Vaspuragan area and the traditions of Agn (Akn).

Madaghjian, Toros M.

1959   *Hushamadean Tomarzayi*. [Memorial of Tomarza.] Beirut, G. Donigian. 628 pp. il., fold. map.

Mostly history of village south of Caesarea. Of folklore interest: Dwelling, household activity, food, costume, pp. 384–400. Marriage, baptism, festivals, pp. 401–448. Fortune telling, etc. pp. 419–431. Games, pp. 432–437. Dialect words and conversation in dialect, pp. 438–452. Proverbs and sayings (195), pp. 441. A few oaths, blessings, good wishes, p. 453. Another dialect word list, pp. 453–503.

Madigian, A.

1914–19 "Groni dzakume ev titsapanutiun esd hamemadagan gronakidutean." [The Origin of Religion and Mythology Based on Comparative Scholarship on Religions.] *HA* 28:129–139, 257–270; 31–32:64–112; 33:1–35.

Origin of religion, positivism, spirit worship.

Madigian, A. *(continued)*
1920   "Titsapanagan urish aztagner." [Other Mythological Factors.] *HA* 34:339–351.

> When Armenian gave birth she left bed and gave birth on earth floor; midwife presented child to father who took child and showed to sun. Mother presented child to mother earth; father to sun and heavenly father.

1922–23   "Ara Keghetsig; hamemadagan knnagan usumnasirutiun." [Ara the Beautiful; A Comparative Critical Study.] *HA* 36:111–121, 226–243, 631–642; 37:116–131. [Notes to be continued, but nothing appears later.]

> Surveys historical sources of story of Ara and Shamiram (Semiramis), also popular tradition and Armenian goddesses.

1923   "Araleznere Hay kraganutean mech." [The Ara lickers in Armenian literature.] *HA* 37:481–495.

> Armenian histories that mention licking dogs to heal wounds. Notes place of dog in ancient times as friend of man, etc. The association of Ara with licking is derived from the legend that when Ara was wounded and died in battle, Semiramis tried to revive him by sending dogs to lick him.

1927   "Aray Keghetsig hamemaduadz urish nmanorinag arasbelneru hed." [Comparison of Ara the Beautiful with Other Similar Tales.] *HA* 40:145–162.

> The legend of Ara the Beautiful is compared with Tamir, Ishtar, Marduk, Osiris, and Isis.

1930   *Ara Keghetsig.* [Ara the Beautiful.] Vienna, Mkhitarian Dbaran. 351 pp.

> The Armenian legend of Ara the Beautiful. This study gives written sources and folklore about Ara and Semiramis and the licking dogs to restore Ara's life. Book also discusses comparable tales, Ara in Greek literature, and the origin of the name Ara.

Madteosian, Vartan
1988   " 'Sasuntsi Daviti' haydnaperman badmutean masin." [About the History of the Discovery of "David of Sassoun."] *B* 146:295–301.

> It is not likely that Servantsian learned about David of Sassoun from written sources. Perhaps there is information in archives not yet studied.

Mahakian, Charles
1935   *History of the Armenians in California.* 97 pp. M.A. thesis, University of California, Berkeley, 1935.

> In the section on social life of Armenians there is brief discussion of family life, marriage customs, but not the details as in the old country.

Mahé, Jean-Pierre

1980   "Origène et la baleine: un fragment pseudo-origénien *Sur Job et le dragon* en traduction arménienne." *REA* n.s. 14:345–365.

        Of special interest is the section "Le Vishap dans la tradition arménienne." *Vishap* is the term used by Armenians for dragon. Also applied to figurative supernatural beings in pagan myths and to monstrous serpents, whales, and metaphorically to the devil and various criminals.

1981   "Six énigmas arméniennes anciennes sur le mythe de l'homme primordial." *REA* n.s. 15:45–57.

        Notes the popular style of the riddles about Adam and attributes them to the period between the 5th and 9th centuries.

1982   "La crime d'Artawasd et les K'ajk' ou le mythe des temps profane." *REA* n.s. 16:175–206.

        Compares the Ardavast legend with other texts and with myths. Also compares with characters in David of Sassoun.

1983   "Echos mythologiques et poesie orale dans l'oeuvre de Grigor Narekac'i." *REA*, n.s. 17:249–270.

        Based on the complete French translation of 1961 *Livre de lamentation* of Gregory of Narek. This well-known Armenian work of the 10th century has many Biblical references, and also elements of Armenian mythology, beliefs about the moon, use of amulets, demons, legends, etc. Examples are given.

1984   "Structures sociales et vocabulaire de la parenté et de la collectivité en Arménie contemporain." *REA* n.s. 18:327–345.

        Armenian kinship vocabulary based on extended family. Kinship words make clear whether relative is from father's or mother's side of family. Kinship roles, especially the bride and specific roles of younger brides. Authority of mother-in-law and father-in-law.

1986   "Siramargn u skahe Haykakan avetaranneri khorannerum." [The Peacock and Goblet in the Armenian Gospel Altars.] *PH* 1:106–112. Russian summary.

        Refers to designs in Gospel manuscripts that have headpieces of peacocks and goblets. Symbolism: peacock is immortality; goblet is reason or divine wisdom, baptism and prophecy. Known even in pagan times.

1986–87   "Remarques supplementaires sur Artawazd et les k'ajk.' " *REA* n.s. 20:557–558.

        Comment on his article (1982) and J. R. Russell's *REA* n.s. 20:253–270. 1986–87.

Maksudian, Nubar
1934   "Araleznere." [Ara Lickers.] *L* 92:339–344.
            Relates to legend about Ara the Beautiful and the attempts of Semiramis to restore him by having dog lick him. Gives information in general about dogs used for this purpose.

1935   "Navasartian done." [The New Year Festival.] *H* 13(3):48–51.
            Navasart was beginning of New Year in ancient Armenia. Royalty and nobles gathered, as did others, and brought fruits and sang to heroes.

1936   "Hetanos Hayasdane." [Pagan Armenia.] *H* 14(4):72–87.
            Gives list of kings of Armenia. First sun worshipers; various Armenian gods in different historical periods. List of planets in Armenian and equivalents in Greek, Babylonian, Assyrian, and Persian.

Malkhasian, Hovhannes
1898–1900   "Hay keghjuki albome." [The Armenian Peasant's Album.] *AH* 3:359–391. il. 6:193–229.
            Various farm implements from Javakhk area, with pictures. Traditions and songs connected with some of them. Vol. 6 shows pictures of household utensils. Describes basic foods, enumerates classes of foods and preparation of some. Mode of life and explanation of utensils.

Malkhasiants, St.
1902   "Arsen arkepiskopos Aytenian." [Archbishop Arsen Aytenian.] *AH* 9:282–284.
            Aytenian made many contributions and did work on folk language. He established the paper *Handes Amsorya*.

1958   *Arakner, avandutyunner, anekdotner.* [Fables, Traditions, Anecdotes.] Erevan, HSSH, GA Hrat. 192 pp. port.
            The work is in dialect of Akhalts. A more accurate title would be "Anecdotes"; a few fables of Aesop are scattered here and there which the compiler notes he heard from his father.

Mansergh, J. F.
1888   "[Armenian Christmas.]" *Notes and Queries*, 7th series, 5:236.
            Armenians keep Christmas on January 6. Also notes Armenian chronology.

Manuelian, P. M.
1980   *Seven Bites From a Raisin.* New York, Ararat Press. 109 pp. il.
            A little over 150 proverbs from A. T. Ghanalanian (1960). Brief introductory comments about Armenian proverbs.

Manukian, M. T.

1963   "Sovetahay kusanakan arveste." [The Art of Soviet Armenian Minstrels.] *PH* 2:31–40.

> Of interest as an example of "invented" folk songs, e.g., "The Kolkhos Shepherd"; "The Girl Heroine."

1976   "Ashugh Shirini ergeri meghedinere." [The Melodies of Minstrel Shirin's Songs.] *PH* 3:117–132. Russian summary.

> Shirin (Ovannes Karapetian) 1827–57. His folk and minstrel songs worthy of being in best rank of songs. The songs are from 18th century and first half of 19th century tradition.

Mardikian, George

1944   *Dinner at Omar Khayyam's*. New York, Viking Press. 150 pp.

> Aside from recipes, some information on background of some types of food, probable origins, and occasion when used. Seldom introduces non-Armenian food.

Mardirosian, Florence

1948   "Armenian Music." *Armenian Review* 1(2):103–108.

> Includes church music (*sharagans*), but pp. 106–108 about folk music collected by Komitas. Also some comments about minstrels.

Mardirossian, N.

1930   "Altarmenische Volksüberlieferungen über Tork, der Gott der übermensch-lichen Kraft." *Archiv Orientali* 2:293–298. il.

> About the power of the superhuman god, Tork.

Marguni, A. V.

1983   "K voprosu o proiskhozhdenii i razvitii siuzhets i zhanre. (Mif-epos-skazka.)" [On the Question of Origin and Development of Subject and Genre. (Myth–Epic–Tale.)] *PH* 1:136–148. Armenian summary.

> Foundation of Armenian folklore. Topics examined for the mythological and artistic interrelated ideas brought about by time and dispersal concepts conditioned by subject and genre construction principles and production of outer forms.

Marguni, Hasmik

1976   "Pokr patmoghakan zhanre banahyusakan akunknere." [The Folklore Sources of a Brief Narrative Genre.] In *Avandutyunere ev gegharvestakan zargatsume*. Erevan, HSSH, GA Hrat, pp. 176–221.

> The brief narrative or novella genre developed from folklore sources such as proverbs, fables, anecdotes, etc.

Markarian, Siran Z.
1931   *A Translation of "The Ancient Beliefs of Armenians," by Avedik Aharonian, with Introduction and Notes.* 47 pp. and 94 [97] pp. M.A. thesis, Columbia University, 1931.
           Biographical information about Aharonian and his work, followed by translation of Aharonian's dissertation that has separate pagination. The bibliography, pp. 86–93, is poorly presented.

Marr, N.
1895–99   *Sbornik pritch Vardana; materialy dlia istorii srednevekevoi Armianskoi literatury.* [Collection of Parables (or Fables) of Vardan: Materials for the History of Armenian Literature.] St. Petersburg, Tip. Impr. Akad. Nauk. 3 v.
           Not seen. Contents: Vol. 1 (635 pp.) gives an account of fable literature in Russian. Vol. 2 (360 pp.) Armenian texts. Vol. 3 (202 pp.) includes some Arabic fables. For a detailed review of this work, see F. C. Conybeare's review in *Folklore* (1899) 10:462–474. Also for a critique see Dashian, H. (1899–1900) in *HA*, v. 13 and 14.

Marr, N., and Smirnov, J.
1931   *Les vishaps.* Leningrad, Impr. "Iv. Fedorov." 107 pp., 24 plates.
           The plates show large stone fish forms discovered by a Russian expedition at Gegham, near Lake Sevan in 1909. Creatures are called *vishaps,* which some consider a synonym for dragon in Armenian. For a review by Ernest Herzfeld, see *Folklore* (1937) 48:101–107.

Marshall, Annie C.
1906   "Armenian Embroideries." *Armenia* 2(1):8–12. Also reprinted in *New Armenia* (1920) 12:104–105.
           Although not illustrated the article describes work done in Marash, Aintab, Urfa, and Constantinople.

1910   "Armenian Industries." *Armenia* 4(5):5.
           About Armenian needle lace and embroidery and ancient designs used. Workers earn money by selling items abroad.

Martinengo-Cesaresco, Evelyn
1886   *Essays in the Study of Folk Songs.* London, George Redway. 394 pp.
           "Armenian Folk Songs," pp. 53–88. Not as much emphasis on folk songs as title suggests. Has some information on the Armenian Catholic Mkhitarist Congregation at St. Lazar, Venice, Italy.

Martirosian, A. A.
1969–72   *Patmutyun ev khratk Khikaray Imastnoy.* [History and Admonitions of Khikar the Wise.] Erevan, HSSH, GA Hrat. 2 v.
           Not seen. This is a critical study of the history and the text.

Marutian, Harutyun

1937 "Hayots avandutayin shtemarannere." [Traditional Armenian Storage.] *L* 7:65–76. il. Russian summary.

    Based on ethnographic material. Mainly concerned with storage of grains for family use. Various styles of 19th and 20th centuries described. Bread storage also mentioned.

Matikian, A. See Madigian, A.

Matindjiane, M.

1907 *Étude sur la poésie populaire arméniennes.* Paris, Gerard Brière. 158 pp. Thesis, Paris, 1907.

    About folk songs for special festivals; themes of love, marriage, émigrés, funerals. Presence of nature in songs. Rhythm and language of songs. Examples given in French translation of songs.

Matossian, Mary Kilbourne

1956 "Armenian Society." *Armenian Review* 9(3):49–63.

    About social and cultural changes in eastern Armenian family life in villages and towns.

1979 "Birds, Bees and Barley: Pagan Origins of Armenian Spring Rituals." *Armenian Review* 32:292–302.

    In pre-Christian times the Armenian year had three seasons with a special festival for each season. For example, growth time patterns of barley later used for St. Hripsime's Day in the Christian calendar.

Maynard, B. W.

1951 "Armenian Needlepoint." *Embroidery*, n.s. 2(1):22–24. il.

    About needle lace, not needlepoint in present usage. Maynard calls it *dentelle de Smyrne*. The illustrations of doily, etc. are typically Armenian needle lace.

Mazian, Florence

1983 "The Patriarchal Armenian Family System." *Armenian Review* 36(5):14–26.

    Interviews with several Armenian immigrants who matured after leaving western Armenia. Gives methodology of study. Power of eldest male, defense and avoidance patterns, marriage (arranged and by choice). Starting period of transitions interrupted by war, 1914–18.

1984 "Armenian Wedding Customs 1914: From Sacred to Profane." *Armenian Review* 37(4):1–13.

    Based on interviews with persons born in Caesarea and one of its villages, Nirsah. About *khoskgab* (binding-word), engagement, pre-wedding parties, ceremony, rituals, and parties. Role of bride after marriage.

Mégavorian, Agop

1894   *Étude ethnographique et juridique sur la famille et le mariage arméniens, précédée d'un aperçu historique.* [Paris] F. Pichon. 126 pp.

First part is about Armenian marriage law. Second part presents conditions under which marriages are contracted. Obstacles to marriage. Celebration of marriage.

Mehrabian, H.

1936   "Gomidas Vartabed ev ir tere Hay erazhshdutean mech." [Gomidas Vartabed and his Role in Armenian Music.] *H* 14(3):65–72. il.

On occasion of 40th day after death of Komitas. Biographical information, education, including the Berlin years and visit to Paris. He collected 3000 folk songs, also contributed to church music. Includes his portrait and choral group in Echmiadzin.

Meinardus, Otto A. I.

1980   "A Stone-cult in the Armenian Quarter of Jerusalem." *REA*, n.s. 14:367–375. il.

Three corner stones in the Church of the Holy Archangels in Jerusalem said to show impression of Christ's arm when he was beaten or when he cried out to witness against hardness of heart of Pharisees. Legend not attached to site before the 17th century.

Melikian, Spiridon

1948–52   *Hay zhoghovrdakan erger ev parer.* [Armenian Folk Songs and Dances.] Erevan, Haypethrat. 2 v. port.

Introduction in Armenian and Russian. Folk songs and dances collected from Sassoun, Aparan, Erevan, Talin, Kirovakan, Tsaghkahovit and nearby areas. Total of 531 songs include music. Some of texts of songs also given in Russian.

Melik-Ohanjanian, K. A.

1964   "Agatangeghosi banahyusakan aghbyurneri hartsi shurje." [About the Question of the Folklore Sources of Agathangelos.] *PH* 4:53–82. Russian summary.

Considerable detailed investigation of the various sources from which were derived the Armenian deities, pagan practices, and folk elements.

1965   "Manuk Abeghian." *PH* 3:3–18. Russian summary.

On occasion of 100th anniversary of Abeghian's birth. Biographical information and his work as a literary figure and folklorist.

Melik-Pashayan, K. V.

1963   *Anahit ditsuhu pashtamunke.* [The Worship of the Goddess Anahit.] Erevan, HSSH, GA Hrat. 163 pp.

Not seen, but there is a review by V. Bdoyan in *PH* 1965 (4):265–268. Anahit of Persian origin; looked upon as mother and love goddess.

Compares with Greek and Assyrian goddesses and gives other comparative information.

1964   "Ervand Lalayan." *PH* 3:42–43. port.
        Biography and survey of Lalayan's ethnographic and folkloristic work. He organized the Armenian Ethnographic Society and collected much folklore. In 1915 he led expedition that collected 1000 folktales and many songs from Armenian refugees from Turkey.

1965   "Stepan Lisitsian." *PH* 4:31–42. port. Russian summary.
        On occasion of 100th year of Lisitsian's birth (text gives 1865, Russian summary gives 1864). Lisitsian was an ethnographer, but also did some folklore work, museum work, and teaching. Died in 1947.

1968   "Sahak Movsisian (Pense)." *PH* 2:163–166. port.
        About life and work of S. Movsesian of Mush who collected folk dance songs and hundreds of sayings. Many of his songs were for dances and weddings. Some of his Turkish and Kurdish songs were never published. He followed scientific method in his collection work.

1969   "Tumanyane ev azgagrutyune." [Tumanian and Ethnography.] *PH* 3:77–84. Russian summary.
        Tumanian was essentially a writer, but adapted some Armenian folktales; he also collected some folklore.

M[elikset]-B[ek,] L.
1925   "O neobkhodimosti sravnitel'nogo izucheniia krest'ianskikh zhilishch Armenii i Gruzii." [On the Need for Comparative Study of Peasant Dwellings in Armenia and Georgia.] *Akademiia Nauk SSSR. Kavkazkii Istoriko-Arkheologicheskii Institut. Tiflis. Izvestiia* 3:109–110.
        Brief description of the structures.

Melikset-Beg, L. M.
1963   "Vratsakan aghbyurnere Sayat-Novayi masin." [Georgian Sources About Sayat-Nova.] *PH* 3:17–44.
        Gives considerable information about Sayat-Nova's life and activities.

Melik-Shahnazarian, G. G.
1928   "Gharabaghi parkeren." [From Customs of Gharabagh.] *HA* 42:552–559.
        Blessings (106) and curses (208) from the Karabagh area.

1928   "Purt kzeln ev kork kordzele Gharabaghum." [Wool Carding and Rug-making in Gharabagh.] *HA* 42:475–478.
        Describes yarn preparation for rug making. On final day when rug ready to release from loom, the rug maker invites women to a party. Pregnant woman is passed through hole made by warp threads, young boy is given

Melik-Shahnazarian, G. G. *(continued)*
shed stick which he uses as hobby horse. He rides in street, the first person he meets, male or female, determines sex of unborn child.

1930   "Hanelukner Gharabaghi parparov." [Riddles in the Gharabagh Dialect.] *HA* 44:357–363.
Gives a preliminary explanation of the dialect and lists 105 riddles.

1930   "Hanelukner Gharabaghi lezvov." [Riddles in the Gharabagh Dialect.] *HA* 44:596–601.
Notes 143 riddles in the Karabagh dialect.

1931   "Niuter Gharabaghi Hay azkutean hamar. Dnayin pzhshgutiun." [Topics for Gharabagh Armenians. Home Medicine.] *HA* 45:246–251.
Treatment suggestions for eyes, teeth, headache, bleeding, coughing, stomachache, abscesses, swellings.

Melik-Shahnazarov, E.
1893   "Iz poverii, predrazsudkovi narodnykh primat Armian Zangezurskogo uezd." [From the Armenian Beliefs, Prejudices and Folk Omens of the Zangezur District.] *Sbornik Materialov dlia Opisaniia Mestnostei i Plemen Kavkaza* 17(2):193–201.
About beliefs in dark powers, celestial powers, and influences of nature. Health care. Foretelling the future; serpents and attitudes towards animals in general and towards people. Religious views, evil eye, pregnancy, birth, marriage, domestic economy, death.

1894   "Svad'by Zangezurskikh Armian." [Armenian Wedding in Zangezur.] *Sbornik Materialov dlia Opisaniia Mestnostei i Plemen Kavkaza* 19(2):220–226.
Describes selection of girl, engagement, wedding, placing boy on girl's lap so she will have a son. Bride sweeps room to clear the way for wealth. Dinner served, etc.

1904   "Iz poverii, predrazsydkov i narodnykh premet Armian Zangezurskogo uezda." [From Beliefs, Prejudices, and Popular Omens of Armenians in Zangezur District.] *Sbornik Materilov dlia Opisaniia Mestnostei i Plemen Kavkaza* 34(3):91–224.
Topics covered as in his 1893 article, but also includes riddles, proverbs and sayings, anecdotes, blessings and good wishes, and curses.

Menevischean, G.
1891   "Ein chinesischer Gebrauch bei den Armeniern." *Ethnologische Mitteilungen aus Ungarn* 2(2–5):55–56.
Notes old Upper Armenian custom of shaving head of child as the Chinese did. Also connects Armenian name Mamikonean to Chinese

Mam-Kun. (NB: About the hair style, see Pawstos Buzandasi, 1989, p. 226 and note 12, p. 331.—AMA)

Mesrop, Vardapet. *See* Ter-Movsesian, Mesrop

Miansarov, M. M.
1868   *Knar Haykakan*. [Armenian lyre.] St. Petersburg, G. I. Bakst. 590 pp. followed by various paging.

    Of folklore interest, pp. 130–185; includes 104 Armenian folk songs used for *vijag* (fortune game). At end of book, on pp. I–XVII, are 529 proverbs and sayings from various sources,

Miklosich, Franz
1878   "Beiträge zur Kenntnis der Zigeunermundarten IV." *Akademie der Wissenschaften, Wien. Philosophisch–Historischen Klasse. Sitzungsberichte* 90:245–296.

    Of interest pp. 281–283 about Gypsies of Armenia; gives 89 words of the Gypsies in Armenian.

Minasian, L.
1986   "'Grung' erki dbakir mi hin darperage." [An Old Variant Printing of the Song "Crane."] *B* 144:338–341.

    History of Armenia shows deprivation of homeland for many. Songs arose expressing longing; one of most famous is "Grung" (Crane). Has appeared in many songbooks since the 17th century. Doubts have arisen about its identity as to whether it is a folk song or not. Here are given nine stanzas of a 1701 manuscript (part missing).

Minasian, L. G.
1972   *Ashugh Margar (Ohan Oghli)*. [Minstrel Margar (Ohan Oghli).] Teheran, "Nurpasha." 437 pp. il.

    Biography of the 20th century minstrel. His song themes were didactic, religious, and humorous; also some love songs. Word list of dialect words.

Minassian, Chaké Der Melkonian. *See* Der Melkonian-Minassian, Chaké

Mirzoev, A., et al.
1892   "Armianskaia skazki, predaniia i legendy." [Armenian Tales, Traditions and Legends.] *Sbornik Materialov dlia Opisaniia Mestnostei i Plemen Kavkaza* 13(2):75–140.

    A dozen items representing the genres noted in the title.

Mirzoyan, I.

1967   "Sayat-Novayi khagherum oktagartsvats mi shark otarazki pareri meknabanakan ports." [An Attempt to Interpret Some Foreign Words Used in Sayat-Nova's songs.] *L* 3:79–91.

In some songs Persian or Azeri words are introduced. Meanings of those words are explained to help clarify interpretation.

Mkhalian, Krikor N.

1938   *Bardizag u Bardizagtsik.* [Bardizag and Bardizag People.] Cairo, Dbaran Sahag Mesrob. 983 pp. il., fold. map.

Folklore material is scattered. Dwellings, furnishings, food, pp. 133–141. Wedding customs prior to 1859, pp. 141–147. Entertainment and games, pp. 752–764. Superstitions and beliefs, pp. 803–812. Sayings, proverbs, expressions (801), pp. 879–901. Special explanations of various expressions, p. 913.

Mkhitar Gosh

1842   *Aragk.* [Fables.] Venice, St. Lazar. 187 pp., front.

Includes 190 fables (pp. 1–164) followed by 23 fables of Olympianos, (pp. 165–187). Mkhitar Gosh was of 12th and 13th centuries. Another edition of this work was published in 1854, but no mention is made that it is a reprint.

1902   "Choix de fables arméniennes attribuée à Mkhitar Gosh." *Journal Asiatique,* ser. 9, v. 19:457–487.

Selection of 48 fables (of 190). Translation is based on Armenian edition of 1842. Some biographical information on Mkhitar Gosh is given.

1907–10   *Tadastanakirk.* [Law Book.] I have not been able to see any original edition, but for a critical study that gives some excerpts, see Samuelian, Kh., 1907–10.

1951   *Arakner.* [Fables.] Erevan, HSSH, GA Hrat. 140 pp.

Commentary and notes by E. Pivazian. Notes that 160 fables are mythical and moral, and have not been studied as much as they should be. Fables are derived from manuscripts; sources indicated. First printed in Venice in 1790 followed by editions of 1842 and 1854.

1957–58   "Bajki." [Fables.] *Przeglad Orientalistyczny* 1:71–72; 2:171–172.

A total of seven fables, translated into Polish by Kazimierz Roszko.

1987   *The Fables of Mkhitar Gosh.* Translated, with an introduction, by Robert Bedrosian. New York, Ashod Press. xi, [80] pp. il.

Of these 190 fables, many use plant and animal motifs. Moral pointed out at end of each fable. Translation from Armenian edition of 1854.

Mkhitarian, K.

1958   *Mer kiughe Tadem.* [Our Village Tadem.] Boston, Hayrenik Dbaran. 256 pp. il.

> About old and recent times of village. Includes some folklore that is scattered in items written by various contributors. Explains that money stuck on forehead of dancer is paid to musicians at wedding, but if fee is pre-arranged, money goes to bride and groom (p. 69).

Mkhitariants, Agh.

1900   *Dagher u Khagher.* [Songs and Dances.] Alexandropol. 260 pp.

> Includes some folk songs and minstrel songs.

1901   "Pshrank Shiraki ambarnerits." [A Fragment from the Granaries of Shirak.] *Eminian Azgagrakan Zhoghovatsu* 1:1–338.

> Includes a variety of genres of folklore: tales, 1500 proverbs, fables, blessings, curses, oaths, riddles. Also family rites and customs, weddings, special festivals, etc. Word list, pp. 303–338.

Mkrtchian, Hasmik

1987   "Hay-Arabakan banahyusakan kaperi patmutyunits." [From the History of Armenian-Arabian Folklore Ties.] *L* 3:54–60.

> Armenian folklore influenced by Arabic, since Arabia dominated Armenia for two centuries. But there are also some Armenian influences on Arab folklore. Mentions David of Sassoun's Katchan king and the City of Bronze. Notes Arab ideas of Mt. Ararat.

Mkrtchian, L. M.

1972   *Armianskaia srednevekovaia lirika.* [The Medieval Armenian Lyric.] Leningrad, Leningradskoe Otdelenie. 388 pp. il.

> The word medieval is somewhat stretched; lyrics date from 15th to 17th centuries. First part of book includes folk songs relating to work, love, lamentations and exile. Also cradle songs.

1982   *"David Sasunskii" Armianskii narodny epos.* [The Armenian Folk Epic "David of Sassoun."] Leningrad, Sovetskii Pisatel'. 358 pp. il.

> Four cycles of the epic David of Sassoun are presented in verse form, with notes.

Mkrtchian, M. S.

1957   *Naghash Hovnatan.* Erevan, HSSH, GA Hrat. 178 pp.

> Life and work of Naghash Hovnatan (1661–1722). A poet but also recognized as an *ashugh* (minstrel) for outdoor performances, though he made some banquet appearances.

Mkrtchian, Manik
1961   *Hay zhoghovrdakan pandukhtutyan erger.* [Songs of Armenian Emigrés.]
            Erevan, HSSR, GA Hrat. 122 pp.
            Songs relating to persons who left home to work for awhile in another
            place, such as Smyrna or Constantinople. Songs grouped by types:
            parting, longing for fatherland, songs of love and longing for family
            members, grief for departure, and miscellaneous songs. Sources are given
            in notes. A word list and a bibliography included.

1979   *Hay mijnadaryan pandukhtutyan tagher.* [Medieval Armenian Émigré Songs.]
            Erevan, HSSH, GA Hrat.
            Not able to see the book, but saw review by A. Sh. Mnatsakanian in *PH*
            1980 (4):273–287. He notes errors, lack of an introduction, and makes
            other objections. A rebuttal by author of book appears in *PH* 1981
            (2):240–253. Russian summary.

Mkrtumian, Ia. I.
1967   "Nekotorye formy soobshchestvi Armianskoi derevene." [Some Forms of
            Community Life in an Armenian Village.] *PH* 4:284–290.
            Work done with help of relatives or with various neighbors in second half
            of 19th century.

Mnatsakanian, A. Sh.
1955   *Haykakan zardarvest.* [Armenian Ornamental Art.] Erevan, HSSH, GA Hrat.
            658 pp. il. (part col.) Russian summary.
            Illustrations derived from old Armenian manuscripts. Symbolism of
            plants, including tree of life; animals, and architectural forms. Each
            ornament documented by source. Bibliography divided by Armenian and
            Russian.

1956   *Haykakan mijnadaryan zhoghovrdakan erger.* [Medieval Armenian Folk
            Songs.] Erevan, HSSH, GA Hrat. 668 pp.
            Introductory essay gives history, development, metrical system, and types
            of songs. Themes: love, patriotism, weddings, social events, dances,
            miscellaneous. Variants also given. Glossary and bibliography included.

1958   "Hayrenneri ev Nahapet Kuchaki masin." [About *hayrens* and Nahapet
            Kuchak.] *PH* 2:234–257.
            The *hayren* is a ballad with a certain metrical verse form of 15 syllables
            and particularly used by minstrels. This is a critique of a work by A.
            Khukasyan (Erevan, 1957). Author claims that some of these verses are
            by Nahapet Kuchak. Gives examples comparing with works of others.

1975   "Ditoghutyunner 'Vardges-Mankan' vipakan hatvatsi veraperyal." [Obser-
        vations Concerning the Article about the Tale "Vardges-Mankan."]. *PH*
        2:212–232. Russian summary.
        > Critique of story in Moses of Khoren's *History*. Concerns date, probably
        > 570–560 B.C., and locale of story. An even earlier date, 3rd century,
        > considered. Supposed to be an epic.

1976   " 'Tukh Manuk' hushartsanneri masin." [About the "Swarthy Youth" Monu-
        ments.] *PH* 2:189–204. Russian summary.
        > The "Swarthy Youth" looked upon as a brave and unknown saint. Older
        > women made visits to monuments and made vows. Practice common in
        > many villages. Origin unknown; associated with water, believed to be
        > very old and passed over into Christianity.

1980   *Hay mijnadaryan hanelukner.* [Medieval Armenian Riddles.] Erevan, HSSH,
        GA Hrat. 522 pp.
        > Have not seen original. The book reviewed in *Lraber* 1981(4):99–102, by
        > Arshaluys Chazinian. Riddles from the Bible and Armenian writers.

1981   "Varazi motive Hay ditsabanutyan ev arvesdi mej." [The Wild Boar Motif in
        Armenian Mythology and Art.] In *International Symposium on Armenian Art.*
        2nd, Erevan, Sept. 12–18, 1978. *Collection of Reports*, v. 1:200–208.
        > Death and resurrection appear in Armenia and other eastern countries with
        > boar as symbol against life. Armenian King Tiridates changed into a boar
        > before accepting Christianity from Gregory the Illuminator.

Mnatsakanian, S. Kh.
1956   *Hayasdani giughakan bnakavayri chartarapetutyune.* [Architecture of
        Armenian Village Dwellings.] Erevan, HSSH, GA Hrat. 241 pp. il.
        > Several Soviet Armenian village dwellings are shown with ground and
        > floor plans. Structures for animals also shown. Floor plans for dwellings
        > show three rooms. Village buildings suitable for meetings and schools are
        > shown. Prominent place given to fountain memorials of various types.

Mokri, M.
1964   "L'Arménie dans le folklore Kurde." *REA* , n.s. 1:342–376.
        > Includes story of Shirin, the Armenian princess who was loved by
        > Khosrov.

Mortillet, G. de
1899   "Rites et usages funeraires." *Revue des Traditions Populaires* 4:566.
        > About a picture by B. Picet entitled "La commemoration des morts chez
        > les Arméniens." Notes that the custom is also followed in Dept. de Haute-
        > Saône.

Moses of Khoren
1961   *Hayots patmutyun.* [History of the Armenians.] Erevan, Haypethrat. 417 pp.
             Introduction, pp. 7–74, by St. Malkhasian, gives biography of Moses of
             Khoren. Discusses the history, sources, the Armenian mythology (or
             tales), significance of the *History*, time of composition, credibility of the
             History, its publication, and various translations. The text is in Armenian,
             followed by notes.

1978   *History of the Armenians. Translation and Commentary on the Literary
             Sources*, by Robert W. Thomson. Cambridge, Mass., Harvard University
             Press. 408 pp. (Harvard Armenian Texts and Studies, 4.)
             Thomson questions that the work belongs to the 5th century and considers
             the work tendentious. This work is important since it is the first time the
             text became available in English.

Mosgofian, K.
1937   "Nmushner Sepasdioy zhoghovrtagan panahusutenen." [Examples of
             Folklore From Sepasdia.] *HA* 5:351–359.
             Various children's verses told either by children or by their mothers.
             Author collected verses from his student days.

Mourier, J.
1888   *Contes et légendes au Caucase.* Paris, Maisonneuve & Ch. Leclerc. 112 pp.
             The Armenian tales, pp. 81–112, do not give sources, nor do the tales
             have titles. Other tales in the book are Georgian and Mingrelian.

1912   *L'Art du Caucase.* 3rd ed. Brussels, Bulens. 252 pp. il., and 148 pp. il.
             First part about religious art; includes costume, ivory carvings, enamels,
             embroideries. Second part about industrial arts, includes some household
             items.

Movsisian, Sahak
1899–1900   "Bulanekh, kam Hark gavar." [Bulanukh, or province of Hark.] *AH* 5:9–
             184. il., map; 6:7–108.
             History, flora and fauna, dwellings, costume, agriculture and implements
             and food. Also includes information about weddings, birth and child care,
             games, names and epithets, folk medicine, death and burial, beliefs,
             superstitions, legends, special festivals, various folk songs, proverbs and
             sayings, fables, and riddles.

Mubayachian. *See* Mubayajian

Mubayajian, Sargis
1911   "Tigran metsi dramnere." [The Coins of Tigranis the Great.] *AH* 21:200–
             212. il.
             Gold and silver coins are described and museum locations noted. Possible
             folklore interest for designs on coins.

1912   "Ezi pashtamunke hin Hayastantum." [Ox Worship in Ancient Armenia.] *AH* 23:114–124.

        Based on archeological evidence relating to agricultural work.

1912   "Hay takavorneri dramnere." [Coins of Armenian Kings.] *AH* 22:198–231; 23:27–67.

        Coins from early times to pre-Christian period.

1913   "Shiraki ashkataryan (kiplopyan) amrotsner." [The Cyclopian Fortresses of Shirak.] *AH* 25:165–188.

        Ruins found in villages of Shirak in 1884 expedition organized by Toros Toromanian.

1913   "Hay takavorneri ev kaghakneri dramnere." [Coins of Towns and Kings of Armenia.] *AH* 24:83–89.

        Coins of Artashat and Kamnagan Towns.

1931   "Vishabazants bashdamunke." [Worship of the non-*vishap* (or Demon cult).] *B* 89:308–319.

        The first word literally means without the demon or dragon, but I cannot grasp the significance of it. Anyway, the article is about the demon or dragon associated with the goddess Anahid who is connected with the Chorukh Basin area. Ancient Anahid tales are associated with water as was the *vishap*.

Mughnetsian, Sh. M.

1981   " 'Goghtan erger' geghagitakan hamakarge." [The Aesthetic System of the "Songs of Goghtan."] *PH* 3:176–186. Russian summary.

        The songs are from Moses of Khoren's *History*. Article points out dynamic images, cosmic scope, and artistic harmony. Examples of songs are in classical Armenian.

Müller, Friedrich

1896   "Armenische Sprache." *Wiener Zeitschrift für die Kunde des Morgenlandes* 10:181–182.

        Gives only four maxims taken from *Toros Akhpar* by K. Servantsian. Maxims are given in Armenian.

Murad, Friedrich

1901   *Ararat und Masis*. Heidelberg, Carl Winter Universitätsbuchhandlung. 104 pp.

        Study of ancient Armenia and literature. Description of Ararat (Masis in Armenian) and the history, traditions, and myths connected with Ararat, such as the flood and Noah in Armenian literature.

Murad-Bablanian, Lillian G.
1986   "The Armenian Dance." *Ararat* 26(1):5–11. il.
            Dance derived from pagan times. Describes steps and style of circle and
            solo dances; times of performance, instruments used in music. Purposes
            of ancient dances.

Muradian, Hrayr
1963   *Sayat-Nova.* Erevan, HSSR. 84 pp.
            On the occasion of the 250th year of the minstrel's birth. Biographical part
            followed by topics of his songs. Excerpts of songs are from the
            compilation by H. S. Hasratian.

Muradian, M. H.
1969   "Komitasi verjin aytselutyune Hayastan." [Komitas's Last Visit to Armenia.]
            PH 4:61–69.
            Komitas had spent many years in Echmiadzin, but had also been to Berlin
            (1896–99); Paris, Switzerland, Vienna, Berlin (1906–07); Tiflis (1905)
            and Baku (1908). In 1908, back to Echmiadzin, but the new Catholicos
            was not sympathetic so Komitas moved to Constantinople in 1910.

1979–80   "Komitasi gortsuneutyune Gostandnopolsum." [Komitas in Constantinople.]
            PH 4:14–24 (1979); 1:115–125 (1980). Russian summary.
            Komitas left Echmiadzin for Constantinople where he organized an
            Armenian choral group and gave concerts, despite some clerical
            objections. Later went to Paris where he attended International Music
            Society meeting and presented papers in 1914. Returned to
            Constantinople and worked on variants of folk songs. In 1915 exiled by
            Turks. Went to Paris in 1916 where he was in hospital until 1935 when
            he died.

1982   "Arevmtahay zhoghovrdakan erazhshtutyune." [Western Armenian Folk
            Music.] *PH* 3:11–25. Russian summary.
            Late 19th century marks beginning of collecting folk music. Komitas went
            to villages and collected 4000 songs, with musical notations. Many lost,
            though 1200 survive. His pupils continued work in some areas. A few
            examples of songs given.

Muradian, Mgrdich
1934   "Sasnoy ashughnere." [The Minstrels of Sassoun.] *B* 92:462–463.
            Minstrels accompanied pilgrims, sang songs of the folk. Names some
            minstrels.

Muradian, P. M.
1961   *Sayat Nova est Vratsakan aghbyurneri.* [Sayat-Nova According to Georgian
            Sources.] Erevan, HSSH, GA Hrat. 119 pp.
            The Armenian minstrel also had songs in Georgian. This surveys Sayat-
            Nova studies in Georgian and his place in Georgian literature. Notes that

the ballad "Stepanos the Tailor" is not by Sayat-Nova, though attributed to him. Need to publish Georgian songs and indicate important readings and new variants.

Muradiants, H.

1898–1900   "Hamshentsi Hayer." [Armenians of Hamshe.] *AH* 4:117–143; 5:361–406; 6:109–158.

Hamshe folk moved from south shore of Black Sea to Georgia. Description of customs and weddings, birth, family life. Moral decline influenced by tobacco workers. Information on folk medicine, death and burial, beliefs, nature worship, saints, etc., superstitions and sorcery, festivals.

Muradjan, Matevos

1968   "Die Entwicklung der armenisch-sowjetischen musik Wissenschaft." *Beiträge zur Musikwissenschaft* 10:3–15.

Folk music development since Komitas; folkloristic activity of Armenians in Soviet Union. Institute for Science and Art is editing works of Komitas and Spendiarov.

Nahapet Kuchak

1912   *Lirika "Aireny."* [Lyrical "Hayrens."] Moscow, "Khudozhestvennaia Literatura." 221 pp.

Translations from Armenian into Russian by various translators. This 16th century poet wrote in the style of Armenian *hayrens* (ballads) and some contend that they should be considered as folklore. Mostly love songs.

1957   *Hayreni karkav.* [Series of Hayrens (Ballads).] Erevan, Haypethrat. 345 pp.

Introductory essay is by Av. Ghukasian. Presents life and work of the author. Linguistic analysis suggests he was from Akn. The types of songs presented 385 love songs, 46 émigré songs, and 22 advisory songs. Some hyperbole in songs, love of nature, and occasional anti-clerical themes. A leading influence on later minstrels.

1974   *Poèmes d'amour.* Translated by Vahé Godel. Paris, L'Association Langues et Civilisations. 47 pp.

Presents 61 verses in the popular musical tradition. Preface gives brief history of the poetic tradition and minstrels.

1976   *Haryur u mek hayren.* [Hundred and one hayren (Ballads).] Erevan, "Sovetakan Grogh." 258 pp. col. vignettes.

Text in Armenian and Russian. Ballads in traditional metrical form of 15 syllables in each quatrain. It is surprising how close the Russian translations retain the form. Various translators named. Also the word-for-word Russian translations are given.

Nahapetian, R.
1973   "Gerdastanakan tune ev kentsaghe Aghdzniki Aznvats Dzor gavarum." [The
            Dynastic Home and the Life of Aghdznik in the province of Aznvats Dzor.]
            Banber Erevani Hamalsarani 1:215–243. il.
                About construction of houses to accommodate extended family. Drawings
                show roof construction, floor plan, and elevation of underground house.
                Significance of *tonir* (sunken hearth) and the good and evil spirits around
                it.

1983   "Zhoghovrdakan havatalikneri hamagarke Hayots entenakan tsisakarut-
            yunnerum." [The System of Folk Beliefs in Armenian Family Ceremonials.]
            L 4: 54–64. Russian summary.
                Customs preserved in Aghdznik. Focus on weddings, birth, and death.

1984   "Aghdznikahayeri amusnakan sovoruytneri avandutyan dzevere." [The
            Traditional Styles of the Wedding Customs of the Armenians of Aghdznik.]
            Banber Erevani Hamalsarani 1:186–194. Russian summary.
                Period from mid-19th century to beginning of 20th century. Gives ages of
                marriage, use of go-betweens, dowry. Rare to get a second wife if first
                wife sterile, yet first wife retains her status and is recognized as mother of
                children of second wife.

1987   "Sasuntsineri entenakan Tsisakargi mi kani hartser." [Some Issues in the
            Domestic Ritual Matters of Sassoun.] *Banber Erevani Hamalsarani* 1:52–62.
                Information from natives of Sassoun who moved to Soviet Armenia.
                About death and preparation of body for burial; special mourners at grave;
                some superstitions.

Nahmad, H. M.
1968   *The Peasant and the Donkey.* New York, H. Z. Wakk. 159 pp. col. il.
                Of the 34 tales, four are Armenian tales taken from translations by Charles
                Downing. Other tales from the Near and Middle East include Persian,
                Arabic, Georgian, Turkish, and Jewish tales.

Nalbandian, G.
1976   "Sayat-Novayi tsatsgagir tagheri vertsanman shurje." [About the Interpre-
            tation of Sayat-Nova's Ciphered Song.] *Banber Erevani Hamalsarani* 2:158–
            166. Russian summary.
                Article is an attempt to show philological information relating to date of
                birth of Sayat-Nova as 1711.

Nalbandian, Louise
1962   "The Khantamour Armenian Collection." *Western Folklore* 21:43–44.
                The collection includes about 1000 titles, and includes some folklore,
                notably a complete file *Eminian Azgagrakan Zhoghovatsu* and *Azgagrakan
                Handes.* The collection is at the University of California, Los Angeles,
                and was donated by Krikor Khantamour, a retired dentist.

Nalbandian, V. S.
1964   "Gnel-Tirityan vipakar avandutyan patmakan himki hartsi shurje." [Regarding the Historical Basis of the Stone-Inscribed Legend of Gnel and Tirit.] *PH* 4:83–100. Russian summary.
            Author believes that the historical basis of the legend in the conflict of King Arshak II and the patriarch Nerses rather than the political conflict Arshak had with the lords.

Nalbandian, Vache
1987   *Sayat-Nova*. Erevan, "Sovetakan Grogh." 96 pp.
            Text in Russian. A biographical essay on the 18th century Armenian minstrel Sayat-Nova. Based on the study done by Georg Akhverdian.

Nalbandian, Zaven
1971–72   "The Prologue of David of Sassoun." *Armenian Review* 24(2):55–61; 25(2):40–42.
            Word-by-word translation in poetical linear style. The second citation is called the "Epilogue" of David of Sassoun.

Narian, M. Kh.
1963   "Ditoghutyunner Sayat-Novayi Hayeren khagheri lezvi masin." [Observations on the Language of Sayat-Nova's Armenian Ballads.] *PH* 3:53–66. Russian summary.
            Sayat-Nova used picturesque language of the people. Also suited choice of words to topic of the song. Brief examples are given.

1974   "Banasirakan ditoghutyunner Sayat-Novayi mi kani khagheri." [Philological Observations Relating to Some of Sayat-Nova's Songs.] *PH* 4:81–88. Russian summary.
            Quotes from three Sayat-Nova songs and questions usage of certain words that are not clear in the light of tradition and history.

1974   "Sayat-Novayi gortsatsats mi kani artahaytutyunneri masin." [About Some Expressions Used by Sayat-Nova.] *L* 2:44–49. Russian summary.

Navasardian, T.
1882–1903   *Hay zhoghovrdakan hekiatner*. [Armenian Folktales.] Tiflis. 10 v.
            I have not been able to see any of Navasardian's volumes. It is said that he was inspired by K. Servantsian's work to collect folktales. Some of the tales have been included in collections of Armenian Folktales. It would be a worthy project if all 10 volumes could be reprinted with notes.

Nazarian, Sh. L.
1978   "Ananun anhatakan ev zhoghovrdakan ergeri tarberakman chapanishnere."
            [The Various Criteria of Anonymous Individual and Folk Songs.] *PH* 2:109–
            116. Russian summary.
            Indicates points to consider in identifying folk songs and individually
            composed songs. Some songs are mistakenly considered folk songs when
            they are not.

Nazarian, Shushanik
1977   *"Krunk" erge ev nra patmutyune.* [The Song "Krunk" (Crane) and its
            History.]
            The song "Krunk" (Crane) is considered the song of songs by émigrés. It
            is 400 years old. Author claims it is not a folk song, but an anonymous
            composed song. Based on style and language the date is placed around
            17th century. There is a 1695 manuscript no. 7717 in library in Erevan.
            Several musical versions, historic traditions, and influences considered.
            (NB: This author may be same as Sh. L. above.—AMA)

Nazariants, Hovhannes
1876–77   *Anekdotner.* [Anecdotes.] Baku, A. Khasapian. 2 v.
            Includes 1126 humorous anecdotes sent to the compiler by 709
            Armenians from various towns in Russian Armenia, Georgia, Baghdad,
            etc. Some are general jokes, some specifically Armenian. Names of
            contributors and their towns are given at end, but in the text no indication
            given of the person who contributed the particular item.

Nazinian, A[rtashes] (sometimes uses only initials A. M.)
1956   *Hay zhoghovrdakan hekiatner.* [Armenian Folktales.] Erevan, Sovet. Grogh.
            142 pp. col. il.
            Collection includes 56 folktales and anecdotes intended for children.

1959–85   *Hay Zhoghovrdakan hekiatner.* [Armenian Folktales.) Erevan, HSSR GA
            Hrat. Vols. 1–13.
            Multivolume collection of folktales. May go to 20 volumes. For
            annotations of volumes seen, see listing under title *Hay Zhoghovrdakan
            hekiatner.*

1964   "Banavech, nvirvats zhoghovrdakan banahyusutyun patmaganutyan
            problemnerin." [Discussion Dedicated to Problems in the Historicity of
            Folklore.] *PH* 3:235–237.
            Brief summary of conference held in Moscow. Date not given, only noted
            "recently."

1967   "Sovetahay banagidutyan antsats ughin." [The Path Traveled by Soviet Armenian Folklore.] *PH* 2–3:87–94.
        Recognizes important work done by individuals in the past. Surveys collecting work done by Soviet Armenian institutions—most outstanding the many versions of David of Sassoun.

1969   *Armianskie narodnye skazki.* [Armenian Folktales.] Moscow, Izd-vo "Detskaia Literatura." 174 pp. il.
        Includes 25 tales intended for children. Introduction notes that often motifs and characters reflect Armenian history and beliefs.

1969   *Lenine Sovetahay banahyusutyan mej.* [Lenin in Soviet Armenian Folklore.] Erevan, HSSH "Gitelik" Ubkerutyan. 25 pp.
        High praise given to the epic "Lenin Pasha." Lenin the savior of the Russian people, yet humble, kind, understanding. Includes some quotations.

1969   "Mets banasteghtse ev zhoghovrdakan banahyusutyune." [The Great Poet and Folklore.] *PH* 3:25–36. Russian summary.
        About the Armenian writer Hovhannes Tumanian and the folklore represented in his works, including a verse version of David of Sassoun.

1990   *Haykakan zhoghovrdakan hekiatner.* [Armenian Folktales.] Erevan, "Arevik." 144 pp. col. il.
        Includes 23 tales; sources of tales not given.

Nelson, Harold
1954   *The Armenian Family: Changing Patterns of Life in a California Community.* 333 pp. Ph.D., University of California, Berkeley, 1954.
        Considerable details about marriage customs and rituals in Fresno, California. Some ancient rituals still used.

Nersisian, Kh. M.
1985   "Perevody eposa 'David Sasunskii' na Angliskii iazyk." [The Translations of the Epic "David of Sassoun" into English.] *PH* 2:174–280. Russian summary.
        Gives brief commentary on following English translations: F. B. Collins (1902); Jane Wingate (1950); Aram Tolegian (1960); Artin Shalian (1964); L. Surmelian (1964); M. Kudian (1970).

1986   "Nekotorye voprosy perevoda slov-realii v eposa 'David Sasunskii' na Angliskii iazyk." [Some Questions of Translation of the Epic "David of Sassoun" into English.] *L* 10:43–52. Armenian summary.
        Uses as examples A. Shalian's *David of Sassoun*, L. Surmelian's *Daredevils of Sassoun*, and M. Kudian's *The Saga of Sassoun*. Compares translations of some passages: reveals differences in choice of words in certain passages and difficulty of finding right words in translation. (NB:

Nersisian, Kh. M. *(continued)*

Author uses name Khandut: I am quite certain she is the same person as Kh. M. Nersisian.—AMA)

Nersisian, V.

1970   "Makdere XIII–XVI dareri Hay taghergutyan mej." [The Epithet in Armenian Verse in the 13th–16th Centuries.] *Banber Erevani Hamalsarani* 3:190–197. Russian summary.

Epithets by writers of the period show evidence of folkloristic origins. Examples are cited.

Nersoyan, Hagop

1966   "David of Sassoun: An Interpretation." *Ararat* 7(3):18–26. il.

Epic discussed from three standpoints: mythological, historical, and socio-political. David's goodness and power against oppression, and David as a savior "of man from his own self."

Nikitine, B.

1934   "Les vishaps: vestiges de l'Arménie paêne." *L'Ethnographie*, n.s. 28–29:109–112.

Refers to N. Marr and J. Smirnov (1931) about large stones in shape of fish and other animals regarded as dragons in area between Erevan, Aragats, and Lake Sevan. Association of goddess Anahit with water.

Nzhdehian, Grigor

1899–1910 "Alashkerti banavor grakanutiun." [Oral Literature of Alashkert.] *AH* 5:185–199; 7–8:437–505; 12:95–103; 13:83–86; 17:49–52; 18:33–36; 19:95–98; 20:108–111.

Vol. 5 has songs for many occasions. Vols. 7–8 children's songs and dance and wedding songs. Vols. 12, 13, 17–20 include 230 proverbs and sayings.

1902   "Paravashunj." [Old Wives' Tales.] *AH* 9:263–271.

Some believe tales are from Bible, but such cannot be verified. Themes include heaven, earth, angels, devils, air, moon, and stars.

1904   "Mamo ev Zine." [Mamo and Zin.] *AH* 11:197–240.

Some consider this a Kurdish-Armenian epic. Translated into Armenian; an Alashkert variant in prose and verse.

Odabashian, A. [or A. A.]

1963   "Nor tarva tonakatarutyan zhamanaki hartsi shurje." [About the Time of the Celebration of the New Year.] *PH* 2:275–280.

In Persia the date of the New Year was in the spring, and Armenians celebrated in the fall in the first month of the calendar, Navasart.

1974   "Amanori tsisakan ergerits." [From the Ritual Songs of *Amanor* (New Year).] *L* 4:43–53. Russian summary

About 12–14 boys circulated around singing songs relating to the New Year. They carried bags or baskets for gifts of food. Songs of good luck followed by *avedis* (good news) and magical songs followed by alleluia. Both words show influence of Christianity.

1974   "Navasardyan tonakhmbutyunneri veraprumnere." [Reliving Navasart Celebrations.] *PH* 3:113–126.

Navasart, old Armenian New Year, also designates name of month in old Armenian calendar. In Christian times New Year was known as Amanor and celebrated in the fall.

1976   "Narodnye verovaniia Armian." [Popular Beliefs of Armenians.] *Kavkazkii Etnograficheskii Sbornik* 6:107–110. il.

From materials of talisman manuscripts of 15th to 19th centuries. The talisman, or *hamayil,* is described and portions of Armenian text are given for fertility, curative measures, and against the evil eye.

1986   "Tiezerasteghtsman araspeli veraprukayin tarrern akhtarkum." [Symbols of Mythological Cosmos in Astrological Texts.] *PH* 3:138–149.

Symbols used are earth, sky, sea, pillar of heaven. Uses fragments of David of Sassoun as examples.

Odabashian, Anya
1987   "Tiezerakan tsare hin Hayots ditsabanakan hamakargum." [The Cosmic Tree in the Ancient Armenian Mythological System.] *L* 10:61–70.

The cosmic tree is established in folklore, ethnography, linguistics, and general historical sources. Appeared in Armenian literary texts, but suffered transformations under Christianity. Still the cosmic tree continues in many manifestations. An interpretative study.

Oganesian. *See also* Hovhannisian

Oganesian, A. L .
1973   "Muzika v drevnei Armenii." [Music in Ancient Armenia.] *PH* 2:61–76. Armenian summary.

Development of musical instruments, though no pictures shown, improved with beginning of theater in Armenia. Establishment of Christianity served as foundation for development of church music and opened Greek-Roman world that played role in cultural life, but lost pagan culture.

Ohanian, Armène
1916   "En Armenie." *Mercure de France* 118:452–465.
              Memories of her childhood. Reflects family life and customs, but clearly
              not peasant life. Locale not named, but notes that preparations made to go
              to Shamakha for the winter.

Olympianos
1842   *Aragk Oghombianu.* [Fables of Olympianos.] Bound in Mkhitar Gosh's
              Aragk. Venice, St. Lazar, 1842. pp. 165–187.
              Includes 23 fables in which animals predominate. A French translation of
              these fables appeared in E. Galtier's article "Les fables d'Olympianos" in
              Bulletin Institut Français d'Archeologie Orientale, Cairo 4:17–30. 1905.

Opie, James
1982   "A Craft is Worth More than Gold. A Traditional Folktale Retold." *Hali*
              5(2):212–213.
              The interesting point of the tale is that the king has to perform the task
              instead of person of lower rank.

Orbeli, Iosip (NB: First name in Armenian Hovseb, or Hovsep.—AMA)
1939   *David Sasunskii, Armianskii narodnyi epos.* [David of Sassoun, the
              Armenian Epic.] Moscow, Izd-vo Akad. Nauk SSSR. xliv, 380 pp. il.
              A Russian edition of the Armenian unified text published on the occasion
              of the 1000th anniversary of the epic.

1939   *Stalin v poezii armianskogo naroda.* [Stalin in the Poetry of the Armenian
              People.] Moscow, Izd-vo Akad. Nauk SSSR. 78 pp. (port.)
              Poems by various Armenian writers in first part. Second part by minstrels
              and story-tellers, all in style of quatrain minstrel songs. Introduction notes
              that Mher, character in David of Sassoun, came out of rock, leaving the
              old regime for the new order. Book offered to Stalin on 1000th
              anniversary of publication date of David of Sassoun.

1956   *Armianskii geroicheskii epos.* [The Armenian Heroic Epic.] Erevan, 143 pp.
              il.
              A study of the Armenian epic David of Sassoun. Includes some excerpts.
              Also published in Armenian in 1956, *Haykakan herosakan epose* (Erevan,
              HSSR GA Hrat.), with added Russian title page.

1956   *Basni srednevekovoi Armenii.* [Fables of Medieval Armenia.] Moscow, Izd-
              vo Akad. Nauk SSSR. 180 pp.
              Text in Russian. Most of 142 fables are from Mkhitar Gosh and Vardan
              Aigetsi. Long essay, about 50 pp., about the fabulists and their themes. In
              1982 another edition was published in Erevan, by Sovetakan Grogh. 109
              pp.

1961   *Sasuntsi Davit; Haykakan zhoghovrdakan epos.* [David of Sassoun, the Armenian Folk Epic.] Erevan, Haypethrat. xliv, 333 pp. col. il.

Introduction presents the contents and structure of the epic, its folk elements, and compares some of the characters from other epics. The text is from the 1939 unified text of the four cycles.

1982   *Fol'klor i byt Moksa.* [Folklore and Life of Moks.] Moscow, Izd-vo "Nauka." 141 pp. il .

Moks area is south of Lake Van and occupied by Armenians and Kurds. Author was there in 1911. His work includes 10 fables, 32 amusing conversations, 12 tales, 163 proverbs, some songs for various occasions, and 51 riddles. A word list is included.

Ordoyan, G. V.

1984   "Mijnadaryan katakayin dimaknere Kilikyan mijavayrum." [Comic Masks in the Cilician Environment.] *PH* 4:117–125. il. Russian summary.

Pictures are from Armenian manuscripts. Mimes of some fables or parables, probably from the Armenian theater of the period of Arab domination. Fable characters known as *johi* who functioned as jesters.

Osgiporig (pseud.)

1847   "Paroyagan hin aradzner." [Old Moral Proverbs.] *B* 5:198–200.

There are 60 proverbs selected from old Armenian manuscripts. Notes that a few are derived from Persian.

1883–84   "Aradzk." [Proverbs.] B 41:57, 154, 318; 42:122.

A total of 18 proverbs presented. Last citation has title "Paroyagan aradzk" [Moral Proverbs].

Ovanesian, Armen

1986   "Two Armenian Romances." *Ararat* 27(2):14–17.

The story of Shirin, an Armenian girl, and her love for Persian Khosrov. The other story about Miroslava, reputed to be the daughter of Samuel the Armenian, king of Bulgaria.

Pachajian, Sarkis K.

1971   *Hushamadean Rodostoyi Hayerin.* [Memorial Book of Rodosto Armenians.] Beirut, Doniguian. 266 pp. il.

Has brief information on dialects, festivals, customs and superstitions, games for boys and girls, engagement and weddings. When girl enters groom's house, sheep or other animal slain; the sacrificial blood satisfies evil spirits so they don't enter house .

Paelian, G. H.
1919   *Songs of Armenia.* New York, Gotchnag Publishing Co. 105 pp.
             Words and music of 51 songs. Musical arrangements by K. H. Aiqouni.
             Texts of songs in Armenian and English, and also transliterated. Includes
             some folk songs; also some Armenian translations of "America" and "Star
             Spangled Banner."

Pakhchinian. *See* Bakhchinian

Palian, Trdat
1911   "Hay ashughner." [Armenian Minstrels.] *AH* 21:236–238.
             A bibliography of Armenian minstrels, singers, and balladeers.

Panian, A. E.
1968   "Obychai izbeganiia y Armian i ego izzhivanie za gody Sovetskoi vlasti." [The
             Custom of Avoidance Among Armenians and its Decline Since Soviet
             Power.] *PH* 2:211–218.
             Study based on village areas. About old Armenian custom that bride
             should not talk directly to her elder in-laws for a year or more, but could
             communicate through children. Table shows usage of custom from 1905–
             1936.

Papajian, Sarkis
1974   "Proverbs Armenians Use." In his *A Brief History of Armenia.* Fresno,
             Armenian Evangelical Union of North America. pp. 122–130.
             These 100 proverbs are given in transliteration and followed by English
             translation, e.g., "Toorsen soorp, nersen sadana," Outwardly a saint,
             inwardly a devil.

Papazian, Dikran S.
1960   *Badmutiun Palu Havav kiughi.* [History of the Palu Village of Havav.]
             Beirut, Dbaran Mshag. 240 pp. il.
             Of folklore interest, pp. 114–139; religious and secular customs, grape
             harvesting, weddings. Pre-1915 recollections of author who considers
             Havav a miniature representative of Armenia.

1963   *Patmutiun Palahovidi.* [History of Palu Valley.] Beirut, Dbaran Mshag. 224
             pp. il.
             Legend of invention of some letters of the Armenian alphabet by Mesrob
             Mashtots at the Palu fortress, pp. 113–118. Taken from *Bazmavep,* but
             date not specified.

Papazian, V.
1898   "Hay poshaner." [Armenian Gypsies.] *AH* 3:74–90. il.; 4:203–275.
             First part general historical information. In vol. 4 about Gypsies who live
             in Armenia but are not Armenians. Their travel guided by symbols along

the way. Information on dwellings, dress, food, occupations (basket and sieve making); marriage and wedding customs.

1898   "Haykakan erazhshtutean masin." [About Armenian Music.] *AH* 3:350–358. il.

Illustration does not identify instruments, and text information not detailed. Notes that *tar* said to be of Indian origin, and that the *saz* is probably Persian.

1901   "Armianskie boshà (tsygane)." [The Armenian Gypsy.] *Etnograficheskoe Obozrenie* 2:93–158.

Relates to Gypsies who live in Armenia. Historical and geographical information about occurrence, numbers, migrations, their life and dwellings, clothing, adornment, food and drink, occupations, language, and character.

1962   "Hay-poshaner ev nrants usumnasirutean kordze." [Armenian Gypsies and the Work of Studying Them.] *B* 60:165–170. il.

Armenian Gypsies scattered, but mostly in Sebastia (Sivas) area. Crafts in which they engage. Some have become sedentary. A short bibliography of studies made about Armenian Gypsies. Photos taken by author.

Paragian, V. J. *See* Barakian, V. J.

Parr, Annie Ruth
1951   *A Study of European Folk Songs Collected in Waukegan, Illinois.* 66 pp. Master of Music thesis, Northwestern University, 1951.

Includes some Armenian folk songs. Not seen.

Parvin, Madeline K.
1988   "The Caucasian Dragon Carpets: Domestic Innovation or Artistic Import?" *Ararat* 29(1):24–28. il.

Dragon carpets usually ascribed to Armenians. Notes controversy about them, but supports Armenian origin; ties to Armenian legends and myths.

Paspati, Alexandre G. [Greek form: Paspates]
1870   *Études sur les Tchinghianes ou Bohémians.* Constantinople, Antoine Koromela. 652 pp.

Armenian Gypsy information based mostly on observations of American missionaries A. T. Pratt and M. Hamlin. Gypsies mostly in Marash, Aintab, Tokat, and Marsovan areas in Turkey. They follow religion of Armenian church. Make baskets and sieves. Language has a mixture of Turkish and Armenian. Large part of book has grammar and vocabulary.

Patkanov, K. P.

1875   *Govor Nakhichevanskii.* [Speech of Nakhichevan.] St. Petersburg, Akad. Nauk. 140 pp. (Materialy dlia armianskikh narechii. Vyp. 1)

Introduction in Russian. Text in Armenian in the dialect of Nakhichevan. Includes five tales and 181 proverbs, and a glossary.

1875   *Mushkii dialekt.* [Dialect of Mush.] St. Petersburg, Akad. Nauk. 71 pp. (Materialy dlia armianskikh narechii, Vyp. 2).

Introduction in Russian, with Armenian examples of dialect. Text in Armenian includes various folklore genres in Mush dialect.

1887   *Tsygany neskol'ko slov o narechiiakh Zakavkaskikh Tsygan: Bosha i Karachi.* [Gypsies; Some Words About Dialects of Transcaucasus Gypsies: Bosha and Karachi.] St. Petersburg, Akad. Nauk. 146 pp.

Gypsies not Armenian, but live in Armenian community; some identify with Armenian church. Do not intermarry. Language uses some Armenian declension endings. Gypsies make baskets and sieves, and tell fortunes (see pp. 76–101).

1908–9   "Some Words on the Dialects of Transcaucasian Gypsies—Bosha and Karac." *Gypsy Lore Society. Journal,* n.s. 1:229–256.

Only first part discusses Gypsies in Armenia; they speak Armenian and follow Armenian faith, but will not intermarry. They catch and tame snakes and exhibit them. Dance with tambourines; go from house to house and entertain. Notes some superstitions.

Patmagrian, A.

1954   "L'Utilisation des éléments folklorique dans le chant liturgique arménien au XII siècle." *International Congress of Orientalists. Proceedings.* 23rd, Cambridge, Eng. 21–28 Aug. 1954. pp. 173–174.

No liturgy when Armenians adopted Christianity. Early minstrel music influenced composition of music for the church.

1955   *The Utilization of Elements of Folklore in the Armenian Liturgical Music in the Twelfth Century.* Paris, Impr. "Le Soleil." 48 pp. Text in French, English, and Armenian.

Notes that folk music is the basis of some Armenian liturgical music. Comparative examples of music are given.

1963   "Hay zhoghovrdakan erge." [The Armenian Folk Song.] *PH* 1:81–92. Russian summary.

Some Armenian church music derived from folk songs; examples given, including melodies.

1973   *Hay erke tareri michits.* [Armenian Song Through the Centuries.] Beirut, G. Doniguian & Fils. 359 pp. il., ports.

> Includes folk songs of various kinds; also minstrel songs and instruments used by minstrels. List of minstrels by names and birthplaces. Komitas, the folk song collector, is discussed. Musical notations included.

Patrik, A. N.

1967   "Patmakan Hay droshnere." [Historic Armenian Flags.] *PH* 1:161–170. il.

> Notes symbolism of Armenian flags in different periods, but no dates; probably through the Cilician period which ended in 1375.

1974–83   *Badmakirk hushamadean Sepasdioy ev kavari Hayutean.* [History-Memorial Book of Sebastia and Armenians of the Province.] Beirut, Dbaran Mshag. 2 v. il., fold. map. Vol. 2 published in New Jersey, by Rozkir Press, but no city named.

> Vol. 2, pp. 59–166, of folklore interest: picturesque expressions, sayings, family life, games, weddings, folk medicine, oaths, blessings, curses. March 1, instead of April 1, called Fool's Day.

1983   *Haykakan taraz.* [Armenian Costume.] 2nd ed. Erevan, "Sovetakan Grogh." 198 pp. il. (part col.).

> Title pages and introduction in Armenian, Russian, and English. Descriptive notes also in three languages. Localities of costumes given.

Patrubany, Lukas

1897   "Beiträge zur armenischen Ethnologie." *Ethnologische Mitteilungen aus Ungarn* 5 :139–153 .

> Most of article about some Armenian gods. Also a metrical analysis of Vahagn's song from Moses of Khoren's *History.*

Pawstos Buzandasi [Faustus of Byzantium]

1989   *The Epic Histories (Buzandaran Patmut'iwnk).* Translation and Commentary by Nina G. Garsoian. Cambridge, Mass., Harvard University Press. 665 pp., 2 fold. maps.

> Work once attributed to Faustus of Byzantium, now presented as work of unknown cleric. Covers period from about A.D. 330–387 and written in late 5th century. Based on oral tradition; evidence in formulas, both epic and spiritual. Includes some legends: Mt. Ararat (pp. 77–78); lion healed by extraction of reed from paw (p. 206); banishment of snakes (p. 207). Use of *gusans* (minstrels) to transmit oral tradition (pp. 52, 529).

Pense. *See* Movsisian, Sahak

Petrosian, A. S.
1988   "Orsortutyune ev orsvadzanere 'Sasna Tsrer' eposum." [Hunting and the
              hunted in the Epic "David of Sassoun."] *PH* 2:226–235.
                  Cites portions from the epic; notes that more animals than birds were
              hunted.

1989   "Gayli pashtamunke Hay zhoghovrdakan havataliknerum." [Wolf Worship in
              Armenian Folk Belief.] *Banber Erevani Hamalsarani* 2:72–80. Russian
              summary.
                  Parts of the wolf used as talisman. Rites to protect animals in farming;
              cure for evil eye; reveal theft, etc. Prevent turning into werewolf. Also
              gives information on place and personal names that include wolf word.
              Neighboring countries also have wolf worship.

Petrosian, Anushavan
1974   "Sheramapahutyan het kapvats orosh tsisakatarutyunner Hayots mej."
              [Certain Rituals Connected with Silk Culture Among Armenians.] *Banber
              Erevani Hamalsarani* 3:41–45. Russian summary.
                  Silk is protected by taking to church to be blessed. Protective measures
              taken for silkworms to ward off evil eye. No gold jewelry worn when
              caring for worms. Magical rituals used when worms not well.

1977   "Metaksi statsman ev nerkman zhoghovrdakan eghanaknere Hayastanum."
              [Popular Ways of Obtaining and Dyeing Silk in Armenia.] *Banber Erevani
              Hamalsarani* 2:241– 246. Russian summary.
                  Period from end of 19th century and beginning of 20th century. Describes
              processing of cocoons and reeling of silk. Natural sources used for dyes.
              Owner fed the workers. Comical songs about food given in relation to
              quality of work.

Petrosian, E. Kh.
1974   "Obrazy zhivotnykh v Armianskom narodnom teatre." [Appearance of
              Animals in Armenian Folk Drama.] *Sovetskaia Etnografiia* 5:131–138.
                  Mainly based on 19th and 20th centuries, though some on earlier periods.
              Goat, bear, monkey, or ape are the animals impersonated by persons in
              costume.

Petrosian, L.
1966   "Gitakan nstashrjan nvirvats Garegin Srvantsyantsi tsnndyan 125-anyakin."
              [On the Occasion of his 125th Birthday Conference Devoted to Garegin
              Srvantsyants.] *L* 2:118–119.
                  Important work of Servantsian for saving treasures of Armenian folklore
              in his various writings.

Petrosian, S. G.

1975   " 'Sasna Tsreri' erek eghbayrnere ev nrants vipasanakan zugahernere." [The
Three Brothers of "Sasna Tsrer" and Their Mythic Parallels.] *L* 9:71–77.
Russian summary.

> The three brothers in David of Sassoun—Mher, Hovan, Verko—have
> their parallels in the sons of the Armenian king Ardashes—Makhan,
> Ardavast, Vruir.

1986   " 'Sasna Tsreri' Oghan-Toghan tsagman." [Origin of Oghan-Toghan in
"Sasna Tsrer."] *PH* 3:195–200. Russian summary.

> Names of two Tsrer characters in David of Sassoun derived from persons
> who lived southwest of Caspian Sea area. Gives linguistic origin based on
> Caucasian Albanian.

Petrosian, Sargis

1981   " 'Vahagni erge' agrostikosneri verakangman ev vertsanman ports."
[Experiment in Reconstruction and Deciphering Acrostics in "Vahagn's
Song."] *L* 4:78–88. Russian summary.

> By arrangement of the song of nine lines taken from Moses of Khoren's
> *History*, the author derives the names Ervant and Nana, the father and
> mother of Vahagn.

1982   "Shirakay ambarki shurj." [About granaries of Shirak.] *L* 9:73–79.
Archeological work reveals old storehouses for grain in Shirak.

Phaphazian. *See* Papazian, V.

Phillips, Jenny

1989   *Symbol, Myth, and Rhetoric: The Politics of Culture in an Armenian-
American Population.* New York, AMS Press. 311 pp. (Immigrant
Communities and Ethnic Minorities in the United States and Canada, no. 23)

> Based on her Ph.D. thesis, Boston University, 1978. The Armenian
> Apostolic Church identified with shared symbols involving myths,
> Gregory the Illuminator, and the church at Echmiadzin. They share
> common legendary heroes. The flag is a symbol of church and political
> party.

Pikichian, H. V.

1988   "Zurnan Hayots kentsaghum." [The *zurna* (fife) in Armenian Life.] *Banber
Erevani Hamalsarani* 2:104–111. il. Russian summary.

> The *zurna*, an old traditional musical instrument among Armenians. Name
> derived from Persian. Information on materials used in making it, and its
> use, usually with a drum. Females not allowed to use or touch it for it is
> considered a phallic symbol. Care of instrument in embroidered bag [no
> doubt made by women!]. In modern usage *zurna* a rude word used as
> substitute for nose. [One source gives English name of instrument as
> shawm.]

Pilibosian, Nuritsa M., and Kesdekian, Avedis

1955   *Hushartsan Yozghatsineru (Yosgad).* [Memorial of Yozgad.] Fresno, Calif.,
M. M. Kasparian. 445 pp. il.
Yozgad also spelled Yozgat. Of folk interest the following: some customs,
pp. 84–90; weddings, births, tooth party, death, proverbs, pp. 96–99;
Turkish sayings used in villages, pp. 100–101; blessings, p. 101;
sayings, pp. 101–103; love songs and lullabies, pp. 103–104; festivals,
pp. 104–105; folk medicine, p. 109.

Pipoyan, Lilit

1983   "Sovetakan Hayastani hyusisarevelyan shrjanneri zhoghovrdakan bnakeli
tneri tibere." [Types of Folk Dwellings of Northeastern Soviet Armenia.] *L*
11:47–54. Russian summary.
Gives illustrations of elevations and floor plans of dwellings.

Piruzian, A. S.

1960   *Armianskaia kulinariia.* [Armenian Cooking.] Moscow, Gostorgizdat. 205
pp. il. (part col.)
There is an Armenian edition, but unable to locate loan copy. Introduction
about Armenian history. Basic and special foods of Armenians. Recipes
arranged by classes of foods; many pictures of preparation and
presentation of foods.

Pivazian, Em. A.

1987   *Mkhitar Goshi "Datastanagrkii" banasirakan knnutyun.* [Philological
Examination of Mkhitar Gosh's Law Book.] Erevan, Erevani Hamalsarani
Hrat. 225 pp.
Not seen, but review by Artashes Shahnazarian in *Lraber* 1988(4):82–85.
Reviewer notes that several persons have studied the law book but have
clouded some issues. Notes that Pivazian has opened new paths to study
of the book.

1989   "Mijnadaryan Haykakan norahayd arakner." [Newly Discovered Medieval
Armenian Fables.] *PH* 1:95–103. Russian summary.
Notes that when N. Marr collected fables of Vartan he had few sources
compared to newly discovered manuscripts containing fables and
parables. Gives some examples.

Plato

1950   *The Republic of Plato.* Trans. by John Llewelyn Davies and David J.
Vaughan. London, Macmillan. Book X:361–370.
Story of Er, the son of Armenis of Pamphylia, killed in battle; 10 days
later body still fresh, comes to life on 12th day and tells of his
experiences. Some identify Er as Ara, the legendary Armenian king.
Consult J. R. Russell's article (1984).

Poghosian, E. *See* Boghosian, Efrem

Poidebard, A.
1929   "Anciennes broderies arméniennes." *REA* 9:239–248. il. (part col.).
        Terminology, materials, techniques, styles, and symbolism are presented.
        Marash work featured.

Poladian, Antranik L.
1969   *Badmutiun Hayots Arabkiri*. [History of the Armenians of Arabkir.] New
        York, Arabkir Union. 1048 pp. il. (part col.) fold. map.
        Of folklore interest, pp. 157–341: about family life, customs, weddings,
        births, death, home remedies, special festivals, songs with music, sayings
        and proverbs in dialect, riddles and superstitions.

Poladian, Sirvart
1942   *Armenian Folk Songs*. Berkeley, University of California Press. 77 pp. port.
        (California. University. Publications in Music, v. 2, no. 1.)
        Based on 253 songs collected by Komitas between 1890 and 1904.
        Musical study of tonality and scales, intervals, ranges, rhythm, form and
        structural, pictorial elements. A review by S. B. Hustvedt in *Journal of
        American Folklore* 1942 (57):153–154. (NB: Poladian's work considered
        one of best about Komitas.—AMA)

1972   "Komitas Vardapet and his Contribution to Ethnomusicology." *Ethnomusi-
        cology* 16:82–97. Includes music.
        Biographical sketch of Komitas who collected 4000 Armenian folk songs
        (including Turkish and Kurdish songs) between 1890 and 1913. He used
        neumes, a kind of music shorthand, to note the tunes. Folk songs by
        peasants show some Arabic and Persian influences. Includes bibliography
        of works by Komitas. Some songs lost because of deportations in 1915.
        Komitas did not collect urban songs. 1200 of folk songs have been
        edited.

Pope, Arthur Upham
1925   "The Myth of the Armenian Dragon Carpets." *Jahrbuch der asiatischen Kunst*
        2:147–188. il.
        Contrary to a number of rug specialists, Pope contends that the dragon
        rugs are from Caucasus, and not of Armenian origin. See some of the
        listings under H. Kurdian, not only for a translation of Pope's article, but
        criticism of Pope's views.

Popescu, Ion Apostol
1967   *Basme Armenesti din Transylvania*. [Armenian Tales from Transylvania.]
        Bucharest, Ed. Pentru Literatura. 214 pp.
        At end of each of the 22 tales, the name, age, and residence of each
        narrator is given. French summaries of the tales, pp. 193–211. Tales
        include traditional ones and also variants that circulate in Transylvania.

Popescu, Ion Apostol *(continued)*
1967   "Les contes de fées, recits et traditions arméniens de Transylvanie." *REA*,
             n.s. 4:377–393.
             Active story telling of Armenian tales is a mixture of Romanian and
             Armenian languages. According to N. Iorga more exploratory work
             needed for Armenian folklore in Rumania. Deep human message in the
             tales.

Porkshian, Kh.
1910   "Nor-Nakhijevani banahyusutyunits." [From the Folklore of New
             Nakhichevan.] *AH* 20:102–107.
             About songs of greeting, e.g., "A Star Arose" with reference, no doubt,
             to Advent.

Powers, Harriet B.
1889   "In Armenian Villages." *Chautauquian* 10:197–202.
             Author visited villages south of Trebizond in mountainous, treeless areas
             where part of houses are underground. Vivid descriptions of household
             arrangements.

Poyacian, Zapel. *See* Boyajian, Zabelle C.

Racinet, M. A.
1888   *Le costume historique*. Paris, Firman-Bidot et Cir. 6 v. il. (part col.).
             In vol. 3 (no pages are given) under the heading "Turquie" there is one
             illustration of a married Armenian woman's costume in Constantinople,
             no. 10. In section "Turquie, Asie Mineure," no. 7 is costume of a Van
             woman, and no. 14 a Christian woman of Diarbekir.

Raffi, Aram
1916   "Armenia, its Epics, Folk-songs, and Mediaeval Poetry." In *Armenian
             Legends and Poems*, ed. by Zabelle C. Boyajian. New York, Dutton, pp.
             125–191.
             Historical information and some examples. Notes some of the legendary
             characters, some examples of proverbs, and folk songs.

1918   "Armenian Epics and Ancient Poetry." *New Armenia* 10:168–171.
             About heroic characters of ancient times, based on Moses of Khoren's
             History.

1918   "Armenian Legends and Epics." *New Armenia* 10:140–142.
             About Armenian heroes from Moses of Khoren's *History*.

1919   "Armenian Hymns, Proverbs, and Folk-Song." *New Armenia* 11:40–42.
             Gives a dozen charm songs used in fortune telling; notes a few proverbs
             and folk songs.

1919   "Fables and Religious Poetry." *New Armenia* 11:107–109.
                About fables of Mkhitar Gosh and Vartan Aigetsi.

Raphaelian, H. M.
1960   *Rugs of Armenia, their History and Art.* New Rochelle, N. Y., Anatol Sivas.
                87 pp. il.
                Emphasis on design motifs reputed to be Armenian; also notes on outside
                influences.

Ratcliffe, Dorothy Una
1933   " 'Armenian' Gypsies Near Marathon." *Gypsy Lore Society. Journal* series
                3, 12:113. il.
                These Gypsies said to have come from Armenia, but they are not
                Armenians.

Redosko, O Yanko le
1984   "The Armenian Contribution to the Gypsy Language." *Ararat* 25(4):2–6.
                Notes 34 western Romany words derived from Armenian. Words are
                nouns and suggest some of the Gypsy activities in the Armenian
                community.

Remizov, Aleksei
1922   *Lalazar; Kavkazkii skaz.* [Lalazar; Caucasian Tales.] Berlin, Izd-vo "Skify."
                311 pp.
                Includes three Armenian folktales.

Renoux, Ch.
1980–81   " 'Les fêtes et les saints de l'église arménienne' de N. Adontz." *REA* n.s.
                14:287–305; 15:103–114.
                About legends of the origin of the Armenian lectionary, but does not
                discuss how the festivals were celebrated. Legends claim origin in
                Jerusalem for festivals such as *Vartavar*, etc. For information about
                background of this article see Adontz, N., 1927–28.

Rohrbach, Paul
1919   *Armenien; Beiträge zur armenischen Landes- und Volkskunde.* Stuttgart, I.
                Engelhorne. 144 pp., 128 plates, fold. map.
                Contributions by various authors, though attention to folklore is slight.
                Photos include scenes of towns, villages, peasants at work, modes of
                land and water transport. Costume photos useful since drawn from
                various sources which would otherwise be difficult to locate.

Rosenberg, Adolf
1905–23   *Geschichte des Kostüms.* New York, M. Weyhe. 8 parts in 5 vols. Plates
                (part col.).
                Volume 5, following page 378, figures 9–12 show Armenian costumes
                from various places.

Runciman, Steven

1955   "The First Crusade: Constantinople to Antioch." In *History of the Crusades*,
            ed. by Kenneth N. Stetton. Philadelphia, University of Pennsylvania Press.
            Vol. 1:280–307.
                Of special interest is p. 303 about Armenian adoption ceremony used by
                Armenian prince Toros to adopt Baldwin. Toros puts on wide shirt that he
                extends over Baldwin's head, and they rub bare chests.

Russell, George, and Amfittheatrof, Erik

1981   "Tired? Nyet!" *Time* 118(15):66. col. il.
                Rock festival from America to Erevan. Sponsored by Armenian Ministry
                of Culture. Enthusiastic response by audience characterized as "rebellious
                answer to the kitschy pop tunes and folk songs the authorities want them
                to hear."

Russell, James R.

1984   "The platonic Myth of Er, Armenian Ara, and Iranian Arday Wiraz." *REA*,
            n.s. 18:477–485.
                Er legend based on Armenian legend of Ara the Beautiful; legend recorded
                by Plato. Armenian legend may have come from Zoroastrian source.

1986   "Bad day at Burzan Mihr: Notes on an Armenian Legend of St.
            Bartholomew." *B* 144:255–267. Armenian summary.
                The apostles Bartholomew and Thaddeus claimed as founders of
                Armenian church, hence the name Armenian Apostolic Church. This
                article notes legend of St. Bartholomew who put out the flame of
                Zoroastrian fire temple at Burzan Mihr.

1986–87   "Some Iranian Images of Kinship in the Armenian Artaxiad Epic." *REA*, n.s.
            20:253–270.
                Based on tale or legend in Moses of Khoren's *History*. The heart as
                symbol of power. Discussion of *kajk* (supernatural braves) and
                comparison with Iranian. Various images of the hunt said to be north
                Iranian. Armenians kept some old Iranian traditions in Christian times.

1987   "Armenian Tales." *Ararat* 28:21–22.
                Translation of three tales from *Haykakan zhoghovrdakan hekiatner*,
                compiled by N. Hakobyan and A. Sahakyan. Erevan Univ. Press, 1980.
                "The Foolish Woman," "The Missing Friday," "The Tale of the Pauper."
                Includes a commentary.

1987   "A Mystic's Christmas in Armenia." *Armenian Review* 40(2):1–13.
                About St. Gregory of Narek's "Song of the Nativity." Of interest for
                explanation of symbolism of some of the gods.

1987   *Yovhannes T'lkuranc'i and the Mediaeval Armenian Lyric Tradition.* Atlanta, Georgia, Scholars Press. 198 pp.

        Based on his B. Litt. thesis, Oxford University, 1977. Lyric tradition from the Parthian *gosan* (minstrel) tradition. Music cultivated in monasteries in Christian period. Includes Armenian text. Notes of special value for explanation of some folk beliefs. Review in *Patmabanasirakan Handes* 1989(4):227–229, by A. N. Ter-Ghevondyan.

1987   *Zoroastrianism in Armenia.* Cambridge, Harvard University, Dept. of Near Eastern Languages and Civilization, and National Association for Armenian Studies and Research. 578 pp. il.

        Some of Armenian gods were from the Zoroastrian pantheon. A number of Armenian customs derived from practices of Zoroastrians. Some persist today. Many useful notes for each chapter.

1988–89   "The Dream Vision of Anania Sirakac'i." *REA*, n.s. 21:159–170.

        Gives historical survey of sun visions. Anania interested in natural sciences, mathematics, myths, astrology. Book of Six Thousand attributed to him as is discovery of flower *hamaspiur*.

1989   "The Book of the Six Thousand: An Armenian Magical Text." *B* 147:221–243. Armenian summary.

        Many versions of book since 13th century. Use of mathematics, botany, theology, astrology for magic. In ancient times 6000 believed to be age of the world. Evil eye symbol: ø. This article a revision and expansion of his article in *Banber Erevani Hamalsarani* 1988(1):85–93, " 'Vetz hazaryak' matyane Hayots mej."

1990   "The Rites of the Armenian Goddess." *Ararat* 31(3):21–24. il.

        About goddess Anahit who was worshipped especially for fertility. Anahit was called "golden mother." Eduard Gulbenkian disputes some of Russell's statements; see "Response to Russell," *Ararat* 12(12):72.

1990–91   "Dragons in Armenia: Some Observations." *Journal of Armenian Studies* 5:3–12. Historical information about dragons in Armenia according to literature. Gives some comparative information.

Rustigian, Stella P.
1982   "Some Notes on Literature Concerning Armenian Rugs." *Armenian Review* 35(4):410–418.

        Not a bibliography, but gives sources to use to get information about Armenian rugs. Lately a tendency to ignore role of Christians in the art of rug making. Paper presented at the 3rd Symposium of Armenian Rug Society, New York, Sept. 25, 1982.

S., A. *See* Sakisian, Armenag

Saakian. *See* Sahakian

Sadoian, Queenie Hagopian
1957   *Armenian Folk Music and Dance: Selected Materials for Use in American Schools*. 163 pp. il.
            Master of Music thesis, University of Southern California, 1957. Includes music and words, in English and Armenian. Also has music for Armenian dances, with description of steps. Has section on Armenian festivals and how they are celebrated. Useful for teachers who want to use ethnic material in classes.

Safarian, K. H.
1989   "Mkhitar Goshi iravagaghakakan hayatsknere." [The Legal-Political Views of Mkhitar Gosh.] *PH* 4:35–47. Russian summary.
            Religious arguments should not lead to enmity. Classes should respect classes; Christian idea that all men are brothers.

Safarian, V. H.
1989   "Mijnadaryan araki zhoghovrdakan tarerke." [The Folk Element of the Medieval Fable.] *Banber Erevani Hamalsarani* 3:114–121. Russian summary.
            Fables selected from Mkhitar Gosh and Vartan Aigetsi, then compared.

Sahagian, Aram
1955   *Tiutsaznagan Urfan ev ir Hayortinere*. [Heroic Urfa and her Armenian Sons.] Beirut, "Atlas" Dbaran. 1368 pp.; 55 pp.; 77 pp. il., fold. map.
            Of folklore interest: pp. 693–709 include a variety of folk songs. Pages after main paging include some proverbs and sayings, good wishes and blessings, folk medicine, and a dialect story. There is also a word list.

Sahagian, G. D.
1909   "Hayots 'Varis' astuadzutiune." [The Armenian Godhead "Varis."] *B* 67:529–535.
            Author believes that "Varis," mentioned in Strabo, was an ancient god of the hunt, also known as Varaz.

Sahakian, A. S.
1981   " 'Patmutiun hatsuneats khachin' zruytse ev nra tipabanutyune." [Story of the Hatsuniats Cross and its Typology.] *PH* 4:153–166. Russian summary.
            Suggests some folkloristic elements about a fragment of the cross.

1982   "Hatsunyats anvaver banavor tarperaknere." [The Unverified Oral variants of the Hatsunyats Tale.] *PH* 3:135–143. Russian summary.
            Tale is related to a piece of wood (the cross) dating from the 7th century and variants appearing up to 19th century. The cross was being carried by a mule; it refused to go beyond the village of Hatsunyats, so legend is said to mean that God intended that the cross remain there.

Sahakian, Hasmik

1961   *Hay ashughner XVII–XVIII dd.* [Armenian Minstrels of the 17th–18th centuries.] Erevan, HSSH, GA Hrat. 465 pp.

        Historical overview of role of minstrel in Armenian culture. Elements of songs about life of people, grief, pain, love and some didactic songs. Names were not given to minstrels until 16th century. Songs arranged under names of minstrels with biographical notes when known. Reviewed by H. Osgian in *HA* 1963 (77):151–152.

Sahakian, V. (also V. Sh.)

1971   "Mets Mheri chyughn est 'Sasna Tsreri' karutsvatski." [Structure of the Branch of Great Mher in "Sasna Tsrer."] *Banber Erevani Hamalsarani* 3:184–192. Russian summary.

        Comparative analysis of the first and second branches of David of Sassoun shows identity of the epic's scheme.

1971   " 'Sasna Tsrer' zhoghovrdakan vepi chyughern est patumneri." [The Branches of the Folk Epic "Sasna Tsrer" According to the Tellings.] *L* 4:66–77. Russian summary.

        Various inclusions of additional tales to the four branches of David of Sassoun have led some to believe that there are three additional versions with three, seven, or 40 branches. Notes Chituni's idea of seven branches.

1971   " 'Sasna Tsrer' zhoghovrdakan vepi ashkharagrakan taratsman ev teghaynatsman khndire." [The Problem of the Geographical Distribution and Localization of the Folk Epic "Sasna Tsrer."] *PH* 2:94–106. Russian summary.

        Location of David of Sassoun is in eastern part of present-day Turkey. Story spread northeast; some versions carried by Armenians who escaped to Russia in 1915.

Saharuni, Kr.

1952   "Khorhtahay iskagan panahyusutyune." [The Essential Soviet Armenian Folklore.] *H* 30(2):15–30.

        Folklore the mirror of the soul of people. Notes forms of folklore: songs, humor, anecdotes, fables, tales, proverbs, sayings, legends, epics.

Sakezian, Armenag. *See* Sakisian, Armenag

S[akisian], A[rmenag]

1920   "Les tapis armeniens." *REA* 1:121–127. il.

        Armenian rugs from the 13th century, etc. Special characteristics and places of production. Reports F. R. Martin's views about rugs.

S[akisian], A[rmenag] *(continued)*
1928   "Les tapis à dragons et leur origine arménienne." *Syria* 9:238–256. il.
                Holds the view that Oriental rugs known as dragon rugs are of Armenian
                origin contrary to Arthur Upham Pope's idea.

1935   "Surp Ghazaruvankin aseghnakords gdornern ev zhaneagnern." [The
                Needlework and Laces of St. Lazar Monastery.] *B* 93:75–78. il.
                Describes Armenian rugs and laces.

1980   "Two Studies on Armenian Rugs," trans. by Lemyel Amirian. *Armenian*
                Review 33(1)4–29. il.
                Contends that the dragon rugs are of Armenian origin contrary to Arthur
                Upham Pope's opinion. Other Armenian supporters are F. R. Martin and
                Prof. F. Sarre. Over 100 notes and citations.

Salmaslian, A.
1969   *Bibliographie de l'Arménie*. New edition. Erevan, Académie des Sciences de
                la RSS de l'Arménie. 463 pp.
                Some folklore items in literature section, pp. 278–308.

Samter, E.
1911   *Geburt, Hochzeit und Tod*. Leipzig, B. G. Taubner. 222 pp. il.
                Armenian information about birth, marriage, and death are scattered in the
                text.

Samuelian, G.
1949   "Totemism Among the Armenians." *Armenian Review* 2(4):54–64.
                Names a number of animals, birds, insects, and reptiles that have been
                objects of worship. Notes that evidences are in creeds, superstitions,
                prejudices, tales, legends; also in names of persons. places, tribal coats of
                arms, taboo animals and food animals.

Samuelian, Kh.
1903   "Arean vrezh ev prkank." [Blood Vengeance and Salvation.] *AH* 10:269–
                303.
                From Armenian customary law; an old practice used by individuals or clan
                against clan. Vengeance strong among people of Zeytun. Notes forms of
                vengeance, and gives examples from David of Sassoun. Also comments
                about Mkhitar Gosh's view.

1904   "Arevangmamb ev gnmamb amusnutiun." [Marriage by Capture or by
                Purchase.] *AH* 12:40–83.
                Based on customary law. Old practice represented war between families
                of groom and bride, hence use of firearms at time of wedding. After
                marriage, bride goes to home of parents for visit; this represents peace
                making. She stays two or three weeks. Purchase represented by gifts
                given by groom's family.

1904   "Hin Hayots iravunke ev nra hetazotutean metode." [Ancient Armenian Law
              and the Method of Studying it.] *AH* 11:5–12.
                  Old Armenian law based on custom, not recorded. Recommends
                  comparative method for study. More revealing to study family life and
                  relations than political life.

1904–6   "Hay entenakan pashtamunke." [Armenian Familial Worship.] *AH* 12:203–
              234; 13:112–130; 14:156–174.
                  A view of Armenian customary law: structure of family. Beliefs about
                  death and soul of departed. Meaning and symbolism of hearth, keeping
                  fire alive. Dualism: good and evil, light and dark. Family saints, guardian
                  angels against evil spirits, evil eye. How to avert actions of evil spirits on
                  occasion of birth, marriage, etc.

1907   "Hayots zharangakan iravunke." [Armenian Inheritance Law.] *AH* 15:68–84;
              16:117–129.
                  Views in Armenian customary law. Paternal head of family. Refers to
                  Mkhitar Gosh's law book.

1907–10   "Mkhitar Goshi tadasdanakirke ev Hayots hin kaghakstsagan iravunke."
              [Mkhitar Gosh's Law Book and Ancient Armenian Civil Rights.] *HA* 21:42–
              47, 78–84, 97–101, 135–139, 206–210, 366–371; 22:48–52, 74–79, 108–
              111, 172–175, 241–245, 270–274, 361–367; 23:38–44, 65–71, 106–109,
              200–212, 239–240, 345–347; 24:77–83, 108–113, 238–241, 277–279, 292–
              299.
                  A critical study that includes some excerpts from Mkhitar Gosh's law
                  book.

1908–10   "Mayrakan iravunke." [Maternal Law.] *AH* 17:126–141; 18:59–90; 19:35–
              58.
                  Views in Armenian Customary law relating to matriarchal society.

1911   "Folklori mijazgayin dashnaktsutyune." [The International Folklore
              Federation.] *AH* 21:34–36.
                  About efforts to establish an International Folklore Federation (Prague,
                  Berlin, Finland, Russia, etc.). Problem of representation of Caucasian
                  folklore. Armenian Ethnographic Society can help.

1912   "Simbole Hay sovoruytnerum." [The Symbol in Armenian Custom.] *AH*
              22:232–245; 23:231–234.
                  Does not list symbols but notes usefulness of them to persons to
                  understand the significance of certain things.

1927   "Kari bashtamunke Hayeri mech." [Stone Worship Among Armenians.] *HA*
              41:435–442, 521–526, 583–508.
                  Spirits in mountains and rocks. Spirit of dead enter rocks, thus tombstone
                  developed. Infertile women pray to phallic stones, rub butter on them in

Samuelian, Kh. *(continued)*
> Murgathat village. In Zangezur province on road from Datev to Prasgot there is a navel stone on which women rub their stomachs. Special rocks for healing children. Legends connected with rocks.

Samuelian, V. T.
1960   "Hay zhoghovrdakan ashkhatankayin erger." [Armenian Folk Songs of Labor.] *PH* 1:119–169. Russian summary.

Samvelian, Kh. *See* Samuelian, Kh.

Sandalgian, Joseph
1917   *Histoire documentaire de l'Arménie des ages du paganisme.* Rome, Impr. du Senat. 2 v.
> Of interest to folklore, vol. 2:565–575, about epic songs of Colthène (Goghtn) and folk songs. Also pp. 591–793 about Armenian mythology relating to pagan gods, sanctuaries, and temples. Information on divination and sorcery. Covers period from 1410 B.C. to A.D. 305.

Sandaljian, Hovsep V.
1901   "Agni, Vahagn vishabakagh." [Agni, Vahagn the Dragon Slayer.] *B* 59:213–217.
> Relates Armenian Vahagn to Agni of the Rig-Veda of India.

Sanosian, A. S.
1989   "Javakhki 'vishap' karakotoghnere." [The Dragon Steles of Javakhk.] *Banber Erevani Hamalsarani* 2:97–102.
> Various persons have described these stones which are considered dragons. Believed to be related to water cult.

Sarafian, Kevork A.
1953   *Badmutiun Antebi Hayots.* [Armenian History of Aintab.] Los Angeles, Union of Armenians of Aintab in America. 2 v. il., fold. maps.
> Of folklore interest: vol. 2, pp. 128–407. Expressions, p. 328; various verses, pp. 329–334; blessings, curses, pp. 334–335; sayings, p. 336; dialect word list, pp. 336–380; recreation, games, toys, pp. 381–384; festivals, pp. 385–397 includes 711 fortune songs; asking for bride, etc. partly in conversational form, pp. 398–401; grape harvesting, pp. 402–404; Aintab minstrels, p. 407. Examples of songs in Turkish since Aintab was a Turkish-speaking Armenian community.

Sargsian, H. V.
1973   "Manrakandakner Komitasi patkerov." [Small sculptures with the image of Komitas.] *L* 1:95–100. il.
> Ten commemorative medals of Komitas, first made in 1966 in Milan for Mkhitarist Congregation of Venice. Other medals made in Soviet Armenia

in 1969, and some in Cairo, Beirut, and the United States to recognize 100th year of birth of Komitas. Descriptive information included.

Sargsian, Kh. S.
1963   "Humanizme Sayat-Novayi khagherum." [Humanism in Sayat-Nova's Songs.] *PH* 1:67–80. Russian summary.
        Sayat-Nova saw injustice of world, had a belief in truth. A singer of freedom: what man does of value, but not his boasting. Excerpts of songs given.

1963   "Sayat-Nova." *PH* 3:99–108. Armenian summary.
        In Russian, about Armenian minstrel Sayat-Nova. His aesthetics directed to common man for justice. Great influence on people of his time; he understood the people.

1963   *Sayat-Nova.* Erevan, HSSH, GA Hrat. 125 pp. Russian summary.
        Sayat-Nova, the Armenian minstrel of the 18th century, performed in Armenia, Georgia, and Azerbaijan. Discusses artistry, his love songs, and his understanding of the common man. Highly regarded by several Armenian authors. His widow burned some of his papers after his death.

Sari, Hov.
1907   "Dura (Parskakan vichakakhagh)." [Dura (Persian Fortune Game).] *AH* 16:66–68.
        Dura is similar to Armenian fortune game. Examples of Persian songs of game are given in Armenian translation.

Sarkisian, Eprem
1948   "Gomidase Echmiadzni jemarani mech." [Komitas at the Echmiadzin Seminary.] *H* 26(3):49–57.
        Author, a Komitas pupil, recalls singing folk songs that Komitas transcribed.

Sarkisian, Harutiun
1932   *Palu, ir sovoruytnere, grtagan u imastagan vijage.* [Palu, its Customs, Education and Intellectual State.] Cairo, Db. Sahag-Mesrob. 568 pp. il., includes music.
        Family customs, weddings, births, festivals, pp. 1–42. Mock trial of a village chief, pp. 25–30 [a practice I have not encountered in other Armenian folklore.—AMA]. Folk music, pp. 285–291. Oaths, good wishes, blessings, curses, prayers, pp. 321–325. Illustrations of clothing and stocking designs, pp. 326–345. Dialect list at end illustrates some of the objects named.

Sarkisian, Nerses
1864   *Deghakrutiunk i Pokr ev Medz Hayk.* [Topography of Minor and Major
             Armenias.] Venice, St. Lazar. 289 pp. il., fold. maps and plans.
                  Based on trip between 1843 and 1851. Brief note on Gypsies in Erzerum,
                  and vocabulary with Armenian meanings pp. 81–82. Gypsies not
                  Armenian but live among Armenians in Erzerum and work there, but do
                  not intermarry.

Sarukhan [no first name]
1925   "Arshag Chobaniani hopeleane." [The Jubilee of Arshag Chobanian.] *HA*
             39:81–87. port.
                  Biographical sketch of Chobanian who was primarily a writer. He also
                  edited a paper and translated some Armenian folk songs into French.

Sassouni, Viken
1980   "Armenian Rugs." *Armenian Review* 33(4):383–410. il.
                  Mostly about Armenian inscribed rugs and Armenian design elements.
                  Table of alphabet and dating system.

1981   "Armenian Church Floor Plan—a Hitherto Unidentified Design in Oriental
             Rugs." *Hali* 4:(1):24–28. il.
                  Floor plans of certain churches shown with illustrations of rugs that have
                  designs resembling floor plans of Armenian churches.

Sasuni, G.
1933   "Davit ev Mher." [David and Mher.] *H* 11(3):174–183.
                  This is part of the epic of David of Sassoun. It was found among the
                  papers of Kegham Der Garabedian of Mush who had received the hand
                  written text from H. Hamamjian in 1910. Sasuni introduced punctuation
                  when he printed the text here, and notes history of this version.

1956   *Badmutiun Daroni ashkhari.* [History of the Daron World.] Beirut, Sevan.
             1252 pp. il., fold. map.
                  Folklore of the Daron area, pp. 430–502. Comments on folklore and
                  dialect words, pp. 430–477; wedding songs, pp. 478–481; children's
                  songs, pp. 489–501; proverbs, pp. 502–507; riddles, p. 508; fable, pp.
                  509–510; verse in Sassoun dialect pp. 510–511; names of some sources
                  of folklore, p. 512.

Sayadian, Harutiun. *See* Sayat-Nova

Sayat-Nova
1963   *Hayeren, Vratseren, ev Adrbejaneren khagheri zhoghovatsu.* [Armenian,
             Georgian, and Azerbaijan Song Collection.] Erevan, Haypethrat. xl, 346 pp.
             il.
                  Collected and edited with introduction and notes by Morus Hasratian.
                  Songs arranged by place, but text in Armenian. Includes a word list, pp.

277–320, and bibliography, pp. 337–342. Reviewed by H. Kurdian in *HA* 1966 (80):119–123.

1963   *Lirika*. [Lyrics.] Moscow, Gos. Izd-vo Khudovzh. Lit. 279 pp. il.
The minstrel's songs are translated into Russian from Armenian, Georgian, and Azerbaijani. Includes glossary.

1969   *Khagher*. [Songs.] Erevan, "Hayasdan". 142 pp.
Includes 63 songs, edited by Sarko Bayazad, but no introductory information.

Scarborough, John
1986–87   "Medieval Armenia's Ancient Medical Heritage." *REA*, n.s. 20:237–251.
Much of Armenian medicine derived from natural products. Also notes plant material for care of horses.

Schawerdjan, Ruben
1958   "Komitas, Sogomon Sogomonjan." *Musik in Geschichte und Gegenwart* 7:1449–1450.
A brief biographical sketch of Komitas; gives his other name also.

Schmitt, Rüdiger
1985   "Zur den alten armenischer Monatsnamen." *Annual of Armenian Linguistics* 6:91–100.
Names of Armenian month names and equivalents in several other ancient languages such as Sogdian, Parthian, middle Persian, etc. Some of Armenian month names are associated with festivals.

Seidlitz, N. von
1889   "Armenische Sprichwörter und Rätsel." *Ausland* 62:807–809.
Includes 90 proverbs and 25 riddles.

Seiffert, M.
1899   "Die armenische Kirchenmusik." *Zeitschrift der Internationalen Musik-Gesellschaft* 1:46–47.
Summary of paper presented at International Music Society meeting at Berlin. Though article about church music, it does mention folk music and its influence on church music.

Seklemian, A. G.
1893   "Armenian Fairy Tales." *Journal of American Folklore* 6:150–152.
In Bitias, the author's birthplace, stories were told in the evenings usually by Gypsy men or Dervishes. They adapted stories to the audience. Gives one tale: "The Youngest of the Three."

Seklemian, A. G. *(continued)*

1897   "The Wicked Stepmother: an Armenian Folk-tale." *Journal of American Folklore* 10:135–142.

   Widowed stepmother sends stepson on tasks to get rid of him so she can fulfill her love for a giant.

1898   *The Golden Maiden and Other Folk Tales and Fairy Stories Told in Armenia.* Cleveland and New York, The Holman-Taylor Co. 224 pp.

   First book of Armenian folktales published in English in the United States. Includes 29 tales. The book has been out of print for many years, but some tales have been reprinted in magazines.

[NOTE: For a number of years the following Armenian folktales, by A. G. Seklemian, appeared in the periodical *Armenia*, a publication not as widely available as its successor *New Armenia*. For the convenience of readers, reprintings of the tales in *New Armenia* after Seklemian's death are noted after the first entry.—AMA]

1910   "[Armenian Folk Tales.]" *Armenia* 4(5):7–11. "The Fisherman's Son." See also *New Armenia* 1923 (20):27–30. *Armenia* 4(7):9–12. "The Water–Child and the Wolf–Child." See also *New Armenia* 1929 (21):13–14.

1911   "[Armenian Folk Tales.]" *Armenia* 4(10):11–13. "Unseen Beauty." See also *New Armenia* 1917 (9):360–361, and *New Armenia* 1929 (21):29–30. *Armenia* 4(10):13–14. "Three Rustic Minstrels." *Armenia* 4(12):8–12. "The Bald-Headed Orphan." *Armenia* 5:15–19, 48–53. "The Snake Child." *Armenia* 5:83–85. "Prince Pari and the Beasts." *Armenia* 5:110–114. "Reed-Maid." See also *New Armenia* 1928 (20):11–13. *Armenia* 5:145–147. "Shapoor, the Hunter's Son." (To be continued.)

1912   "[Armenian Folk Tales.]" *Armenia* 5:174–177. "Shapoor, the Hunter's Son." *Armenia* 5:212-216. "The Bird of Luck." *Armenia* 5:238–240. port. "The Betrothed of Destiny." *Armenia* 5:275–276. "The Shepherd and the Shepherdess." See also *New Armenia* 1925 (17):7–8. *Armenia* 5:304–306. "Nahabed's Daughter." See also *New Armenia* 1925 (17):43–44.

1912   "[Armenian Folk Tales.]" *Armenia* 5:340–342. "The Man and the Snake." See also *New Armenia* 1925 (17):28–29. *Armenia* 5:378–379. "Father Myriad." See also *New Armenia* 1924 (16):91–92. *Armenia* 6:23–25. "Reynard and Bruno." *Armenia* 6:118–122. "Julita." See also *New Armenia* 1924 (16):59–61.

1913   "[Armenian Folk Tales.]" *Armenia* 6:185–187, 216–219. "The Youngest of the Three." See also *New Armenia* 1925 (17):58–61. *Armenia* 6:279–284. "Zoolvisia." See also *New Armenia* 1924 (16):73–76. *Armenia* 6:337–340. "The Poor Widow's Son." See also *New Armenia* 1924 (16):42–44. *Armenia* 6:378–379. port. "Simon, the Friend of Snakes."

1914   "Folk Tales of the Near East." *Oriental World* 7:119–125. "The Adventures of Mirza."

Semerdjian, M. [signed with pseudonym: Zeytuntsi]
1900–1903   *Zeytuni ants'ealen ev nergayen.* [From the Past and Present of Zeytun.] 2 v. in 1. Vol. 1 published in Vienna, Mkhitarian Dbaran, 1900. 160 pp. Vol. 2, published in Paris, 1903. 239 pp. il., fold. map.
>   Of folklore interest, vol. 2, pp. 123–127; 134–150. Information on foods, family customs, baptism, marriage (includes detailed cost). When there is death, some of clothing of deceased taken to grave and there is weeping and lamentation. This not done when soldier dies, for it is said he is happy in his glory.

Servantsian, Karekin [NOTE: I have adopted this spelling of the name from the many listed in the Preface. A cross-reference has been made only for the spelling used by the U.S. Library of Congress: Srowandztiants.—AMA]
1874   *Krots u prots ev Sasuntsi Tavit gam Mheri Tur.* [Written and Unwritten and David of Sassoun or Mher's Door.] Constantinople, Dbakrutiun E. M. Dndesian. [Pages not known.]
>   The citation above is taken from facsimile title-page that appears in author's *Erker* [Works], Vol. 1, published in Erevan, HSSH, GA Hrat, 1978, pp. 35–116. Includes brief folklore sketches and observations, for example, p. 52 has the anecdote "Holy Well," and a crane legend is on p. 75. On pp. 89–110 is "Sasuntsi Tavit gam Mheri tur."

1876   *Manana.* [Manna.] Constantinople, Dbakrutiun, E. M. Dndesian. 456 pp.
>   The first part, almost 100 pages, is picturesque, like a guided tour of the town of Van and the various folk activities along the way. There are nine folktales, a number of songs for various occasions, riddles, bird language, reverse language, magic, and amulets. There is also a word list of village vocabulary. This work has been reprinted in Servantsian's *Erker* [Works], vol. 1, pp. 117–364 (1978).

1949   "Hazaran bulbul." [Thousand-Throated Nightingale.] *Armenian Review* 2:152–154
>   This tale has been translated by J. G. Mandalian. Tale about a king who builds three churches, but a stranger declares they lack a nightingale, so king sends his three sons in quest of the bird. The youngest son finds the bird.

1949–50   *Hamov-hodov.* [With Flavor and Fragrance.] 3rd ed. Paris, Impr. Araxes. 2 v.
>   I have not seen the first edition, published in 1884 in Constantinople. In 1904 a second edition was published in Tiflis. A recent printing appears in Servantsian's *Erker* [Works], vol. 1, pp. 365–586, published in Erevan (1978). The first volume includes descriptive material of villages visited by the author who gives some observations of folk life. Also includes 19

Servantsian, Karekin *(continued)*
　　　　　　　　folktales. The second volume has seven folktales. Also includes a variety
　　　　　　　　of folk songs for various occasions and some proverbs. A dialect word
　　　　　　　　list in vol. 2, pp. 176–208.

1982　　　　　*Toros Akhpar*. [Brother Toros.] (In his *Erker* [Works].) Erevan, HSSH, GA
　　　　　　　　Hrat. pp. 180–545.
　　　　　　　　Vol. 1 of this title was published in Constantinople in 1879. Because of
　　　　　　　　government delays, vol. 2 was published in Constantinople in 1884. This
　　　　　　　　work, requested by the Armenian patriarch and approved by the Turkish
　　　　　　　　government, is a survey of many towns and villages where there were
　　　　　　　　Armenian communities, number of inhabitants, churches, etc. Mainly
　　　　　　　　descriptive, but now and then author suggests places that should be
　　　　　　　　investigated for folklore material.

Setian, Ralph
1971　　　　　"Some Armenian Folk Maxims." *Ararat* 12(1):31.
　　　　　　　　A list of 20 proverbs and sayings.

Sevak, Paruyr
1966　　　　　"Erp e tsnvel Sayat-Novan?" [When was Sayat-Nova Born?] *PH* 2:88–114.
　　　　　　　　Several dates have been suggested between 1711 and 1724 as the birth
　　　　　　　　date of Sayat-Nova. The author tries to establish 1722 by studying the
　　　　　　　　minstrel's songs and the cryptograms in some of the songs.

1969　　　　　*Sayat-Nova*. Erevan, HSSH, GA Hrat. 498 pp. facsim.
　　　　　　　　Much uncertainty about birth date of Sayat-Nova; 1711 to 1728
　　　　　　　　suggested. Author gives considerable space to the question by examining
　　　　　　　　the songs (pp. 13–117) and establishes birth date as 1722. Rest of the
　　　　　　　　book is a critical study of the minstrel's creative work interspersed with
　　　　　　　　biographical information. Notes extensive (pp. 369–482) but difficult to
　　　　　　　　use since no pages given to connect with the text, and text numbers to
　　　　　　　　notes are so small that they are difficult to pick out. The bibliography (pp.
　　　　　　　　483–498) mostly Armenian and a few Russian.

Shahaziz, E.
1901–2　　　"Nor Nakhijevane ev Nor-Nakhejevantsik." [New-Nakhichevan and the
　　　　　　　　Inhabitants of New-Nakhichevan.] *AH* 7–8:5–102. il., 9:5–82.
　　　　　　　　Historical information and information about churches of the area.
　　　　　　　　Customs, weddings, birth and baptism, death and burial discussed in
　　　　　　　　vols. 7–8. Vol. 9 includes rites and customs of special festivals. For
　　　　　　　　Christmas gives songs that end each line with *avedis* (greeting).
　　　　　　　　Witchcraft, superstitions, beliefs, and crafts and occupations also noted.

Shahinian, A.
1976   "Vayots Tsori vishap-kotoghnere." [The *vishap* Steles of Vayats-Tsor.] *PH*
            1:286–289.
                    Refers to N. Marr and Ia. I. Smirnov work (1931) about *vishap* stones in
                    fish shapes, or bull; believed to be related to water worship. Author found
                    two *vishap* stones converted to cross stones in a village.

Shahnazarian, A.
1912   "Prof. Grigor Abrahamian Khalatian." *AH* 22:249–263.
                    Memorial service organized by Armenian Ethnographic Society.
                    Biographical information and list of works of Khalatian, who did so much
                    work in ethnography and folklore.

1913   "Garegin episkopos Srvantdyani erkere grakan tesutyun." [Literary View of
            the Writings of Bishop Garegin Servantsian.] *AH* 24:111–116; 25:85–107.
                    Lecture given before the Armenian Ethnographic Society on occasion of
                    20th year of Servantsian's death.

Shalian, Artin K.
1964   *David of Sassoun: The Armenian Folk Epic in Four Cycles.* Athens, Ohio,
            Ohio University Press. 377 pp.
                    In blank verse. Based on 1939 unified text published in Erevan.

Shamlian, Deacon Zohrab
1980   "The Development of Armenian Music from the Fifth Century to the
            Fifteenth." *Armenian Review* 33(2):145–161; 33(3):269–279. Includes
            music.
                    Translated by Anahid Kechichian from various issues of the periodical
                    Sion, 1965–66. Mostly about church music, but includes some
                    information about folk music and minstrels. Also some information on
                    musicians.

Sharbkhanian, Pavel
1967   "Manuk Abeghian." *Erevani Hamalsarani Lratu* 1:32–34. Russian summary.
                    Biographical information about M. Abeghian and his work, including
                    folklore.

Sharf, A.
1982   "Animal Sacrifice in the Armenian Church." *REA* , n.s. 16:417–449.
                    Armenian word for animal sacrifice is *madagh,* which means to tender.
                    Tradition established by Gregory the Illuminator, adapted from pagan
                    times. At Easter, a lamb or other animal may be used. *Madagh* may also
                    be used for other special events, including dedication of altar. Rules are
                    given for selection of animal, preparation, etc. Food is distributed to all of
                    those who are present.

Shaverdian, A. I.
1989   *Komitas.* Moscow, "Sovetskii Kompozitor." 318 pp. ports.
          A study of the life and work of the folk song collector Komitas. He has
          high place in musical history and Armenian musical culture. Works of
          Komitas and a bibliography. A wide range of photos of Komitas from
          childhood and through his career.

Sheohmelian, Ohannes
1982   *Three Apples From Heaven: Armenian Folktales.* Saddle Brook, New Jersey,
          Ararat Press. 133 pp. il.
          These 25 tales have been selected from various volumes of Armenian
          folktales. Dialect words and phrases from Kurdish, Turkish, Persian, and
          Arabic are dropped and English equivalents given. Book is intended for
          young people.

Sherents, G.
1885–99   *Vana saz havakatsuyk.* [The Collection of the *saz* of Van.] Tiflis. 2 v.
          This is a scarce item that I have not been able to locate, but it is mentioned
          quite often in footnotes. It contains folk songs, tales, sayings, and riddles
          from the area of Van. A brief selection from vol. 1 is given on pp. 185–
          186 of G. Grigorian's *Hay zhoghovrdakan vipergnere* . . . (1986). The
          saz is a musical instrument.

1902   "Garegin episk. Sruantstiants." [Bishop Garegin Servantsian.] *AH* 9:272–
          281.
          About life, work, and publications of Servantsian. On occasion of 10th
          anniversary of his death.

Shipley, Alice
1987   "Wedding in Dikranagerd." *Ararat* 28(3):25–26. il.
          Childhood memory of a wedding that took place in early 20th century.
          Notes use of henna, and some old practices and their adaptations.

Shvod (pseud.). *See* Deroyan, Mardiros Shvod

Sidal, K.
1939   *Sasna Dzrer.* [Daredevlis of Sassoun.] Philadelphia. 113 pp.
          A variant told by Sarkis Baghdasarian. Sidal renders it in rhymed couplets
          and introduces a few changes in the story.

Simeonian, Arsen Av.
1957   "Gomidas Vartabed ev ir tshnaminere." [Gomidas Vartabed and his Enemies.]
          H 34:(11):47–56.
          Komitas, the folk-song collector, had enemies in Echmiadzin. He went to
          Constantinople where he also had enemies who said that he used
          nationalistic songs in concerts.

1969   *Gomidas Vartabed*. Boston, Haig H. Tumayan. 101 pp. ports.

On the 100th anniversary of birth of Komitas. About his life and creativity as a collector of folk music, researcher, and teacher. Explains his notation system. The legacy of his work. His benefactor Alexander Mantashian.

Simonian, H. A.

1988   "Mijnadaryan mi norahayt zruyts." [Newly Discovered Medieval Tale.] *PH* 1:193–201. Russian summary.

The tale is called "The Story of Abdl Jafar," the youth and the girl Chemillay who took each other, i.e., married. Two versions found: one in Vienna in Mkhitarist Library, the other in Istanbul in Holy Angels Church. Text of A printed, and footnotes give variant words and phrases of B. Some similarity to Arabian Nights. Story in prose and verse.

Sinclair, Salinda

1931   "The Span of Life." *The Golden Book Magazine* 13(78):55.

Supposed to be an Armenian legend: cat, dog, donkey, monkey asked how many years they need. What is left over given to man who attains 70 years and gets a place in his son's house. There he provides functions of animals above for the children. (NB: Seems more like a fable than a legend.—AMA)

Siruni, H.

1928   "Hay arvesdin ev mdkin hedkere Rumanots mech, 10 arasbelnerum entmechen." [Remnants of Armenian Art and Thought in Rumania from Among 10 Legends.] *H* 7(1):45–52.

There is a tale of Arjish Abbey in 47 stanzas. Another tale in verse about an Armenian building that demands body of live girl in foundation.

Skinner, Joseph

1940   *The Alexander Romance in the Works of Armenian Historians*. 404 pp. Thesis, Ph.D., Harvard University, 1940.

Have seen abstract only in *Summaries of Theses*, 1940, of Harvard University Graduate School of Arts and Sciences, pp. 204–209 (pub. 1942). Compares Alexander legend in Mss 1664 at Echmiadzin Library and Venice text of Moses of Khoren's *History*.

Sköld, Hannès

1925   "Comment se forment les légendes." *REA* 5:137–139.

Refers to Pliny and Moses of Khoren. Stories brought by travelers cannot be denied by listeners, so they do not dispute. Once six fingers a sign of royalty is accepted, in time can change to persons with six hands.

Soghomonian, Soghomon. *See* Komitas, Vardapet

Solakian, A.
1910   "Vana banahiusutiunits." [From the Folklore of Van.] *AH* 19:99–114.
            Mixture of folklore genres: prayers, fortune songs, children's games and
            rhymes, riddles, curses, blessings.

Srabian, Levon
1960   *Kghi*. 2nd ed. Antelias, Lebanon, Dbaran Gatoghigosagan Hayots Medzi
            Dann Giligioy. [Press of the Catholicos of Cilicia.] 72 pp. fold. map.
            Folklore material of the Kghi area is scattered in the text. Snakes, p. 11;
            respect for ants, p. 12; name day celebration, p. 28; numskull stories, pp.
            34–35; moonstone and evil eye, p. 42; folk medicine for children, p. 45;
            death customs, pp. 45–46; Lent, p. 50–51; evil spirits, p. 52.

Srapian, Armenouhi
1969   *Hay mijnadaryan zruytsner*. [Armenian Medieval Anecdotes.] Erevan,
            HSSH, GA Hrat. 413 pp.
            A collection of anecdotes derived from Armenian manuscripts of the 13th–
            18th centuries. Religious, national, and historical types include clergy,
            women, palace life, folk ideals, etc.

1981   "Aradzi zhanrayin embrnume mijnadarum." [Medieval Genre Concept of the
            Fable.] *L* 9:61–70. Russian summary.
            Wide scope terminology included edifying fables, proverbs and sayings,
            myth, tales, anecdotes. Later more narrow meaning for fable.

Srowandztiants. *See* Servantsian

Steinmann, Linda K.
1987   "Shah Abbas and the Royal Silk Trade, 1599–1629." *British Society for
            Middle Eastern Studies. Bulletin* 14(1):68–74.
            Of special interest since Armenians were in the silk trade. During period
            1600–1617 Shah Abbas sent Armenians as emissaries to courts of Venice,
            Tuscany, and Spain. They took silk samples so rulers could send
            merchants to trade in Persia. Not all of the article is about Armenians.

Stepanian, G. Kh.
1969   "Komitase Kostandnupolsum." [Komitas in Constantinople.] *PH* 3:96–110.
            il. Russian summary.
            Komitas spent 1910–15 in Constantinople. Organized large choir and
            gave concerts. Restrictions on singing national songs until 1908
            constitution. During Balkan war went to Berlin, returned in 1913. Exiled
            by Turks in 1915; later returned, but not the same man.

Stepanian, Hovag
1944   "Ashugh Chivanin ev ir sdeghdzakordzutiune." [Ashugh (Minstrel) Chivani
           (Jivani) and his Creations.] *H* 22(3):38–48.
               Life and work of 19th century minstrel on the occasion of the 33rd year of
               his death. Some examples of his work are given.

Stone, Michael E.
1986   "Holy Land Pilgrimage of Armenians Before the Arab Conquest." *Revue
           Biblique* 93(1):93–110.
               Armenians devoted to pilgrimages since the 4th century. Traveled in
               groups; went for penance, prayer and gathering relics. Mt. Sinai and
               Jordan River were favored places.

Surmelian, Leon
1955   "Magic Carpets." *Holiday* 18(5):61–62, 65, 67, 69–72. col. il.
               Part of this of interest for describing the making of Oriental rugs in a
               family setting by the author's cousin.

1964   *Daredevils of Sassoun, the Armenian National Epic*. Denver, Alan Swallow.
           279 pp. il.
               Translation of the epic David of Sassoun's four cycles in prose, but
               Surmelian has tried to retain the poetic feeling.

1968   *Apples of Immortality: Folktales of Armenia*. Berkeley and Los Angeles,
           University of California Press. 319 pp. il.
               The 40 tales, including a few anecdotes, are selected from volumes of
               Armenian folktales, and a few from Servantsian's *Hamov-Hodov*.
               Reviewed in *Journal of American Folklore* 1970 (83):85–86 by Hugh
               Jansen.

Sutherland, James K.
1964   "The Music of Asia Minor." *Strad* 74:412, 415, 417, 443, 445, 447.
               Notes Armenian dance and songs. Includes modes.

Svazlian, V. G.
1963   "Sargis Haykunu kyankn u gortse." [The Life and Work of Sargis Haykuni.]
           PH 1:151–162. port. Russian summary.
               Haykuni was a teacher and a folklore collector. His nationalistic interests
               led to imprisonment for short periods in Turkey and Russia. Collected
               folklore in various localities. In 1878 he met K. Servantsian.

1969   "Musa Leran Hay zhoghovrdakan banahyusutyune." [The Armenian Folklore
           of Musa Mountain.] *PH* 1:201–206.
               Gives some selections of sayings in dialect, and some riddles. A lullaby is
               given in dialect, then in standard Armenian. Notes émigré items.

Svazlian, V. G. *(continued)*
1989   "Sargis Haykunu kyankn u zhoghovrdagitakan gortsuneutyune." [Sargis
             Haykuni's Life and Folklore Scholarship.] *L* 4:70–77.
             In his early years Haykuni dedicated to improve the lot of Armenians in
             Turkey. As in other countries, nationalism and ethnic identity had a role in
             promoting folklore. He began to collect folklore and published in various
             journals.

Sys, T. Ivanov V.
1973   "Obrazets fol'klora Armian Podalis." [An Armenian Folklore Specimen of
             Podalis.] *PH* 3:252–254 . Includes music.
             About an Armenian folk song sung in Podalis. Gives metrical scheme.
             Some evidence of feeling of Ukrainian songs.

Szeskus, Reinhard
1970   "Komitas in Berlin." *Beiträge zur Musikwissenschaft* 12(2):121–132.
             Komitas spent the years 1896–99 studying music in Berlin. Subjects
             studied and names of professors are given.

1970   "Komitas—Musikforscher und Patriot." *Musik und Gesellschaft* 20:245–247.
             Musical studies of Komitas in Armenian folk music and church singing.
             Use of polyphony in Armenian folk music.

Szongett, Kristof
1892   "Armenischen Volksmärchen aus Siebenbürgen." *Ethnographische Mitteil-
             ungen aus Ungarn* 2:218–220.
             The story "Májrey vêrtin jev usape; Mutter, Sohn und Drache" is given in
             Armenian transliteration followed by German translation.

1893   "Märchen des Siebenbürgen armenier." *Ethnologische Mitteilungen aus
             Ungarn* 3:88–91.
             The tales "Gové," "Die Kuhe," "Gachine," and "Das Beil" are given in
             Armenian transliteration, then in German translation.

1893   *Szamosújvar, a Magyar Ormeny Metropolisz.* [Szamosújvar, a Magyar
             Armenian City.] Szamosújvar, Todorán. 272 pp.
             Not seen. Reviewed by H. Wlislocki in *Ethnologische Mitteilungen aus
             Ungarn* 1893 (3):177–178. According to review there is some information
             about Armenian folklore in the town.

1897   "Armenisches Märchen aus Siebenbürgen." *Ethnologische Mitteilungen aus
             Ungarn* 5:58–59; 110–112.
             The first citation gives the story "Irek enguze," "Die drei Nüsse." The
             second citation is the story "Malace," "Des Blei." Both stories are first
             given in Armenian transliteration, then in German translation.

T., A.
1883   "Khungianos erkich Garnetsi." [Khungianos, Singer of Garni.] *B* 41:97–110.

About the late 18th and early 19th century minstrel; his life and some of his songs reflecting his suffering.

T., A. B.
1911   "The Armenian Christmas and New Year." *Armenia* 4(8):4– 7. See also *New Armenia* 1928 (20):60–62.

Gives some history of selection of January 6 as date of Christmas that is mostly a religious celebration. The New Year involves more merriment, feasting, etc.

Tabagiants, S., et al.
1894   "Armianskie skazki." [Armenian Tales.] *Sbornik Materialov dlia Opisaniia Mestnostei i Plemen Kavkaza* 19(2):155–219.

Seven tales collected by various teachers from various villages. The last story is "Istoriia Khikara v Echmiadzin" [Story of Khigar at Echmiadzin].

Tahmizian, N. K.
1969   "Komitase ev Haykakan khazeri vertsanutyan khndire." [Komitas and the Question of Developing the Armenian Neumes.] *PH* 4:30–48. Russian summary.

Includes modern musical notation but does not give equivalent neumes. Komitas provided a "neume-key."

1969   "Komitasi 'Shar Akna zhoghovrdakan erger' zhoghovatsum." [The Komitas Collection of the "Series of Akn Folk Songs."] *L* 11:7–26. Russian summary.

Author points out that some of the Akn (Agn) songs Komitas vocalized were originally urban songs that came into folklore of Akn when some of the Van population migrated to Akn in middle ages.

Tarayan, S.
1898   "Hay zhoghovrdi arhestagortsutiune." [The Crafts of the Armenian People.] *AH* 3:3–71.

Based on early 19th century practices: home crafts, traveling craftsmen, work by men and women. Establishment of guilds. Caucasus, Caspian, Black Sea, and Euphrates River areas studied.

Tarbassian, Hratch A.
1975   *Erzerum (Garin): Its Armenian History and Traditions.* Translated from the Armenian by Nigel Schahgaldian. [No place], The Garin Compatriotic Union of the United States. 270 pp. il.

Folk items appear on pp. 70–73 and 78–83: proverbs and sayings, blessings, curses, riddles. A few folk songs and dances with music. There are also costume pictures.

Tashin, H. *See* Dashian, H.

Tashjian, Nouvart
1903   *The Priscilla Armenian Needlepoint Lace.* Boston, The Priscilla Publishing
            Company. 36 pp. il.
                The word "needlepoint" somewhat misleading. Directions are given for
                making needle lace for edgings and insertions as well as doilies. Pub-
                lished later as "Armenian Lace" by Nouvart Tashjian, edited by Jules and
                Karthe Kliet. Berkeley, California, Lacie Publications, 1952. 36 pp. il.

Tashjian, Virginia A.
1966   *Once There Was and Was Not: Armenian Tales Retold.* Boston, Little,
            Brown. 85 pp. il.
                Includes seven tales; title taken from a common opening formula of
                Armenian folktales.

1971   *Three Apples Fell From Heaven: Armenian Folk Tales Retold.* Boston, Little,
            Brown. 76 pp. il.
                Nine tales; title taken from a common closing formula of Armenian
                folktales.

Tavtian, S.
1906   "Kavari 'sher'er." [Provincial Lamentations.] *B* 64:350–352.
                Lamentations given for various specific persons in a family.

Tcheraz, Minas
1893   "Notes sur la mythologie arménienne." *International Congress of Orientalists*,
            9th, London, Sept. 5–12, 1892. *Transactions* 1893 (2): 822–845.
                Beliefs about celestial bodies, nature, cult of ancestors, various spirits,
                and magic, including the Book of the Six Thousand.

1893   "Saiat-Nova, sa vie et ses chansons." *Royal Asiatic Society. Journal.* pp.
            497–508.
                Life and work of Sayat-Nova. Notes some excerpts of Akhverdian's
                work about the minstrel concerning musical instruments, beauty and love,
                and didactic elements. (NB: G. Akhverdian supposed to be authority on
                Sayat-Nova, but I have been unable to locate a copy of his book.—AMA)

1901   "La légende d'Alexandre-de-Grand chez les Arméniens." *Revue de l'Histoire
            des Religions* 43:345–351.
                Tcheraz heard the legend from an illiterate Armenian in Constantinople
                who had heard it from grandfather in Agn village in Armenia. Notes that
                Alexander had a daughter.

1912   *L'Orient inédit; légendes et traditions, arméniennes, grecques et turques.*
        Paris, Ernest Leroux. 328 pp.
        Mostly Armenian folklore; Biblical and historical persons, followed by 25
        tales, including two versions of Cinderella, and some animal tales. Also
        includes some customs, superstitions, and mythology.

1917   "Saiat-Nova." *New Armenia* 9:91–94. port. of author.
        About the Armenian minstrel tradition and Sayat-Nova, the 18th century
        minstrel. Notes minstrel contests.

1929   "The Wonderful Twins: An Armenian Folk-tale." *New Armenia* 21:45–46.
        Tale adapted from M. Tcheraz's French version. Of three sisters, the
        youngest marries king and promises him twins: boy with moon on head,
        girl with sun on head. Jealous sisters substitute dogs for twins and
        abandon them. Eventually truth prevails.

Tchituny. *See* Chituni

Tchobanian, Archag. *See* Chobanian, Arshag

Tchukasizian, B. L. *See* Chukasizian, B. L.

Teica, Nicolae
1971   *Vitejii din Sasun: epopee populara armena.* [David of Sassoun; Folk Epic of
        Armenia.] Bucharest, Minerva. 397 pp.
        Translation of David of Sassoun into Rumanian. Introduction is by Victor
        Kernbach who gives brief historical background. All four cycles are
        presented in verse form. Includes a glossary.

Ter-Ghevondian, A. N.
1965   " 'Ara ev Shamiram' araspeli mi artsaganke Arab patmich Masuda mot." [The
        Echo of the Legend "Ara and Shamiram" in the Arab Historian Masud.] *PH*
        4:249–253.
        The Armenian legend of Ara the Beautiful has had several versions. The
        one by Masud, at the time of Bagratid rule, bears Armenian stamp. The
        story is so widely spread that Arabs also used it.

1978   "Aghjik Taroni zruytse XII dari Arapakan aghbyurum." [Saga of the Girl of
        Taron in a 12th Century Arab Source.] *PH* 3:265–269.
        An Armenian tale that dates from the 9th century and was translated in the
        12th century. Notes history of the work and compares with some
        elements of David of Sassoun.

Ter-Hovannisian, Gabriel

1901–2   "Haykakan sovorutyunner." [Armenian Customs.] *AH* 7–8:113–204; 9:83–116.
>   Vol. 7–8 about festivals and some songs connected with them. Family life, weddings, lullabies. Vol. 9 includes children's rhymes and games with variants in some villages. Also some riddles and tongue-twisters.

Terlemezian, Rupen

1923   "Gomidas Vartabed." HA 37:360–374, 445–462, 528–548.
>   Biographical information about the prominent Armenian folk song collector Komitas. Brief excerpts given of his folk songs.

1924   *Gomidas Vartabed.* Vienna, Mkhitarian Dbaran. 96 pp. port.
>   Biographical information about Komitas, description of some of his folk music—its intimate relation to situations when sung, e.g., kind of work, dance, etc. Quotes some of views of Komitas about folk songs. He had collected about 3000 songs that were in files of the Armenian patriarch in Constantinople. Great contribution of Komitas.

Ter-Minasian, Vahan

1893   *Angir dprutiun ev aragk.* [Unwritten Literature and Fables.] Constantinople, K. Baghdadian. 288 pp.
>   Introduction of 106 pp. about Armenian literature, its oral transmission, with some examples. Includes 167 fables designated by source from Vartan to Khigar. Some without designation.

Ter-Movsesian, Mesrop

1897   "Nakhapasharmunkner Eghishe patmakri kanonnerum." [Superstitions in the Rules of Eghishe the Historian.] *AH* 2:295–299.
>   Superstitions not ascribed to Eghishe, but some self-seeking person used Eghishe's name to give authenticity.

1907   "Ejmiatsin ev Hayots hnaguyn ekeghetsiner." [Echmiadzin and Armenia's Ancient Churches.] *AH* 15:85–128. il., 16:133–204.
>   Historical information. Most of illustrations are of ancient church ruins.

1910–13   "Haykakan manrankarner." [Armenian Miniatures.] *AH* 20:5–32; 21:61–82.
>   Information about many manuscripts examined; also about Roslin the illustrator.

1913   "Haykakan artsanagrutyunner." [Armenian Inscriptions.] *AH* 25:61–84.
>   Information about inscriptions on several monasteries and churches associated with them.

Ter-Mowsesjanz, Parasdan

1892   "Das armenische Bauerenhaus. Ein Beitrag zur Culturgeschichte der Armenier." *Mitteilungen der Anthropologischen Gesellschaft in Wien* 22 (n.f. 12):125–172. il.

> Armenian domestic architecture in villages; interior floor plans, drawings of household furnishings and utensils. Armenian translation in *HA* 1893 (7):42–47, 105–111, 190–192, 283–237, 311–316, 353–358, with title "Hay kiughagan dune." Also published with same title in Vienna, Mkhitarian Dbaran, 1894. 103 pp. il.

Ter-Sarkisiants, A. E.

1972   *Sovremennaia semia u Armian.* [Contemporary Family Life Among Armenians.] Moscow, Izd-vo "Nauka." 204 pp. il.

> Study derived from villages of Soviet Armenian districts. Of special interest is the chapter (pp. 108–147) about marriage and family rites. Pictures show domestic architecture, including one interior scene, and clothing.

Terzian, Paul

1900   "Religious Customs among Armenians." *Catholic World* 71:305–316, 500–512. il.

> Author was Catholic bishop in Adana. Describes baptism, betrothal, life after marriage, and funerals. Essential details are given.

Teymurazian, N. A.

1957   *Komitas (Soghomonian Soghomon Gevorgi) bibliografia.* [Bibliography of Komitas (Soghomonian Soghomon Gevorgi).] Erevan, HSSR. 111 pp. front. (port.).

> A chronological bibliography of 681 items arranged as follows: printed musical items; articles by Komitas; compositions and items edited by Komitas; books about Komitas; articles about Komitas (1891–1920 and 1921–1957). Russian articles about Komitas (1902–1957). Careful citations; many articles from Armenian magazines and weekly papers. A patient undertaking, considering lack of reference indexes.

Thomajan, P. K.

1969   "Armenian Proverbs." *Armenian Review* 22(1):46–117.

> Notes 13 proverbs in English translation.

Thompson, Harold W.

1949   "Proverbs and Sayings." *New York Folklore Quarterly* 5:296–300.

> Proverbs not identified by country except one as Armenian and gives Sirvart Poladian as informant.

Thomson, R. W.
1976   *History of the Armenians. See* Agathangelos, 1976.

1976   "Number Symbolism and Patristic Exegesis in Some Early Armenian
            Writers." *HA* 90:118–138.
                Considers various numbers, e.g., number three the first perfect number
                representing Trinity; four, the elements; twelve, the time, etc. Information
                derived from Armenian theological texts. Compares parallels in Greek or
                Syriac texts known to Armenians.

1978   Moses Khorenatsi. *See* Moses of Khoren

1979   "Architectural Symbolism in Classical Armenian Literature." *Journal of
            Theological Studies*, n.s. 30:102–114.
                Based on printed sources of classical Armenian writers about Church of
                the Holy Cross on the island of Aghtamar in Lake Van. Symbolism
                expressed in theological terms.

1979/80   "Armenian Variations on the Bahira Legend." *Harvard Ukrainian Studies* no.
            3/4:884–895.
                Speculates that one Armenian variant of this legend concerning
                Muhammed may have a connection with the opening of the Armenian epic
                David of Sassoun.

Tixeront, J.
1913   "Le rite du matal." [The Rite of Animal Sacrifice.] *Bulletin d'Ancienne
            Littérature et Archéologie Chrétiennes* 2:81–94.
                About the Armenian animal sacrifice, *madagh*. Only pure animal first
                offered at Easter. Animal is decorated, and there are prayers and reading
                from the Bible. Later other animals used, and sacrifices were made for the
                dead and saints. People shared in consumption of the meat. Mention of
                the ritual made in Georgia, Syria, and Iberia.

Tixeront, L. J.
1888   *Les origines de l'église d'Edesse et la légende d'Abgar; étude critique.* Paris,
            Maisonneuve et Ch. Laclerc. 201 pp.
                According to one version of the legend a letter from Christ to the
                Armenian King Abgar was carried by the apostle Thaddeus, who with
                Bartholomew had brought message of Christianity to the Armenians.

Tolegian, Aram
1961   *David of Sassoun, Armenian Folk Epic.* New York, Bookman Associates.
            140 pp. il.
                First English translation of the third cycle of David of Sassoun. Used
                version of Tumanian published in Tiflis in 1901. Translation is in verse
                form. Bibliography divided by language.

Topalian, Parunag
1943   *Hayreni kiughs Okhu.* [Okhu My Native Village.] Boston, Hayreniki Dbaran.
            181 pp., map.
            Mostly memories of author's village life, or things he heard about some
            events and persons. Folklore is scattered in the narrative. Of special
            interest is p. 16 about buffalo fights that were handled as contests between
            chosen sides. Sometimes bulls or rams used. Some notes about festivals
            and weddings.

Toporov, V. N.
1977   "Ob otrazhenii odnogo Indoevropeiskogo mifa v drevne Armianskoi traditsii."
            [About the Reflection of an Indo-European Myth in Armenian Tradition.] *PH*
            3:88–106. Armenian summary.
            Refers to the Indo-European Trita and the Armenian Vahagn. More study
            needed on the structure of both. Study based on Indian, Iranian, and
            Russian folktales. Three-fold establishment of the world; hero goes to
            lower world, conquers giant, gains success and riches. Remnants evident
            in Armenian Vahagn myth.

Torlakian, B. G.
1976   "Hamshenahayeri taraze XIX dari verjerin." [The Costume of the Hamshe
            Armenians in the Latter Part of the 19th Century.] *PH* 3:145–150. Russian
            summary.
            Pictures of costumes for men and women. The Armenians of Hamshe
            were originally from Trebizond area and relocated in Crimea.

Toromanian, T.
1910   "Ejmiatsni tachare." [The Cathedral of Echmiadzin.] *AH* 19:105–188. il.
            About antiquity and architecture of first Armenian church built in A.D.
            301. Study based on historical information (no remains of the original
            building exist). Notes persons who had visited the building. Author's first
            visit in 1908. Includes pictures and floor plans.

1911   "Gavit ev zhamatun hnaguyn ekeghetsineru mej." [Courtyard and Chapel in
            Ancient Churches.] *AH* 21:5–33.
            Many changes in floor plans over centuries. Historical approach to why
            changes were made.

1912   "Ani kaghak te amrots?" [Ani Town or Fortress?] *AH* 22:61–84; 23:5–26.
            Historical approach to periods when various rulers and crafts pursued.
            Architectural development.

1912   "Usumnasireli nyuter Hay chartarapetutyan hamar." [Worthy Themes for
            Study in Armenian Architecture.] *AH* 22:113–116.
            Study of old structures in ruins in areas near Alexandropol from pagan
            times. Also study of some old churches. (NB: Alexandropol became
            Leninakan and recently went back to its original name, Gumri.—AMA)

Tourian, Kevork G.
1904   "The Armenian Christmas." *Armenia* 1(3):38–45.
            Historical background of choice of January 6 as the Armenian date for
            Christmas. The holiday is mainly religious; includes church rites, also
            visits.

Tsitsikian, A. M.
1966   "Drevnie istoki Armianskoi smychkovoi kul'tury." The Ancient Sources of
            Armenian Bow Making.] *L* 1:37–38. il. Armenian summary.
            Establishes Armenian bow making through pictures in old Armenian
            works. Summary gives no date.

1981   "Drevnie izobrazhenie smychkovogo instrumenta iz raskorok Dvina." [The
            Old Image of Stringed Instruments from the Excavation of Dvin.] *PH* 3:224–
            242. il. Armenian summary.
            Dvin, an ancient capital of Armenia. Musical instrument dates from 9th to
            10th centuries, thus predating use of *kamancha*.

Tumanian, Hovhannes
1944   "Sasuntsi Davite." [David of Sassoun.] In his *Zhoghovrtagan erker*. Venice,
            St. Lazar. pp. 51–83.
            Abridged version of David of Sassoun in verse.

1945   *Le geste de David le Sassouniots*. Geneva, Éditions de la Frégate. 76 pp.
            Translated by Armand Gaspard who also wrote the introduction in which
            he gives historical background and commentary on the epic David of
            Sassoun.

1945   *Sayat-Nova*. Erevan, Haypethrat. 86 pp. il.
            Consists of comments and articles about the minstrel between 1912 and
            1916. Notes how little is known about Sayat-Nova during his clerical
            years. Criticizes Briusov's translations of some of Sayat-Nova's songs.
            Includes seven-line verse Tumanian wrote about Sayat-Nova. It is
            impossible to convey the feeling of the original, but here is a poor attempt:
            He came with dance/ Went with a moan, Sayat-Nova/ He came with song/
            Left with a wound, Sayat-Nova/ He came with love/ Went with a sword,
            Sayat-Nova/ May he remain with love, Sayat-Nova. (NB: It is said that he
            was slain with a sword.—AMA)

1951   *Sasuntsi Davit*. [David of Sassoun.] Beirut, Olympic Press. 59 pp.
            Abridged version of the epic David of Sassoun in verse.

1963   *Sayat-Nova, hodvatsner ev charer*. [Articles and Essays About Sayat-Nova.
            Erevan, HSSH, GA Hrat. 97 pp.
            Selections are on different aspects of Sayat-Nova's life. Notes indicate the
            occasion for which some of the articles were written.

Turian, Eghishe
1933   *Hayots hin grone, gam Haygagan titsapanutiun.* [Ancient Religion of the
           Armenians, or Armenian Mythology.] Jerusalem, Dbaran Srpots Hagopiants
           [Press of St. James]. 157 pp. port.
               After some general matters about schools of thought on mythology, the
               author tells about Armenian deities, their functions and characteristics.
               Influence of Persia and Greece. Historical myths and legends. Glossary
               of Armenian peasant words (pp. 101–105) and some superstitions
               connected with them.

Türkmen, Fikrat
1982   "Türk-Ermeni aşik Edebiyati iliskileri." [Turkish-Armenian Relations in
           Minstrel Culture.] *Osmanli arastirmalari* 3:13–20.
               Author considers Turkish-Armenian relations old, concentrating on
               minstrels.

Utudjian, Edouard
1965   "Un palais neutragé sur le Mont Ararat." *Connaissance des Arts* No. 155:70–
           75. il.
               Remains of civil architecture in which there are some Armenian elements.
               Believed that at one time an Armenian fortress to which palace was later
               added. Designated as Citadel of Ishak Pasha of 12th century. Castle
               constructed in 1786.

Uvezian, Sonia
1974   *The Cuisine of Armenia.* New York, Harper & Row. 412 pp. il.
               Armenian recipes from various regions, but also some Middle East areas
               where there are similarities. A glossary and sources of ingredients are
               given. Also some suggested menus.

Vagramian, Violet
1973   *Representative Choral Works of Gomidas: An Analytical Study and
           Evaluation of the Minstrel Style.* 232 pp. Part of text in Armenian. Ph.D.,
           University of Miami, 1973.
               Have seen *Dissertation Abstracts* 34A:2689 only. Gives biographical
               information. Discussion of folk song arrangements and lecture
               demonstrations on sacred and secular music. Compositional style studies.

Vahe, M.
1906   "Samoshayvar." *AH* 18:91–105.
               A travel account about Armenian community Samoshayvar, in Hungary.
               Tells of dwellings, occupations, customs, beliefs, and education.

Vantsian, G.
1901   "Armianskie Tsygany." [Armenian Gypsies.] S*bornik Materialov dlia Opisaniia Mestnostei i Plemen Kavkaza* 29(1):45–70. (NB: This citation has part 1 in two sections, both called part 1, each starting with page 1.—AMA)
            Distribution of Gypsies in Alexandropol and nearby areas, and some in northern Turkey. These Gypsies called Armenians, but really are not. They have a free life style, make drums, sieves, cymbals, toys in exchange for supplies. They also do blacksmith work and mend household items. Only one Armenian known to have married a Gypsy girl.

Varandyan, Emmanuel
1938   *The Well of Ararat.* New York, Doubleday, Doran & Co. 343 pp.
            Although this is a novel, it mirrors the family life and some customs of Armenians in a Persian village. The focus is on wedding customs.

Vardan. *See* Vartan, Aigetsi

Vardanian, Anahit
1980   "Zhoghovrdakan hekiatnere Hovh. Tumanyani steghtsagortsakan tesadashtum." [The Folktale in the Creative Range of Hovh. Tumanian.] *L* 4:52–64. Russian summary.
            Tumanian, a literary figure of late 19th and early 20th centuries, was familiar with Grimm and Andreyev and other folklorists. Through announcements he asked Armenians to send him tales without changes, yet when he selected for publication he shaped tales into literary style. This study based on archive material.

Vardanian, L. M.
1967   "Perezhitkii instituta initsiatsii y Armian." [Survivals of Custom of Initiation Among Armenians.] *PH* 4:292–296.
            Concerns customs relating to marriage up to beginning of 20th century. Male unmarried youths with groom-to-be, shave him, kill rooster, and feast on it. Describes dressing of groom. Girls have henna for bride, and dress the bride.

Vardanian, S. A.
1979   "Deghagitutyune hin Hayastanum." [Pharmacology in Ancient Armenia.] *PH* 2:179–194. Russian summary.
            Medieval knowledge of plants, animals, minerals used in curing or alleviating diseases. Based on work of Amirdovlat of Amasia.

Vardanian, Svetlana
1971   "Banahyusakan nyuter Lernayin Gharabaghi." [Folklore Topics in Mountainous Gharabagh.] *L* 8:88–93. Russian summary.
            In 1860s various Armenians collected folklore in Karabagh. From 1967 to 1970 the author collected many examples of songs that had been almost

forgotten. The humorous stories of Pul Pugh have changed somewhat over period of time as have other genres of folklore. Some are abbreviated. A popular theme is the mother-in-law and daughter-in-law.

1974   "Tigran Navasardyane banaget-banahavak." [Tigran Navasardian as folklorist and folklore collector.] *L* 5:42–48.
            Navasardian's early education followed by study of engineering in Geneva. Interested in folklore collecting in 1880. He had a strong feeling for preservation of folk materials as part of national heritage. He published 10 volumes of *Hay zhoghovrdakan hekiatner* [Armenian Folktales]. His activities after 1903 not noted.

1980   "Banahavak Poghos Muradian." [Folklore Collector Poghos Muradian.] *PH* 3:301–303.
            Muradian was one of Navasardian's field workers who collected folklore. He was very careful to note name of narrator, sex, age, and origin, and how skilled the narrator was, and he evaluated the narrator's memory. Author gives no date for collector; he was educated in village, then went to Constantinople, later taught in Erzerum. Much of his collected material still in manuscript form.

Vardanian, V.
1973   "Inch en 'tueleats' [tveleats] ergere?" [What are the "enumerated" Songs?] *Banber Erevani Hamalsarani* 3:203–208. Russian summary.
            Concerns meaning of the word "enumerated" songs, a word derived from "number." Various interpretations given by various writers. Author considers it an enumeration of deeds. (NB: See R. W. Thomson's note 14, page 120 in Moses of Khoren's *History of the Armenians* (1978).— AMA)

1980   *Komitas.* Kiev, Muzichna Ukraina. 76 pp. port.
            Ukrainian work on the life of Komitas, the folk song collector. Notes education in Echmiadzin, later in Berlin. Gave concerts in Paris. Exiled by Turkey in 1915, later spent final years in Paris hospital.

Vardanian, V. G.
1974   "Grigor Khalatiani namaknere." *See* Khalatian, Grigor, 1974.

Vardumian, Gohar
1977   "Hin Haykakan ditsarani hamakargume." [The Classification of the Old Armenian Pantheon.] *L* 8:68–77. Russian summary.
            Although author does not consider her classification absolute, she thinks it presents a better picture for further research.

Vartan, Aigetsi

1825   *Choix de fables de Vartan en arménien et français.* Paris, Dondey-Dupré et
            Fils. 96 pp.
                These 45 fables are edited and translated by J. A. Saint-Martin. They date
                from the 13th century. Most involve animals, though humans and plants
                have a place..

1895–99   *Sbornik pritch.* [Collection of Fables.] *See* Marr, N., 1895–99, who gives
            not only Vartan fables but also Arabic fables, and an account of fable
            literature.

Vartanian, A.

1912   "Professor Kr. A. Khalatiants." *HA* 26:193–198. port.
                Obituary article about Khalatian's life and work. He first studied medicine
                for two years, then turned to literature.

Varvarian, H. S.

1955   "David of Sassoun." *Armenian Review* 8(1):79–87.
                This translation is about the attempt to capture David to take him to Egypt,
                but the version translated is not specified.

Varzhabedian, Mamigon

1912   *Hushigk Zeytuni.* [Memories of Zeytun.] Marzuan, Nerso u Srabian. 404 pp.
            il.
                Mostly historical, but brief part, pp. 21–33, gives information about food,
                baptism, engagement, wedding, funerals.

Veradzin, M.

1931   "Hay poshanere Pokr Asioy mech." [Armenian Gypsies in Asia Minor.] *H*
            9(6):132–141.
                Gypsies in Turkey are included; Turkish and Armenian-speaking Gypsies
                in some villages up to 1896. Turkish government recognized them as
                "Ermeni Rum."

Villa, Susie Hoogasian (*See also* Hoogasian, Susie)

1948   *A Study of the Style, Narrator Technique, and Motifs of the Armenian
            Folktale.* 228 pp. M.A. thesis, Wayne State University, 1948.
                Not seen.

1966   *100 Armenian Tales and their Folkloristic Relevance.* Detroit, Wayne State
            University Press. 602 pp.
                Tales were collected in 1940–42 from immigrant Armenians in Delray, the
                industrial section of Detroit. Brief biographies of informants. Comparative
                studies. Index of motifs based on Stith Thompson's *Motif-Index of Folk
                Literature.* Bibliography and notes included.

Villa, Susie Hoogasian, and Matossian, Mary K.
1982   Armenian Village Life Before 1914. Detroit, Wayne State University Press.
                197 pp. il., map.
                    Information on family life and customs given by immigrant Armenian
                    informants whose biographies are noted. Glossary of some Armenian and
                    Turkish words are followed by notes and bibliography. (NB: In the
                    illustrations the famous monastery of Surp Garabed, St. Garabed, is
                    designated as St. Charles! A gross error.—AMA)

Volland [no first name]
1907   "Aberglauben in Armenien und Kurdistan." *Globus* 91:341–344. il.
                    Superstitions to ward off evil. Illustrations show: depiction of animal head
                    of church entrance, caricature of devil, jewelry pendant with special
                    ornament, and page from Armenian amulet (*hamayel*).

Vosgiporig. *See* Osgiporig

Vostrikova, P.
1912   "Muzyka i pesniia y Aderbeidzhanskikh Tatar." [Music and Song Among the
                Azerbaijan Tatars.] *Sbornik Materialov dlia Opisaniia Mestnostei i Plemen
                Kavkaza* 42(2):1–39. il.
                    Of special interest are pp. 1–20 that describe musical instruments used in
                    the Caucasus, including Armenia. Illustrations of individual instruments
                    are given.

1912   "Skazki zapisanniia v Elizavetpol'skoi gubernii." [Tales and Writings in
                Elisapetpol province.] *Sbornik Materialov dlia Opisaniia Mestnostei i Plemen
                Kavkaza* 42:(2):1–169. (NB: These pages follow pp. l–39 noted in the
                preceding citation of 42(2).— AMA)
                    There are 14 Armenian tales, pp. 20–84. Narrator of each tale is noted,
                    also place where tale was told.

Wallis, Wilson D.
1923   "Some Phases of Armenian Social Life." *American Anthropologist*, ser. 2,
                25:582–584.
                    Information from Armenians in Fresno, California, in 1919. Marriage
                    regulations, kinship terms, and inheritance.

Waterman, Richard A ., et al.
1948   "Bibliography of Asiatic Music. Fifth Installment. D. Christians. 3. Armen-
                ians." *Music Library Association. Notes*, ser. 2, 6:122–128.
                    There are 121 items, mostly liturgical music, though some folk music,
                    including Komitas. Includes citations in English, French, German,
                    Russian.

Wesendonk, G. G. von
1924   "Über georgisches Heidentum." *Caucasica* 1:1–109.
        Although about Georgian paganism, includes considerable material about
        Armenian comparisons.

Weyh, Wilhelm
1912   "Die syrische Légende der 40 Märtyrer von Sebaste." *Byzantinische
        Zeitschrift* 21:76–93.
        Doubts that the 40 testaments in Greek were translated from Syriac.

Widengren, Geo.
1905   *Die Religionen Irans*. Stuttgart, W. Kohlhammer Verlag. 393 pp.
        Of interest here is part of Chapter VI which gives historical information on
        relation of Armenia and Asia Minor: worship, sacrifice, and religious
        terminology, pp. 174–196.

Wilhelm, Eugene
1908   "Analogies in Iranian and Armenian Folklore." In *Spiegel Memorial Volume*.
        Bombay, British India Press, pp. 65–81.
        Notes that Armenians always under foreign influences, especially Iran.
        For example, legend of Rustum-i-Zal. Similarity of beliefs about light
        (good) and darkness (bad); ideas of heaven, immortality of soul, sun
        worship, veneration of moon, fear of certain animals.

Wilson, Vivian, and Covington, Dorothy
1991   "Armenia—in the Shadow of Ararat." *Counted Thread* 17(2):3–6. il., map.
        Describes and illustrates a form of embroidery known as Marash work.
        Gives instructions.

Wingate, J. S. [also Wingate, Jane S.]
1910   "Armenian Stories." [i.e., Folktales.] *Armenia* 4(6):11–12. Page 11 "The
        Bride of the Fountain"; p. 12 "The Wise Weaver." *Armenia* 4(8)14–15. Pages
        14–15 "The Foolish Man"; p. l5 "The Three Brothers."

1910   "Armenian Folk-Tales." *Folk-Lore* 21:217–222.
        Gives some preliminary information about Armenian folktales and the
        contribution of K. Servantsian to folklore. Author's translation of "The
        Foolish Man" is on pp. 220–222.

1910   "Armenian Folk-Tales." *Folk-Lore* 21:365–370 "Brother Lamkin"; 370–371
        "The Magpie and his Tail"; 507–511 "The Thousand-noted Nightingale."

1911   "Armenian Folk-Tales." *Armenia* 4(9)15–17.
        "Brother Lamkin."

1911   "Armenian Folk-Tales." *Folk-Lore* 22:77–80 "Ten-thousandfold"; 351–361 "The Adventures of a Prince" [original Armenian bears no title]; 476–481 "The Dreamer"; 481–484 "The Daughter of the Village Patriarch."

1912   "Armenian Folk-Tales." *Folk-Lore* 23:94–102 "The Perfidious Mother"; 220–223 "The Fortunes of a Prince and the Wise Fox."

1912   "Armenian Folk-Tales." *Folk-Lore* 23:471–472.
         A short collection of 19 riddles.

1928   "Armenian Folk-Tales." *New Armenia* 20:42–44. Page 42 "The Bride of the Fountain"; pp. 42–43 "The Wise Weaver"; pp. 43–44 "Brother Lamkin."

1930   "The Scroll of Cyprian: An Armenian Family Amulet." *Folk-Lore* 41:169–187.
         The scroll, 3-3/4 inches wide and 4 yards long, belonged to Prof. V. H. Hagopian of Anatolia College, Marsovan, Turkey. The translation also includes deeds of Saint Cyprian.

1949–50   "David of Sassoun." *Armenian Affairs* 1:271–286.
         This translation is based on Armenian text of 1939. This is Book One, in verse, of Sanasar and Baghdasar. The work seems more like an adaptation than a direct translation. Footnote mentions that soon her entire translation will be available. (NB: I have not seen further mention of continuation.—AMA)

1949–50   "God Gives to the Giver." *Armenian Affairs* 1:82–83.
         An Armenian tale translated from Servantsian's *Hamov-Hodov*.

Winkler, Gabriele
1982   *Das armenische Initiationsrituale. Entwicklungsgeschtliche und liturgievergleichende Untersuchung der Quellen 3. bis 10. Jahrhundersts.* Rome, Ponti Inst. Studiorum Orient. 476 pp. (Orientalis Christiana Analecta 217.)
         Originally Ph.D. thesis, Munich University, 1977. Information on baptism rituals derived from various sources, including commentaries and manuscripts. Reviewed by M. Topalian in *HA* 1983 (97):165–178.

Wlislocki, Heinrich von
1889   "Parallele zu einen Afrikanischen Märchen." *Zeitschrift für Vergleichende Litteraturgeschichte und Renaissance-Litteratur*, n.f. 2:449–451.
         Refers to Robert W. Felkin (1887/8). This article translated by K. K into Armenian in *HA* 1890 (4):139–140.

Wlislocki, Heinrich von *(continued)*
1891	*Märchen und Sagen der Bukowiner und Siebenbürger Armenier.* Hamburg, Verlagsanstalt und Druckerei A. G. 188 pp.

> The 63 tales are based on information from Armenians in Bukowina and Transylvania. Some tales retain Armenian feeling, some show European influence. Includes some notes on customs, and lists 95 proverbs and sayings. There is some information about the book in *HA* 1891 (7):22–23.

Wolohojian, Albert Mugerdich
1964	*The Romance of Alexander the Great: English Translation of the Armenian Version of the life of Alexander of Macedon by Pseudo-Callisthenes.* 292 pp. Ph.D. Thesis. Columbia University, 1964. *Dissertation Abstracts* 26:1972.

> This thesis later appeared as a book with the title *The Romance of Alexander the Great by Pseudo-Callisthenes*, New York, Columbia University Press, 1969. 196 pp.

Woman's Day. Needlework Dept.
1956	"Armenian Needle Lace." *Woman's Day* 19(11):66–70. il.

> Description of how the lace is made.

Yardemian, Dajad
1990–91	"Ortan garmir 'kermez,' gam Haygagan garmir nerg." [The Red Color "Kermez," or the Armenian Red Color.] *B* 148:292–329; *B* 149:79–125. English summary.

> Historical background of Armenian carpets using the red color from certain insects. Gives Armenian and Arabic sources.

Yerem. *See* Erem

Yeremian. *See* Eremian, Aram

Zarian, A. K.
1989	"Khachkareri khorhrdanshannerin ev Mitrayakanutyune veraberogh patkeragrakan hartser." [Cross-Stone Symbols and Questions Concerning Mithraic Iconography.] *PH* 1:202–219. il. Russian summary.

> Sun and moon looked upon as gods, then Christianity made sun the church and moon the Virgin Mary. Plant and animal figures in cross-stones; some Mithraic elements Christianized.

Zartarian, R.
1910	"How Death Came to Earth; an Armenian Folk-Lore." *Armenia* 4(1):4–5. Translated by Bedros A. Keljik.

> World a paradise of everlasting beauty; the old ever rejuvenated. A stranger tells man his years limited to number of hairs his hand can cover on an ox. Man tries to cover ox with body, but hands hang on side of ox.

1917   "The Bride of the Lake; a legend." *New Armenia* 9:59. port.
            A tryst of lovers discovered by husband of bride; he strangles her.
            Midnight turbulence of lake ever after.

Zatikian, Haykanush
1982   "Eghanaki kankhagushman zhoghovrdakan hnarnere est erknayin erevutneri."
            [Folk Methods of Weather Forecasting According to Extra-Terrestrial
            Phenomena.] *L* 11:75–83. Russian summary.
            Physical pain in humans; behavior of animals, birds, insects, and plants
            as indicators of weather and seasonal changes.

Zelinski, S.
1898   "Tsragir tghaberki ev noratsin mankan fizikakan dastiarakutyan masin nyuter
            havakelu." [Plan for Collecting Subjects on Birth, Infancy, and Physical
            Education.] *AH* 3[Suppl.]:73–79.
            Plan directed to women; 59 questions.

1898   "Tsragir hivandutean ev bzhshkutean masin niuter havakelu hamar." [Plan to
            Collect Subjects about Sickness and Healing., *AH* 4[Suppl.]:97–106.
            Notes 78 questions for persons and 32 questions for domestic animals.

1898   "Boyseri gortsatsutiune Erevani nahangum." [Use of Plants in the Province of
            Erevan.] *AH* 4:177–202.
            Wild and domesticated plants with common Armenian names and
            scientific names (some Russian names also). Notes how used—raw,
            cooked, or as herbs. A number of footnotes give details on preparation of
            foods.

Zelvys, Vladimir Ilyich
1988/89   "A First Look at Armenian Maledicta." *Maledicta* 10:245–246.
            Lists a number of curses relating to sexual organs and actions.

Zeytlian, Sona
1973   *Musa leran zhoghovrtagan hekiatner.* [Folktales of Mount Musa (Mount of
            Moses).] Beirut, Vahe Sethian Press. 733 pp. il.
            Tales recorded in dialect of the area, but recorded because of variants. Age
            of narrator given. The 100 tales arranged as follows: magical, moral,
            ingenious and satirical, animals, customary life. Nothing indicates
            background of compiler nor any note about where original records are
            filed.

Zeytuntsi. *See* Semerdjian, M.

Zinjirjian, V.
1978   "Hayastani antik darashrjani erkatya gyughatntesakan gortsiknere." [Iron
           Farming Implements of Armenia's Ancient Period.] *PH* 1:265–271. il.
                Study based on archeological discoveries in Garni, Armavir, Artatasht.
                Probably dates from second and first centuries B.C.

Zurabian, Zhanna
1983   "Haykakan erazhshtakan folklori u 'arajnayin' intonatsion tarrere."
           ["Primary" Intonation Elements of Armenian Musical Folklore.] *L* 7:50–58.
           Russian summary.
                Gives several examples of music in modern notation.

Index

Abandonment of aged: Ghaziyan, A., 1977

Abeghian, Manuk: Abeghian, Ardashes, 1948, 1955; Ghanalanian, Aram Tigrani, 1959, 1963, 1966, 1985; Harutyunian, S. B., 1965, 1970; Melik-Ohanjanian, K. A., 1965; Sharbkhanian, Pavel, 1967

Abgar. *See* Legends about: *Abgar*

Abovian, Khachatur: Ghanalanian, Aram Tigrani, 1941, 1985; Lalayan, Ervand, 1897

Adoption: Bedrosian, Robert, 1984; Ghltchian, A., 1912–13; Runciman, Steven, 1955

Advice: Aghayan, M., 1959; Ayvazian, Abraham H., 1893; Gevorgian, S. A., 1980

Afion Karahisar. *See* Folklore, by place or type: *Afion Karahisar*

Agathangelos: Melik-Ohanjanian, K. A., 1964

Aged. *See* Abandonment of aged

Aghtamar: Bartikian, H., 1962; Billeter, Erika, 1966; Bryer, A.A.M., 1960; Burton, Richard, et al., 1958; Der Nersessian, Sirarpie, 1965; Frasson, Giuseppe, 1987; Thomson, R. W., 1979

Agn. *See* Folk songs, by place or type: *Agn*; Folklore, by place or type: *Agn*

Agni (of Rig Veda): Sandaljian, Hovsep V., 1901

Aharonian, Avedik (or Avedis): Erevantsian, B., 1930; Markarian, Siran Z., 1931

Ahikar: Dashian, H., 1899; Tabagiants, S., et al., 1894

Ahikar (text): Conybeare, F. C., et al., 1913; Martirosian, A. A., 1969–72

Aintab. *See* Folklore, by place or type: *Aintab*

Akhtamar. *See* Aghtamar

Akn. *See* Agn

Aladjalov, Constantin: Kurdian, H., 1952–53

Alashkert. *See* Folklore, by place or type: *Alashkert*

Alexander the Great. *See* Legends about: *Alexander the Great*

Amanor: Bdoyan, V., 1977

Ambrosia. *See* Legends about: *Ambrosia*

Amulets and talismans: Bezhkeuk-Melikian, L., 1968; Der Nersessian, Sirarpie, 1936; Esaian, S. A., 1968; Feydit, Frédéric, 1986;

Odabashian, A. A., 1976; Volland, 1907; Wingate, J. S., 1930

Anagrams: Anonymous, 1890

Anahid (or Anahit): Aharonian, A., 1960; Arvanian, Veronica, 1954; Chaumont, Marie-Louise, 1965; Chituni, Dikran, 1911; Khachatrian, Zh. D., 1985; Melik-Pashayan, K. V., 1963; Mubayajian, Sargis, 1931; Russell, James R., 1990

Anania of Shirak: Russell, James R., 1988–89

Anecdotes: Harutyunian, V. A., 1976; Kalashev, Aleksandr, 1889; Kazanjian, Hovh., 1898; Lalayan, Ervand, 1903; Malkhasiants, St., 1958; Nazariants, Hovhannes, 1876–77; Srapian, Armenouhi, 1969

Ani: Toromanian, T., 1912

Animal sacrifice: Conybeare, F. C., 1901; Girard, M. D., 1902; Pachajian, Sarkis K., 1971; Sharf, A., 1982; Tixeront, J., 1913

Aparan. *See* Folklore, by place or type: *Aparan*; Folktales, by place: *Aparan*

Arabkir. *See* Folklore, by place or type: *Arabkir*

Ararat. *See* Folktales, by place: *Ararat*

Ara the Beautiful. *See* Legends about: *Ara the Beautiful*

Architecture. *See* Art and architecture

Ardavast. *See* Legends about: *Ardavast*

Armenia, history: Agathangelos, 1976; Moses of Khoren, 1961, 1978; Pawstos Buzandasi, 1989

Armenian alphabet. *See* Legends about: *Armenian alphabet*

Armenian Catholics. *See* Catholics

Armenian Ethnographic Society. *See* Folklore societies

Armenian Gypsies. *See* Gypsies

Armenian language. *See* Language

Armor: Esaian, S. A., 1962

Arshag. *See* Legends about: *Arshag*

Art and architecture: Amirbakian, R. J., 1989; Arakelian, B. N., 1978; Billeter, Erika, 1966; Brambilla, Mario Giovanni, 1974–76; Burton, Richard, et al., 1958; Carswell, John, and Dowsett, C.J.F., 1972;

Pawstos Buzandasi, 1989; Servantsian, Karekin, 1874 (rep. 1978)

Soviet Armenia and Soviet period. *See* Folklore, by place or type: *Soviet Armenia and Soviet period;* Folk songs, by place or type: *Soviet period*

Stone cult in Jerusalem. *See* Legends about: *Stone cult in Jerusalem*

Storehouses: Marutian, Harutyan, 1937; Petrosian, Sargis, 1982

Sun: Alojian, H., 1909; Arutiunian, S. B., 1976; Davtian, K. S., 1967; Esaian, S. A., 1968; Israelian, H. R., 1967; K., A., 1929; Russell, James R., 1988–89

Superstitions: Chantre, Ernest, 1891; Ghaziyan, A., 1983; Haigazn, Edouard, 1895; Hamamchian, E., 1897; Lalayan, Ervand, 1895; Melik-Shahnazarian, G. G., 1928; Ter-Movsesian, Mesrop, 1897; Volland, 1907

Surmelu. *See* Folklore, by place or type: *Surmelu;* Folk songs, by place or type: *Surmelu*

Swastika: Ezekian, A. M., 1908

Symbolism: Ajello, Roberto, and Borghini, Alberto, 1989; Amirbakian, R. J., 1989; Babayan, F. S., 1967; Billeter, Erika, 1966; Conybeare, F. C., 1907; Demirkhanian, A. R., 1982; Frasson, Giuseppe, 1987; Gevorgian, N. Kh., 1984; Hakobian, Grigor, 1965; Hatsuni, Vartan, 1910; Khachaturian, V. A., 1977; Mahé, Jean-Pierre, 1986; Mnatsakanian, A. Sh., 1955; Odabashian, A. A., 1986; Patrik, A. N., 1967; Phillips, Jenny, 1989; Pikichian, H. V., 1988; Russell, James R., 1986–87; Samuelian, Kh., 1912; Thomson, R. W., 1976, 1979; Zarian, A. K., 1989

Szamosújvar. *See* Folklore, by place or type: *Szamosújvar*

Tadem. *See* Folk dances, by place: *Tadem;* Folklore, by place or type: *Tadem*

Talismans. *See* Amulets and talismans

Tarku: Adontz, N., 1927

Taron. *See* Daron

Tasks to win bride: Collins, F. B., 1924

Tatev. *See* Folklore, by place or type: *Tatev*

Theater. *See* Folk drama and theater

Tiflis. *See* Folklore, by place or type: *Tiflis*

Time: Hatsuni, Vartan, 1910

Tiridates: Ablian, Eprem, 1895. *See also* Legends about: *Tiridates*

Toasts: Arutiunian, S. B., 1971

Tokat. *See* Folklore, by place or type: *Tokat*

Tomarza. *See* Folklore, by place or type: *Tomarza*

Tombs and tombstones. *See* Death and burial

Tonir. *See* Hearth

Tonir, Holy. *See* Legends about: *Tonir, Holy*

Tork: Bartikian, H., 1963; Mardirossian, N., 1930

Totemism: Samuelian, G., 1949

Traditions: Arkayik, 1908–10; Carnoy, E. Henry, and Nicolaides, J., 1967; Ghanalanian, Aram Tigrani, 1979; Haigazn, Edouard, 1895

Transformation into animal: Agathangelos, 1976; Kouymjian, Dickran, 1978; Krappe, Alexander H., 1949; Mnatsakanian, A. Sh., 1981

Transylvania. *See* Folk dances, by place: *Transylvania;* Folklore, by place or type: *Transylvania;* Folktales, by place: *Transylvania*

Trdat. *See* Tiridates

Trebizond. *See* Folklore, by place or type: *Trebizond;* Proverbs and sayings, by place: *Trebizond*

Trees: Avdalbekian, S. T., 1964

Tsitogh. *See* Folklore, by place or type: *Tsitogh*

Tukh Manuk: Mnatsakanian, A. Sh., 1976

Tumanian, Hovhannes: Melik-Pashayan, K. V., 1969; Nazinian, Artashes, 1969; Vardanian, Anahit, 1980

Turkish language. *See* Language

Tvyal erger. *See* Enumerated songs

Twin cult: Israelian, H. R., 1980

Unfortunate lovers. *See* Mam and Zin

Urban folk songs. *See* Folk songs, by place or type: *Urban*

Urfa. *See* Folklore, by place or type: *Urfa*

Urts. *See* Nurts

Utensils. *See* Household utensils

Vahagn: Dumézil, Georges, 1938; Iakobson, R., 1982; Petrosian, Sargis, 1981; Sandaljian, Hovsep V., 1901; Toporov, V. N., 1977

Van. *See* Folklore, by place or type: *Van;* Folk songs, by place or type: *Van*

Vanatur, V.: Bdoyan, V., 1977

Varanda. *See* Folklore, by place or type: *Varanda;* Folk songs, by place or type: *Varanda*

Varaz (or Varis). *See* Boar

Vardges Mankan: Mnatsakanian, A. Sh., 1975

Vardik family. *See* Folk songs, by place or type: *Vardik family*

Vartan, Aigetsi: Abeghian, Manuk, 1970; Dashian, H., 1899–1900; Orbeli, Iosip, 1956; Raffi, Aram, 1919